STAIRWAYS
to
HEAVEN

25-09-19

Lorna's writing has touched so many people across the world. Here, just a few share their thoughts on the books.

'Through Lorna's books, and open-mindedness, you feel like you've just met your best friend whom you've known all your life. She has the gift of connecting with all her readers, and for those lucky to be in her presence, this connection is magnified tenfold.' Martha

'An angel herself, Lorna's words have not only enlightened my life but enriched it as well. I feel loved more then ever by my Angels and know I am never alone. This book will change your life!' Cristina, New York City

'Inspirational, exhilarating and moving.' Órla

'This book changed the way I think. I am open to angels now and talk to them all the time, I also passed these books to my family and friends who loved them just as much. Lorna you're my hero.' Irene, Omagh

'Thank you, Lorna, for your beautiful story.' Kim, Wisconsin

'Lorna's understanding of who God is, as revealed through her experiences with angels, is the God I always hoped He would be. Bigger than one religion, more forgiving, with a sense of humour and immeasurable love. *Stairways to Heaven* is a source of comfort and hope.' Claire

'Your books have been inspirational at a time of great difficulty. You have made me realise I should listen to my angels and that I'm not on my own.' Louise, Stratford-upon-Avon

'*Stairways to Heaven* made me feel me a beautiful connection to you, to my angel, to love itself and more importantly, to hope. I really feel inspired by your message.' Janny, Mexico

'Nothing will ever give you more comfort than reading this book.' Mary, Kilmarnock

'Before reading your books my thought was that angels were true but too far away from me, now I talk everyday with them and I feel that they never leave me.' Gisella, Italy

'Thank you for your courage to share your life.' Ela, Poland

'The impact that *Angels in my Hair* has had on my life is simple – I don't worry any more. Life is very uncertain for me at the moment, but I'm just going with the flow, doing what I can, but knowing that I am being looked after and that all will be well in the end. Such peace of mind is priceless, thank you.' Jenny, Powys

'Being a young person (18) I find not many people my age know about what there is out there and how much help there is on offer to us all. I tell my friends everything I know, and even if they don't believe me, I know they are still listening and absorbing that information, which hopefully has some kind of positive impact. Lorna Byrne has given me that extra knowledge and comfort that I can now share around.' Zeria, London

'Lorna, your books helped restore my faith. You have given me comfort knowing that my dad was not alone when he passed away. I can't begin to explain how much you have helped me. Thank you so much for writing these books.' Orla, Derry.

'Through your book you helped me to have more faith, to be a more spiritual person, to be more patient. I'm sure I found you because my guardian angel guided me to you and wanted me to learn from you that he is with me always.' Adriana, Costa Rica

'Thank you and the angels with all my heart and soul Lorna. When I think of my guardian angel which is more and more often these days, I feel like my heart smiles.' Mary

'These books will open your eyes if your heart is willing.' Andria

Lorna Byrne has been seeing and talking to angels since she was a baby. Now that her family is raised, she talks openly about what she has learned. She lives quietly in rural Ireland. She is the author of the international bestseller *Angels in My Hair* which has been translated into twenty languages. *Stairways to Heaven* is her second book.

For more information, visit www.lornabyrne.com

Lorna Byrne
STAIRWAYS to HEAVEN

CORONET

First published in Great Britain in 2010 by Coronet
An imprint of Hodder & Stoughton
An Hachette UK company

First published in paperback in 2011

12

Copyright © Lorna Byrne, 2010

The right of Lorna Byrne to be identified as the Author of the Work has
been asserted by her in accordance with the Copyright, Designs and
Patents Act 1988.

A CIP catalogue record for this title is available from the British Library

ISBN 978 1 444 70660 4

Typeset in Sabon MT by Palimpsest Book Production Limited,
Falkirk, Stirlingshire

Printed and bound in the UK by CPI Group (UK) Ltd, Croydon, CR0 4YY

Hodder & Stoughton policy is to use papers that are natural, renewable
and recyclable products and made from wood grown in sustainable forests.
The logging and manufacturing processes are expected to conform to the
environmental regulations of the country of origin.

Hodder & Stoughton Ltd
338 Euston Road
London NW1 3BH

www.hodder.co.uk

Dedication

I dedicate this book to everyone who has listened to God and the angels and played their part.

Contents

The Secrets of Your Guardian Angel

In this special chapter I want tell you as much as I can about guardian angels, so as you will be able to know and communicate with your guardian angel better.

You have a guardian angel – whether you believe it or not. Your guardian angel is a gift from God and is there to help you. I'd like to help you to enjoy more the wonderful comfort, joy and help that this gift can bring.

Your guardian angel loves you. You are precious to it. You are the most important person in the world to this angel.

I see angels every day and have done since I was a baby. I see them as plainly as I see people on the street. For the first few years of my life I saw a guardian angel standing behind everyone. Then suddenly one day I no longer saw a guardian angel standing there – instead I saw, for the most part a bright light, like a beam of light, stretching up behind each person. An angel; called Mitha, explained to me that they had closed down in order to protect me.

The truth is that the brightness of the open guardian angels was just too much for me. It hurt my eyes and disorientated me enormously. Guardian angels are brighter than other angels. The light was often so strong that it made it very hard for me to see the person they were guarding. Angel Mitha told me that God had wanted me to see and experience guardian angels in their full glory, so as I knew what they looked like and would be able to tell people about them, but that from now on only certain guardian angels would open up for me, and even then only for a few moments. Most days at least one guardian angel will open up and show itself to me in its full beauty.

Since that day I have never seen any person without that beam of light that is their guardian angel behind them. It's about three feet behind them and stretches from their feet way up over their head. Its height and width can vary, but this doesn't mean that one guardian angel is better than another.

I am continually amazed at the number of people who doubt they have a guardian angel. Many are happy to accept that other people might have a guardian angel, but doubt that they have one themselves.

I was in Philadelphia in the United States last summer doing a signing and as I chatted to people and signed books I looked down at the queue. I could see the light of a guardian angel behind each and every person there, and the shop was full of other angels too. As I was saying goodbye to a woman an angel tapped me on the shoulder, and pointed down the queue saying; 'There is a mother and child there who are very nervous'. I looked in the direction the angel pointed, but I couldn't see them. Suddenly a guardian angel rose up above the people and the other angels, as if it become taller temporarily. 'Here we are!' it said.

I could see this very, very beautiful guardian angel, but I still couldn't see a mother or child. The guardian angel was a bright emerald green colour of different shades. Its wings seemed to be moving gently, as if there was a breeze, and its face radiated gentleness, kindness and love. Without words I asked whether this was the guardian angel to the mother or the child?

The angel replied 'I am the mother's guardian angel. My name is Rosalet.'

It was a little while before I got to see the mother and daughter. I kept talking with people and signing books and then there was another tap on my shoulder.

'Do you see now?'

I looked straight ahead and I could see a mother and daughter a few places back in the queue. The mother was quite small, dark and pretty, probably about thirty, and her daughter was six or seven-years-old with beautiful brown eyes.

'Yes, I see them' I replied without words. I knew something was wrong, and yet I felt great joy. I prayed that whatever their problem was, it would be healed.

When it was their turn, they walked towards me looking nervous. The child was clinging to her mother. Behind both of them I could see the light of their guardian angels. I invited the mother to sit down on the chair beside me and the child stood between the mother and me. The little girl's eyes kept going anxiously from her mother, to me and back to her mother. The mother never took her eyes off me.

'We are probably not meant to be here,' she whispered nervously. 'We were unsure whether we would be allowed to come into the shop,' she continued.

I was confused and reached out to take her hand asking 'Why?'

The mother looked at me and said in a small voice, 'because this is a Catholic shop and we are Jewish.'

Up to that moment I hadn't even noticed that it was a Catholic shop and I was shocked that someone of any religion would think that they weren't welcome. 'Why would you think that?' I asked

At that moment the light of the guardian angel behind each of them opened up so as I could see their guardian angels fully. The two guardian angels touched each other by the finger tips and formed a protective circle with my guardian angel around the three of us, as if to shield us from everyone.

The mother looked at me with tears in her eyes. 'Lorna, maybe God hasn't given us Jewish people a guardian angel?' she said, still talking in a very hushed voice.

I reached out to them both and took their hands, saying urgently, 'Don't you know that every single human being has a guardian angel. This is a gift from God. It doesn't matter what religion you are or even if you have no beliefs at all.' I gave them a big smile. 'Of course you both have guardian angels. I can see them both behind you as clearly as I can see you.'

The little girl's eyes lit up with excitement as I described her guardian angel to her: 'Your guardian angel has a big smile and is looking down at you with such love. Your angel is giving me a female appearance, like that of a girl. Your angel is dressed in the most beautiful flowing robes of sky blue and silver.'

'I really have a guardian angel!' the child said with delight.

I described the mother's guardian angel for them too.

We sat there for a peaceful moment, then the little girl's big brown eyes welled up. She looked at her mother, 'Ask her about daddy's guardian angel, Mummy,' she implored.

The mother looked at me and explained with sadness in her eyes that her husband had died suddenly a year or so before. What added to their pain, she added, was that he had been alone when he died.

'Your daddy wasn't alone' I said reassuringly to her daughter. 'His guardian angel was right there with him all the time. His guardian angel took his soul to heaven.'

The little girl and mother hugged each other. The little girl said with delight, 'My daddy had a guardian angel, and I have one too!'

'And so has your mum,' I added smiling.

As they left happily I thanked both of their guardian angels for guiding them to come to see me that day, despite their fears. I was very moved, though I was still shocked to think that they could think they didn't have a guardian angel because of their religious faith. We are all God's children and God has given each and every one of us a guardian angel that never leaves us for one second. We are never alone. Our guardian angel is always with us and is the gatekeeper of our soul.

Your guardian angel is one of the most precious gifts that God has given you. Why not use this gift? Your guardian angel is there only for you and wants to help you in every area of your life. If only we would realise how much our guardian angel can help us, our lives would be so much easier.

If your guardian angel is already an active part of your life, that's wonderful, but ask your guardian angel for lots more. If you haven't yet started asking for help, start now. Just ask – it's as simple as that. Even if you are very cynical about the idea that you have a guardian angel, what have you to lose? Asking your guardian angel empowers your guardian angel to help you. Later in this chapter I'll show you how to deepen your communication with your guardian angel.

Guardian angels help us in so many ways. Last week I was walking past the local boys' school as they came out at the end of the day. There was a group of about eight, fourteen- or fifteen-year-olds surrounding and jostling a tall boy. They were shoving him around and jumping on him. The light of his guardian angel opened behind him for a moment. The angel was very tall and strong looking and was dressed in armour. I was allowed to hear what he was saying to the boy: 'Keep cool, don't let them rattle you, don't fight back, turn it into a joke'. The light of the other boys' guardian angels didn't open up, but I know they would have been trying to ease the situation too. The boy being bullied started to laugh, and the other boys started to laugh too. Then they walked off down the street as if nothing had happened.

That night I was visiting a friend in hospital, and an elderly man in a bed nearby started to have difficulty breathing, wheezing and clearly panicking. His guardian angel opened up behind him and I watched as it reached its arms around and touched the man's chest to ease his breathing. A few moments later a nurse walked in and said, 'You're alright now, its passing.'

When someone is feeling sad or depressed I will often see the guardian angel wrap its wings around them to comfort them. One day walking through a park I saw an angel reach out its arm from behind the person it was guarding and slowly open a hand in front of them. From this hand emerged a light about the size of a golf ball and, when the guardian angel took away his hand, the light remained there floating, glowing brightly. The guardian angel smiled at me and told me that it was a light of hope. I often see such a light around someone who is depressed. The light could be as small as a one cent coin or as big as a tennis ball, and it could be in front of them or to either side, not moving, always at about eye level. I have never seen more than one of these lights of hope with an individual. I know the person doesn't see this light, but I also know it helps them to reconnect with the hope inside of themselves.

Your guardian angel never leaves you – not even for a second. This is one of the reasons that a guardian angel often has to call in other angels to help. They do this all the time. On the main shopping street in Dublin the other day I saw a man with a disability walking along with the help of a walking frame. On each side of him his guardian angel had two angels helping him to walk.

Some of the things I see make me laugh. Recently I saw a man out jogging. I could see the light of his guardian angel behind him, but in front of him, running backwards and giving him encouragement, was another angel.

There are millions of unemployed angels, and your guardian angel can call them in to help you. There are teacher angels for everything under the sun, and lots of different types of angel. Just remember to ask you guardian angel to call them in to help. It's very simple: talk to your guardian angel as you would a friend and ask it for help. Ask it to let a teacher angel in to help you with whatever it is that is concerning you. You could say, for example, something like, 'Guardian angel, please send me a teacher angel to help make me a better driver.'

God has chosen your guardian angel especially for you. Your guardian angel only comes to this earth with you. Your guardian angel has been appointed by God especially with the task of guiding you through your human life, and has never been to earth with any other soul, and will never come to earth with another soul. This is one of the things that make the relationship between you and your guardian angel so special and unique.

While writing this chapter I have been asking lots of questions about guardian angels and I have been learning lots more about them. Last week I was out walking and Angel Michael came and walked beside me. He said he was going to tell me more about how guardian angels are chosen. We sat down together on a big stone and Michael held my hand saying, 'God is going to take your soul to heaven for a moment'.

I found myself in an enormous corridor with thousands and thousands of guardian angels streaming past. Unlike when I see them on earth, they didn't each have a person standing three steps in front of them, but I knew they were guardian angels because guardian angels look different to other types of angels.

One guardian angel came and stopped beside me and Michael told me we were to follow. We followed this angel for some distance and it was as if all the other guardian angels disappeared allowing me to see this one clearly.

Suddenly we found ourselves in a vast space with what Michael told me were unborn souls – souls that were to be conceived and born on earth, but hadn't yet. These souls were so beautiful! I haven't words to describe them. They were extremely bright, but, unlike with souls that I see on earth, I could see no human appearance whatsoever. I have never seen so many souls gathered together in the one space.

The guardian angel walked among these souls and the souls seemed to turn to it. I was almost overwhelmed with emotion as I realised that these souls were waiting for their own guardian angel, and were turning to this guardian angel as if saying, 'Is this mine? Has my guardian angel arrived?' We walked on and on through the sea of souls, following the guardian angel.

Then suddenly the guardian angel stopped beside a soul, and it was as if there was an explosion of love between the soul and the guardian angel as they encountered each other for the first time. The guardian angel and the soul embraced each other tightly. I have never seen a guardian angel and soul embrace in that way here on earth.

I watched with tears in my eyes, feeling the enormous love between them, as Angel Michael explained that God had chosen this guardian angel for this soul. I wasn't shown it, but Michael told me that God had also called the guardian angel into His presence and indicated which soul the guardian angel was to be with for eternity, which soul it was to become the gatekeeper for.

I asked Michael how God decides which guardian angel each of us is given, but I have not been given any answer, so I have no idea how and why they are chosen. Perhaps in the future I will be told more.

I watched the soul and the guardian angel for another few moments, deeply moved by how joyful they were at being together.

I turned and asked Michael whether the soul was to be conceived shortly, but he shook his head, explaining that God had not yet chosen the time, that it might be years – even centuries – but that in the meantime the guardian angel and soul would be together in heaven, learning about the joys and challenges that they would face together when the soul was conceived.

Suddenly I found myself back sitting on the big stone with Michael beside me. As we sat there we talked a little more about guardian angels, and Michael told me that guardian angels are angels who have been specially chosen by God to mind us. We are very precious to God because we have been made in His image. We each have a soul that is a speck of God's light. This soul is very precious to God; that's why He has given us each a guardian angel to help to bring the soul safely back to Him in Heaven. Guardian angels don't have souls and one of the reasons they never leave us is that they love being in the light of our souls – the light of God.

All guardian angels were created by God as guardian angels. They have been never been any other type of angel – and never will be. Michael also told me that guardian angels have been created with all the skills and knowledge they need and don't get any special training, even if they are going to mind someone through a very challenging life, or someone who is is physically or emotionally disabled in some way. We all have only one guardian angel each. I have never seen two guardian angels with any human being. When I see twins each has its own guardian angel. I asked Michael about this. He said 'Of course, Lorna, each twin must have their own individual guardian angel. You must remember: twins are often separated'. Each twin is guided through life, individually by their own personal guardian angel, but the guardian angels of twins have a closer relationship than any other guardian angels. Sometimes when I see twins, particularly twins who are children, I will see one of the twin's guardian angels looking at the other twin with a look of such love and tenderness, and then back at the child it guides. It is very rare to see guardian angels reach out to each other, but I have seen it with the guardian angels of twins. It is so beautiful to see.

Sometimes you might, for example, hear someone call a granny who has died an angel. This is an expression of affection and love and the angels tell me they are very happy when they hear it said – but it's not actually true. This granny is not an angel. No person who has lived on this earth becomes an angel.

An Archangel cannot be any individual's guardian angel. God has given Archangels wider tasks that relate to all humanity and, because of this, He has made them available to be called on by any of us. You or anyone anywhere in the world can call on an Archangel for help. Your guardian angel is only in one place at a time – with you. An Archangel can be in many places at one time. So when people tell you they have a particular relationship with an

Archangel – they may well be right, but that archangel is not their guardian angel. It is, of course, their own guardian angel that allows the Archangel in at times to help them.

Much as you might love your dog or cat, it doesn't have a guardian angel. No animal does. That doesn't mean, though, that angels don't help in the care for animals. Your guardian angel may attract your attention to your pet if something is wrong with it. Recently while I was sitting on a bus, I saw a dog that had just been knocked down. There was a man caring for the dog and beside him was an angel petting the dog and helping him care for it.

People always want to know what their guardian angel looks like. The truth though is that even if a guardian angel sometimes opens up its light to show me a human appearance, this appearance can change on different occasions. Take the guardian angel of Luke, a young man who I meet regularly and whom I like a lot. The appearance of his guardian angel seems to change each time we meet. One day I met him and as the light opened up I was a shown a very tall and elegant female appearance. The angel on this day seemed to be dressed in a modern and fashionable style, in colours of crimson, purple, mauve. On this day Luke told me about his problems with his girlfriend.

Another time we met for coffee and Luke's guardian angel gave me the appearance of a very broad and strong male. It was almost as if he was ready for battle, as if wearing some sort of soft body armour in a gold colour. Most of the time the appearance a guardian angel gives represents something of what the person needs at that moment within their life. At his time Luke was struggling with a bullying boss. The guardian angel appearance represented strength because this is what Luke needed that day.

I don't fully understand why guardian angels take on different appearances when they appear to me on different occasions but I think it's to help me to understand more fully the person in front of me and what is going on for them at that time. And so as I can share this description with the person it may also be so as they will understand that their guardian angel has the strength and skills to help them in the way they need to be helped.

The last time I ran into Luke on the street, he told me life was good, that he and his girlfriend were happy and that he had a new boss. As he talked, his guardian angel opened behind him and didn't give me an appearance of being either male or female. The guardian angel was large and elegant with a very bright face. Its colour was creamy and seemed to reflect other colours faintly.

In general guardian angels don't reflect age and don't age with people, but occasionally a guardian angel may give an appearance of a young adult. I have never yet been shown a guardian angel with an elderly appearance.

You cannot touch your guardian angel, but your guardian angel can touch you and occasionally people will feel this. Your angel can touch you anywhere on your body, and in general it's a signal to give you comfort, to give you reassurance that your guardian angel is there beside you. For example, I often feel my guardian angel messing my hair or pulling it. That's why I called my first book *Angels in my Hair*. It feels so real to me when my guardian angel does this that I often put my hand to my head to tidy my hair. Sometimes a guardian angel will take someone's hand, This can be felt in different ways – as warmth or cold, as tingling, or as a reassuring pressure. A young girl recently asked me whether if she turned around fast, could she step on her guardian angel or walk through it? No matter how you try to do this, you can't. You can't step on anyone else's guardian angel either.

The only emotion I have been seen a guardian angel show is love. I have never seen a guardian angel angry or annoyed or frustrated. I feel that at times they *should* be frustrated with us, but they seem to have endless patience and they never ever give up on us. They never, ever stop communicating with us. I have never seen a guardian angel sad – but I have seen a guardian angel pouring love and compassion on the person that guardian angel is caring for was sad. Guardian angels know and understand our emotions and help us to cope with them, but they have no emotions of their own, other than love. Some other types of angels have great senses of humour and mimic people and play and have fun, but I have never seen a guardian angel doing this. The only expression of emotion I have seen is a smile of love.

Guardian angels don't have friends in the way we do. The guardian angels of your family and friends know each other, but very rarely communicate with each other in the way we humans do. If I am walking down the street and four guardian angels with a group of people open up altogether, I will not see them communicating with each other in any way. To the best of my knowledge my own guardian angel has never communicated with my daughter Megan's guardian angel, even though they are both in the same house much of the time.

The exception to the rule comes into play if you ask your guardian angel to ask another person's guardian angel to mind them, or to help in some way. The communication then is automatic. As soon as you ask, the message is conveyed. It's not as if your angel has to tell the other person's guardian angel the message. That's another of those things that's a little hard for us humanly to understand.

If you are in need – and particularly if you have asked for help – your guardian angel can send for a teacher angel to help you with, for example, your computer, or to give you patience with your children. There are teacher angels for everything. Your guardian angel will send for the teacher angel, but will not need to explain anything. The teacher angel will already understand the issue. Your guardian angel can let a teacher angel, as I've already mentioned, but also an Archangel, or any other type of angel or soul to communicate with you, but if your guardian angel says 'No' then it cannot come in. As far as you are concerned, it's the boss.

I remember one occasion talking with a girl who was stressed out about exams, and I could see a teacher angel alongside her guardian angel. Another teacher angel came along, but her guardian angel didn't let it in, and told me without words that it was not yet time for this second teacher angel. This second teacher angel left with no trace of human emotions such as resentment, or irritation. Angels don't have any ego. They don't take anything personally. Their love is unconditional. They are simply here to help us.

I don't believe that any one guardian angel is better than any other. I have never seen anything to indicate that one is superior to another. When someone has what seems to others to lead a happy and successful life, it's not because they have a better guardian angel. If someone feels his or her life is a disaster, it's not because they have an incompetent guardian angel.

We have free choice. Our guardian angels are always there whispering in our ears, trying to get us to listen. Your guardian angel knows your life story, the possible paths your life could take and the choices you face. It does its best to prompt you to make the right choice, even if it may not seem like the easy one at the time. In my experience life is much easier and happier when we listen to our guardian angel but we have free choice and neither your guardian angel nor any other angel is allowed to interfere with it. The truth is none of us should blame our guardian angels when things don't turn out as we wanted.

As I say, your guardian angel never leaves you even for one moment. Your guardian angel is there whatever you are doing – no matter how intimate and private you might think it is. Guardian angels don't look on these things the way we do. Your guardian angel sees you body, but, being honest, is much more interested in the light of your soul.

When you sleep your guardian angel is right there with you, and prays over you while you sleep.

Your guardian angel has no physical needs. Your guardian angel doesn't sleep or need food or drink, doesn't get tired or bored, is constantly alert and focused on you.

As I have said, your guardian angel is with you from before you are conceived. Often when I am out and about I see a pregnant woman and will catch a glimpse of her baby inside of her as she passes by. Sometimes what I see is so tiny, but regardless of how tiny, I see the light of the guardian angel, right there with the baby. I get such joy from seeing this. I always say a quick prayer that that baby will grow healthy and strong and will listen and be aware that his or her guardian angel is there with it through life.

Your guardian angel knows when you are going to die, and will be there with you holding on to your soul, ready to take it from the human body when death comes. When I see someone who is terminally ill their body looks to me as if it's becoming a little translucent because the person's guardian angel has moved closer so as the guardian angel and the persons soul are almost touching.

At the moment you die you will see your guardian angel and all your fears will disappear. Remember, you are going home. Remember too that no one has ever, or will ever, die alone. Their guardian angel is always there with them.

When your guardian angel takes your soul to heaven, your guardian angel will stay there with you for a while. Then over time, when you have been in heaven a while, your guardian angel will start to come and go, so you will no longer be together all the time in the way you were on earth. Angel Michael has told me that when your soul and your guardian angel part in heaven, your guardian angel spends time praying for your family and loved ones who are still alive. Isn't it wonderful to know that the guardian angels of all our family members who have died, and those of all our ancestors are in heaven praying for us?

I find it strange when people ask me how to communicate with their guardian angel. That's because I have been talking to my guardian angel since I was a baby, and to me it's as natural as talking to my daughter. I talk to my guardian angel all the time. My best friend.

So for me it is a very natural process, but meeting people all around the world I am finding that it seems to be a big issue for many.

Just say hello to your guardian angel, acknowledge that is there – even if you still have your doubts that your angel exists. Start to talk to your angel as you would a friend. You can talk silently, or out aloud if that feels right, depending on the situation.

People sometimes ask me if I pray to my guardian angel. I pray only to God, not to any angel. But I do ask my angel to help. I remember learning the prayer to the guardian angel that so many children in Ireland and elsewhere learn. It's beautiful:

> Angel of God,
> My guardian dear,
> To whom God's love commits me here,
> Ever this day,
> Be at my side
> To light and guard,
> To rule and guide.

The day we learnt this was one of the best days ever in school. I was about five years old and it was the first time I had ever heard an adult – in this case my teacher – acknowledge that guardian angels exist, and can help us. I was jumping for joy inside as I watched the other little girls and boys learning this prayer and asking their guardian angels for help.

Although that's how it's generally known, I have never actually considered this *a prayer* to my guardian angel – just another way of asking for help. If you like it you can use it, but talking to your guardian angel as a friend works just as well.

Ask your guardian angel to help you to strengthen your belief that your angel is there and can really help you. You can ask your angel anything. Ask for a sign – but choose one that is very simple. Remember, your guardian angel cannot leave you for one second, so may need to involve other angels or people to deliver that sign. Choose a sign that's simple but that you will recognise: someone giving you a flower, finding a feather, a particular person phoning you or someone who has been unfriendly to you giving you a smile. You could also ask you guardian angel to touch you – it does touch you – and to keep touching you somewhere on your body until you recognise its touch.

Keep pestering your guardian angel until you get a sign. Watch out for it. Be alert. You might ask for a flower, for example, and you might assume this means a rose and so miss the child who picks a buttercup in the park and offers it to you as you walk past. We often miss the signs that our guardian angels give us – even the ones we have asked for!

My phone rang the other day. I rarely answer my phone unless God's angels tell me to do so. This day they did tell me to answer. A woman introduced herself and told me she had been at a book signing and met me after waiting many hours. She told me that on that day she had asked me to ask her guardian angel to give her a sign that her angel was there. But her guardian angel wasn't giving her any signs, she complained. I started to laugh and said,

'Is my not answering this phone a sign? How did you get the number anyway?'

She explained that after the signing she had rushed to catch a train and jumped into a taxi. She got chatting with the driver about having just met me. The taxi driver told her he knew me and had driven me on occasions. He mentioned that he had my telephone number, and offered it to her.

I started to laugh again. 'You got into a taxi with a driver who knew me personally, and had my telephone number? He was probably the *only* taxi driver in Dublin who had my number. Didn't you think getting into his taxi was a sign? Didn't you think his offering you my telephone number was a sign?' I asked. 'Your guardian angel has given you loads of signs. You just haven't recognized them.'

The woman at the end of the phone hemmed and hawed. She still felt her guardian angel had given her no sign. I repeated all the signs to her: getting into a taxi with a driver who knew me, him offering it her the number, and me answering the phone, which I seldom do. Despite my spelling it out I'm not sure that she did see the signs. I actually suspect she thought her guardian angel was going to appear to here: something that is so, so rare. I don't know why I see angels and others don't, but if you are going to wait for you guardian angel to appear to you in order to have a relationship with your angel, you may be waiting a very long time. And in the meantime you will be missing out on this incredible gift.

Your guardian angel speaks to you all the time through

your thoughts and feelings. Learn to recognize and listen to these feelings. When you start to get an instinct that you should do something, that's often your guardian angel communicating with you. Perhaps you are painting a room in your house, and you get the feeling you should move that tin of paint. But you don't, and later on you knock over the paint. That will have been you guardian angel trying to warn you. Try and learn to do what your guardian angel is telling you without hesitation. Recognize those times when you don't and give yourself a pinch and promise that next time you will listen. Often we will get an instinct to do something and will reject it. We shouldn't always think we know better.

Your guardian angel also speaks to you through other people. You could be standing at a bus stop and a stranger says something to you that reminds you of something you need to do, or could help with a decision you need to make.

You can't actually talk directly to another person's guardian angel. But just ask your guardian angel to ask that person's guardian angel for help and the message will be conveyed automatically. I am meeting more and more mothers who tell me that they are asking their guardian angel to ask their children's guardian angels to help them – and that this is giving them great peace of mind. When you ask your guardian angel to ask another's guardian angel to help, you are empowering that guardian angel to help that person. That person may not believe in angels, may not have a relationship with his or her guardian angel but through your asking, you give it's guardian angel more power to intervene – although not as much as if the person guarded has asked him or herself.

You know your guardian angels name whether you know it or not! You knew it as a child and have probably forgotten it, so it's now time to remember.

Guardian angels' real names are very long – sometimes more than a hundred letters. They also include letters that don't exist in any human language. I know that before you were conceived you and your guardian angel will have spent time shortening its name, and also taking out those letters we don't use in order to make it pronounceable.

Your guardian angel will do everything to prompt you and nudge that name back into your mind. The angels have told me to help you too and to tell you: 'It's the name that you love that is in your heart.'

For some people – particularly children – I only have to say that and they will automatically remember the name. Adults, though, are much slower and frequently reject the name that comes to them, saying to themselves it couldn't be that! They may think the name that has come to them is silly, or not good enough for their guardian angel. Children have no such worries and have told me of guardian angels with names such as Stinky, Puddleboots, Fishy and Ireland. Remember, in heaven, you and your guardian angel agreed on this name.

Take a little time out and ask your guardian angel to help you remembering this name. Don't be afraid to let your guardian angel get closer to you. Take that little bit of time and space for you and your guardian angel to get closer. You could be anywhere – at the kitchen sink, out walking, on the bus, cooking dinner or sitting relaxing. Just for a few moments think of nothing else but your guardian angel. Your angel is right there with you and it already knows that you are trying to remember the name.

Try and become like a child again. Suspend any cynicism or doubt. Don't allow all the conditioning that has happened to you throughout your life become a hindrance. Reach back to your childhood and see what memories or thoughts come up. Maybe the name will be suggested by a favorite song, a pet or a family member. Bringing things into your mind is one of the ways that your guardian angel communicates with you.

Or you could find yourself very attracted to a particular flower or tree or animal. This could be your guardian angel giving you a clue as to its name. Perhaps it has never dawned on you before that you have always been attracted by a particular name or word. Let it dawn on you now.

You may wish to know your guardian angel's name because it makes you feel closer, but for them it's all the same if you just call them 'Guardian Angel'. For them the important thing is to communicate with them. They also tell me that if you want a name, but can't remember it, you can choose a new one and put it into your heart and your guardian angel will accept that name forever, such is the unconditional love your guardian angel has for you.

Chapter One

My friends, companions and teachers

An angel stepped through the trees and the light surrounding this angel grew brighter and brighter. The angel had a human appearance. He was tall and elegant. He was radiant, his face gold in colour and his eyes gleaming with light like pearls with light shining through them would. His clothes were draped over him but as he moved not a fold changed. A golden sash was wrapped around his waist and around his neck hung a necklace made of round gold links with one large green sapphire at the V point. As with all angels his feet didn't touch the ground. He was surrounded by golden birds in flight and on the ground around him were all kinds of birds – crows and jackdaws and all kinds of little birds including robins, sparrows, finches and tits.

Suddenly, light exploded from the sapphire, with incredible rays of light and energy, shooting in all directions. At the same time the small birds suddenly lifted from the ground, flying towards the angel. Then they flew into the rays of the emerald-green sapphire and finally into the sapphire itself. There the birds disappeared.

The angel now walked towards me and opened up his wings and moved them gently. They were enormous and incredibly beautiful. I could see each individual perfect feather. They varied in size from enormous feathers to small ones. All the feathers were white but a tint of gold reflected from each feather. Angels don't always have wings and the wings don't always give the impression of feathers, but I knew this angel was different. Because this was the Bird Angel. I had last seen him shortly before my husband Joe had died. Joe had only been dead a few months and I was missing him terribly. I was so thrilled though to see the Bird Angel – and to know that he had come to comfort me as I was sitting on my own on a log in woodland near my home.

The Bird Angel now knelt down in front of me and wrapped his enormous wings around me. I could feel the touch of his wings around my body. As I snuggled into the Bird Angel I felt so peaceful. I whispered to him, 'Thank you for coming to comfort me.'

He whispered back, 'Every time you see a bird, I want you to think of me and smile.' I could feel the Bird Angel unwrapping his wings slowly from around me. Then he put his hand under my chin and raised my head up; his eyes were smiling at me, alight with such tenderness and love, his face glowed gold. There was no need for more words.

The Bird Angel stood up slowly, saying goodbye as he let go of my hand. He started to move back slowly and as he did so he grew enormous in size and, once again, his enormous wings opened up. The wings started moving, beating swiftly and smoothly with a rhythm that sounded like a drum. He started flying upwards gradually and then he stopped and hovered. The area of the radiant light that shone from him was full of birds. Then the Bird Angel and all the birds disappeared into the light.

* * *

I see angels all the time. I cannot remember any time I have not seen angels. From the very moment I opened my eyes after I was born they were there – even though at the time I did not know they were angels. When lying in my cot as a baby, I would see them around my mother. I would be playing, trying to catch them but I never could. I see them as clearly as I see my daughter sitting across the dinner table from me, and I talk with them as I talk with other people, but I can also communicate with them without words. To me there has never been a day when I haven't seen angels. For me it is the most natural thing to see them. Angels are my best friends and companions. The angels told me when I was quite young that I should keep what I was seeing a secret, so I didn't even tell my parents or brothers and sisters. I don't know why God has chosen me in this way. I don't think I'm better than anybody else. In fact, when I was a child the doctors told my parents that I was retarded. I'm certainly not perfect. I'm just an ordinary person, and an ordinary person with learning difficulties at that. But He did choose me and He sent His angels to teach me. When I see an angel I want to stop and stare. I feel like I am in the presence of a tremendous power.

When I was younger, the angels generally adopted a human form – to make it easier for me to accept them. Now that's no longer absolutely necessary. The angels I see do not always have wings, but when they do I am sometimes amazed by their form. Sometimes they are like flames of fire, and yet they have shape and solidity. Some angels' wings have feathers like the wings of the Bird Angel.

When angels have a human appearance – with or without wings – their eyes are one of their most fascinating features.

Angel eyes are not like human eyes. They are so much more alive, so full of life and light and love. It's as if they contain the essence of life itself. Their radiance fills me completely.

I have never seen an angel's feet actually touch the ground; when I see one walking towards me, I see what looks like a cushion of energy between the ground and their feet.

I may have been seeing angels since I was a baby, but I have never lost the sense of wonder that I feel when I see them – and I hope I never do. They give me such enormous joy and I feel so privileged. I get great pleasure out of seeing angels intervening and helping in our ordinary lives and then sometimes I am given a wonderful angelic spectacle that seems to have no purpose other than for my enjoyment.

Recently my daughter Megan took me to a Viennese waltz concert. As we entered the large concert hall I had to take my glasses off as the place was so bright with the abundance of angels there. As the orchestra came out and took their seats, rows upon rows of angels came out with them. The angels were a translucent pearl colour that seemed to reflect the light. They were tall and slender and moved with elegance, I could faintly see closed wings. Each angel carried a musical instrument and when the orchestra played the angels played too. Underneath the music of the orchestra I could faintly hear the harmony that the angels were playing. The conductor was surrounded by angels who seemed to be waving their own batons of light in the air, imitating him. When the dancers came out on to the stage angels streamed out with them. There were many more angels than dancers and they mimicked them gracefully. At times the angels helped to lift a dancer or helped the dancers to whirl around.

It was glorious to see. At the end the angels applauded themselves before streaming out into the hall mingling with the departing audience.

Sometimes the angels show me glorious things like this – simply for my pleasure.

Angels are my friends, my companions and my teachers – and there are some who are with me a lot, particularly Angel Michael, Angel Hosus and Angel Elijah.

Angel Michael is in fact Archangel Michael but I didn't know that when I first met him as a very young child. He is the angel who is around me most often – apart from my guardian angel whom I am not allowed to talk about. Angel Michael always gives me the appearance of a handsome man. His age changes but he always stays between twenty and forty.

Angel Hosus first appeared to me when I was at school; he gives the appearance of an old-fashioned schoolteacher with a gown and a funny-shaped hat. He is full of knowledge and wisdom and can be very serious at times but is great at cheering me up. He gives me confidence. He started all those years ago in school when I felt very stupid and that I didn't belong, and he helps me now when I'm writing and doing interviews.

Angel Elijah appears at crucial points in my personal life. Elijah always gives the same appearance, very tall and broad, and a rusty amber colour. He has a forceful strength and can become angry and always appears to be on the move. He gives me the power and strength to battle in my life. I chat about everyday things of life with Angels Michael and Hosus but not with Elijah.

Sometimes I am shown human souls and when this happens

I feel very privileged. The soul, which is located in the body, filling the shape of the entire body, moves forward. Most souls stay within the physical body during sleep but very occasionally they may move slightly outside the body. The soul as it is shown to me has a resemblance to the person. It's not identical though, it doesn't have all the same features and it's as if the person is physically perfect. When I am shown a soul it means something spiritual is happening, but the person may not be aware of it. When I am shown it doing so I am filled with an enormous joy and peace and a certainty that God is taking care of everything.

I also see spirits every day, the spirits of people who have died and gone to Heaven. People sometimes think that the presence of a spirit means something is wrong. This is not generally the case. Often a spirit comes back to give a loved one support. Sometimes they come back just for the joy of being in this world again for a little while. When I was a young child I used to play with the spirit of my brother Christopher, who died before I was born. Christopher helped me to learn the difference between spirits and angels.

Chapter Two

Elijah's prophecy comes true

When I was ten years of age I met Angel Elijah for the first time. I was standing by a river; I was fishing with my da and had wandered off. Angel Elijah walked across the water to where I was standing. I had never seen an angel walking on water and it fascinated me. He showed me a vision – it was as if he had pulled back a curtain. He showed me a handsome young man walking along a tree-lined street. As I watched, Angel Elijah told me that I would fall in love with this young man, whose name was Joe, that we would marry and have children, but that Joe would fall ill and that we would not grow old together.

I give out to the Angel Elijah for telling me this at the time. I was only ten and it seemed very unfair to be told that we wouldn't get old together. It happened just as Angel Elijah had said. Joe applied for a job in my father's petrol station – where I worked – and we fell in love, bought the little cottage in Maynooth and got married. Even before we were married, Joe's health started to deteriorate in little ways. I used to alternate between begging God and the angels to make him better and giving out to them for letting this happen.

After we were married he had one health problem after another. Over the years he became a diabetic and then the diabetes affected his heart, leading to heart surgery. For the last ten years of his life he was bed-bound most of the time. Towards the end he suffered a lot of strokes. Despite Joe's illnesses we were very happy together and had four children: Christopher, Owen, Ruth and our youngest, Megan. Joe died at home on the morning of 26 March 2000, having kept his promise to stay alive for Ruth's and my birthday the day before. He was only 47. Our youngest child was only four.

In the last weeks of Joe's life, I would watch angels wrapping a spiritual blanket around him as he was sitting in his chair. The blanket was bright and looked like cotton wool. They were fixing it around him. The angels were so loving and so gentle with him. I could see that they were trying to help his body to be less sore, to ease his pain. Every so often Joe would struggle to get out of the chair, insisting that he could do it on his own, and that I didn't need to help. I would watch the angels helping him sit up, walking with him, helping him to keep his balance as he walked into the bedroom or bathroom, ensuring he didn't fall. Sometimes it looked so funny I would have to smile. I would always get up and follow Joe, despite the help the angels were giving him. Sometimes the angels would turn around and tell me it was OK, they could do it! On one particular occasion Joe's guardian angel told me it was very important for Joe to keep his dignity.

The night before Joe died I woke up many times in bed and turned to Joe, who was sleeping beside me, to check he was OK. I knew the angels were going to take Joe's soul very shortly. Joe's beautiful guardian angel, who had loved and cared for Joe so tenderly throughout his life, and particularly in recent years, was no longer behind him in the usual way. His guardian angel glowing incredibly bright and radiant had moved through Joe's body and was holding his soul. The first time I had woken up Joe's guardian angel had told me I must not touch Joe in case I disturbed him. Each time I woke up I would just look at Joe with tears in my eyes and then his guardian angel would tell me to go back to sleep and I would fall asleep instantly. An hour or so later I would wake again. I was last woken about seven that morning by the Angel Michael. Joe was no longer breathing. His soul, looking so beautiful and perfect and accompanied by his guardian angel, was already moving away towards a beautiful light, towards a stairway to Heaven. I wanted to call out, 'Joe, come back to me. I need you!'

I wanted so desperately to ask God to allow Joe to stay, but knew I couldn't, that the answer would be no. Archangel Michael touched my lips and I couldn't speak. The room was now crowded with angels. My special angels – my friends and teachers – were there, but this was no consolation. The tears were running down my cheeks. I felt completely numb as I held Joe's body in my arms. I felt the Angel Michael put a spiritual blanket around me and he whispered in my ear, telling me to call the children, and an ambulance.

Even though you may know a loved one is going to die, even if they have been very ill, it doesn't make it any easier. I was devastated, torn apart and seeing the pain and hurt in my children made it worse. They were trying to comfort me and I was trying to comfort them. Being surrounded by angels didn't make any difference.

When the ambulance men arrived, they tried in vain to revive Joe. I stood there watching, in shock and trembling.

I could see the ambulance men were trying desperately to revive Joe. They kept saying, 'It's not working.' Finally in desperation they lifted him up on a blanket and rushed him into the ambulance to take him to the hospital. Christopher and I followed the ambulance in a taxi. Owen stayed at home with Megan, who was still sleeping and didn't yet know what had happened to her father.

At the hospital Christopher and I were put into a little room. At times, I got a glimpse of Christopher's guardian angel wrapped around him, comforting him. Angel Michael held my hand all the time. Time passed but I have no idea how long. Then the door opened and a woman doctor came in and told us what I already knew. Joe was dead. She said she was very sorry. There was nothing they could do.

I have no memory of getting home. We all sat, devastated, round the kitchen table, drinking tea but deriving no comfort from it. Megan sat on my knee distraught repeatedly sobbing, 'I want to see my daddy.' Megan had been fast asleep when her dad died that morning. She hadn't even woken with all the commotion of the ambulance men. I knew her guardian angel hadn't allowed her to wake. She was only four and couldn't understand what happened, she couldn't understand that her daddy had gone to Heaven.

I remember at one stage that day wondering where Megan was and going looking for her and finding her in the bedroom under the blankets of her dad's bed, with her guardian angel bent over her, comforting her and soothing her. Another time that day she turned on me, furious at me for not having woken her that morning.

People kept coming to the house, offering their sympathies. The older children and I discussed whether we would bring Joe's body home before the funeral or allow Joe to be laid out in the funeral home in Maynooth. Because of Megan we decided the funeral home would be the best and Christopher rang the undertaker and arranged everything. As I walked into the funeral home I saw Joe's open coffin in the middle of the room. There were angels standing around the coffin. I felt relieved and spoke to the angels without words, thanking them for not leaving Joe alone. I know it was only Joe's human body in the coffin, but I was still grateful to these angels for this little comfort.

I was devastated even though I knew Joe's soul was still alive and had gone to Heaven escorted by his guardian angel. I knew he was with his family, my dad, and friends that had gone before him. I know it is only our human body that dies. Because we have a soul we live on. Despite knowing and believing all this I was still numb with grief.

Owen lifted Megan up and she looked into the coffin at Joe. As she did, the light of Megan's guardian angel opened up for a moment and said to me without words, 'Megan doesn't quite understand that her daddy is gone to Heaven.' Megan walked around the room as the rest of us stood there in silence looking at Joe. Ruth commented that he looked so peaceful.

Back home, the boys and Ruth asked Megan whether she would like to put a gift into her dad's coffin before it was taken to the church the next day. She went off to her bedroom and drew a picture for her dad.

Late the next afternoon we went to the funeral home. This was the last time any of us were going to see Joe's body before the coffin was closed. When we arrived the funeral undertaker was already there. The room was full of angels and the light behind each of my children opened up showing their guardian angel. But that was little comfort. I felt so numb, and I knew my children did too. We were all trying to be strong for each other, and especially for Megan. Ruth and I wrapped Joe's rosary beads around his hands. Megan stood on her toes and held on to the coffin with one hand so that she could look in at her dad's body. She carefully put the picture she had drawn and her favourite yellow teddy in beside him. We all had our own mementoes to put into the coffin with him: Christopher, a pack of cigarettes and a deck of playing cards – they had always loved playing cards together; Owen, his own Gaelic football jersey and his red Liverpool scarf; and Ruth, a ring and a letter. Watching my children saying their last goodbyes to their father and putting their precious and emotional gifts into the coffin beside him I thought my heart would break. They looked so pale and their eyes so full of tears. I felt so helpless, unable to comfort them.

The night before, in bed, I had written a letter to Joe. I had sobbed gently, so no one would hear me as I wrote. Archangel Michael was sitting on the bed beside me but I was ignoring him. Then he called my name and I looked up at him, unable to say a word. Michael touched my hand and said, 'I will bring that letter to Joe in Heaven.'

Now I put my letter into the coffin with Joe and, as I did, Angel Michael whispered in my ear, 'Lorna, I will make sure that Joe receives everything that has been put into the coffin in Heaven.'

It was very hard for me and the children knowing that once the coffin was closed we would never see Joe's physical body again. It was so very hard for us – and I know it is for everyone who has lost a loved one. Just try and remember – as I tried to remember – that your loved one is not dead, that because they have a soul we live forever. We will all meet our loved ones when it is our time to die and leave this human body behind.

Chapter Three

A wailing cry

After Joe's death, life was very stressful for me. I was trying to cope but it was very difficult, even with all the support from God and the angels. The silence in the house would have been too much to bear without the angels to talk to. Almost every time I was alone in the house or Megan was asleep in bed the angels would visit. There were times when I would tell them to go away and leave me alone, that I didn't want their company. They never went far though and now and then I would catch a glimpse of an angel.

Megan missed Joe terribly and cried a lot. Sometimes she would come over to me for a hug, saying she was feeling very sad. One day, when Megan was playing with her toys and I was busy pressing clothes she started to cry softly. I stopped what I was doing and looked up – the room filled with angels and the light of her guardian angel opened up. She looked at me and we communicated without words. We talked of my little daughter's pain and sorrow. I rushed over to console Megan and as I embraced my child she started wailing. It was a cry from the very depths of her being. It was unlike anything I had ever heard before – a piercing, shrieking sound with one note holding the same high pitch for a very long time. It was very frightening to hear. At one moment the glass in the windows started to vibrate, and I was afraid they were all going to shatter. I cried out to the angels to help. Everything else went quiet suddenly – except for Megan's wailing. Can you imagine silence in its infinity and yet within that silence hearing only one sound – the very loud wailing of a young child? The depth of her sorrow was almost too much for such a little one to bear. As the angels embraced us we were surrounded by bright white lights. I could soon feel the warmth and love of angels start to soothe her. As she quietened the silence became unbelievable. The light of the angels started to fade and the room slowly came back to normal. As I sat there on the floor holding Megan, she fell asleep in my arms.

After a little while I picked her up, put her on the couch and covered her gently with blankets. I quietly went out of the room and closed the door. I called my angels. Michael walked into the room first followed by Hosus, then Elijah and many more. I cried out, 'What just happened?'

'Sit down, Lorna,' Michael said. 'You must remember Megan had her dad beside her twenty-four hours a day. For her whole lifetime he was always there. She is missing him desperately.'

'Is she going to cry in that way again?' I asked in desperation as I sat down at the table.

Angel Hosus, standing at the window, said, 'Yes she is.' He replied, 'We can't stop it!'

'Why not?' I asked, as I got up from the table.

Hosus came over and stood in front of me. 'Lorna. This is a part of Megan's life, part of what she needs to go through for her development.'

I looked at Hosus and the other angels there. 'I do understand. It's just so hard to see her pain. I've watched Megan push the bedroom door open and seen all her energy drop as she looks in and sees her dad is not there, and seen her drawing a picture and running into the front room to show it to him, thinking he will be sitting in the chair in front of the fire as he used to be.'

I felt terribly sad. 'I guess all I can do is give her lots of love,' I continued. 'I know the guardian angels of Christopher, Owen and Ruth are working hard, that they are in communication with their friends' guardian angels. They are getting great support from their friends. Will you thank their guardian angels for me?'

'Of course we will,' Angel Michael said, as he reached out and took my hands. 'Their friends are listening to their angels.' The angels disappeared.

Megan started school in Maynooth that September. It was the same junior school her sister Ruth had gone to, so Ruth had told her all about the school and the teachers. I was delighted to see her going off to school but I was worried about how she would cope. Sometimes she would come home from school very sad and upset. Her little friends would be talking about things they had done with their dad and mum at the weekend. Then they would ask Megan about where she went at the weekend with her dad and mum. She found it hard to tell her friends that her dad had died and gone to Heaven. Then of course there were days like Father's Day when they would all make cards for their fathers in class. I knew all this was getting too much for her and I prayed to God and the angels for help.

The angels tried to cheer me up too. One cold winter's morning I was walking back from having taken Megan to school. I enjoyed walking back by the canal in Maynooth as it was more peaceful than the road. I've always liked that stretch of the canal, there is always something to see: lots of ducks, and a pair of swans nest on an island in the middle of the man-made harbour there. Normally there's only that one pair of swans there, except for the year or so after they hatch their young. Some years no cygnets survived. As I walked that day there was only the pair of swans around. I passed a few people at the beginning of my walk home but then, as I walked along the little path, I seemed to have the place to myself. As I turned the corner at the edge of the harbour I saw there were lots of swans – perhaps twenty. I was surprised, but didn't think too much about it. Then an angel told me to stop.

The canal water seemed to change and become like glass. 'What is happening?' I said to the angels around me. 'Look at all the light around the swans, they are glowing and getting whiter and whiter.' One of the swans glided gracefully over in my direction. Then I realised that the others were following it, they were swimming one after another in a curved row. I looked again and it was as if they were forming the letter S. I watched with fascination. As the leader reached the bank, it waddled up on the grass and came towards me. One by one the other swans followed. I wondered what was going on. I stepped back and stood in the middle of the path. They surrounded me. Then some of them made a circle around me. They were so close to me that they were nearly touching me. Then around this circle other swans made another circle. The remaining two swans stood outside the circles – one behind and one in front of me – as if they were on guard. The swans in the circles stretched their bodies and necks up to the sky, which made them taller than I was. They stretched out their powerful wings and gently fluttered them. They made a beautiful melodious sound and moved their wings in time to their song. It was a high-pitched but mellow sound. It was hypnotic and soothing. I was enchanted. Despite their size and the power that I knew swans had, I wasn't in the least bit afraid. I stayed very still; they were so close to me that I was afraid that if I moved even the slightest little bit I would hit off one of them and make it fall and get hurt.

I have no idea how long we stood there but then the swan standing guard in front turned and walked to the bank and into the water and the outer circle left next in graceful formation like actors leaving a stage. The swans in the circle nearest me were the last to go, and it was fascinating to see how they lowered their bodies gracefully without touching me, stepped back and then went to the water. Eventually all the swans were back in the water, gliding gracefully on the canal.

Everything was back to normal. I thanked the angels. It was a sight I think of every time I walk that stretch of the canal. The angels were showing me just how strong the connection is between God's other creatures and man and were reminding me yet again of the wonder of this world.

One morning, when Megan was at school, I went for a walk out towards a wonderful little church called the Lady Chapel. Nowadays you can't go for a walk along those roads because there is too much traffic, but they were quieter then – I think that morning only one car passed. It was a frosty morning but not raining and every now and then the sun would peep out from behind the clouds. I was enjoying the fresh air and as I walked I prayed and asked God for miracles. There was a lot on my mind – particularly Megan of course but also other people who had come to see me over the weeks before.

I had just turned left on to a quieter road when I heard my name being called, and a voice telling me to hurry up. I looked up the road and I could see a beautiful angel. I recognised this angel straightaway even though she was a long way up the road. It was Angel Elisha. She was standing in the middle of the road, and looked so beautiful – the light of the sun seemed to be shining on her. I ran towards her. 'Where have you been, Angel Elisha?' I asked as I reached her. She didn't answer me but she walked for a short distance beside me. We stopped at the gateway of a field. The light of the sun was shining on us both and I no longer felt the chill. I just stood there looking at her as she spoke. She hadn't changed. The first time she had appeared to me was when she stepped from the mirror in the toilets in the garage in Rathmines where I worked. I find it very hard to describe her. She had a human appearance, but the impression she gave was of beautiful feathers of light.

Angel Elisha now raised her right hand and lifted my chin, saying, 'Lorna, do you remember the Brennan family who came to visit you when Joe was alive?' I nodded. 'Do you remember Granny Brennan's offer to you?' I nodded again. 'God wants you to say yes to Granny Brennan.'

I was shocked. The Brennan family had come to visit me some years before, looking for help. Joe was very ill at the time. Very unusually the angels told me to introduce Joe to the family when they were there in the house. The angels rarely allowed me to involve Joe. Joe was reluctant to meet the Brennans as he was very sick at the time and had difficulties walking, but I persuaded him. We all sat at the kitchen table, Maura Brennan, her mother – whom I always called Granny Brennan – Maura's husband and four of their children. I soon learnt there were more children at home. The Brennan family had prepared and brought a picnic so we sat at the table eating and chatting. Before they left that evening they invited Joe and myself and our three children (Megan wasn't even born at this time) to go and have dinner with them a few Sundays later.

After they had left that day Hosus told me, 'You are going to become good friends with this family. They are going to play a very important role in your own future, Lorna. You will become great friends and your friendship is very important to both families.' Hosus was right – this was the beginning of a long friendship, one of my few friendships, as the angels have always kept me from making friends. I don't really understand why.

Elisha had asked me whether I remembered Granny Brennan's offer – of course I remembered the offer. That first Sunday years ago we had gone to have dinner with the Brennans and after dinner Granny Brennan had taken me to see an old farmhouse she owned up the road. She offered me the house as a gift. She suggested we might like to move and live there at some stage in the future. There was an old man living in it, but he wasn't there that day. Granny Brennan told us she couldn't give us the house while the man was there, but that when he moved on she would be happy to give it to us.

'Wouldn't it be lovely if you lived down here in Johnstown

– just up the road from us!' she said. 'I would love to be able to do this for you and Joe, Lorna. That's a promise and I never break my promises!' I fell in love with this old farmhouse! It reminded me of the old house I had lived in as a child in Old Kilmainham. The roof had fallen in but I still had my fond memories of it. Maybe I got my love of old houses from that first home of mine? Joe commented on how peaceful it was.

Now Angel Elisha was suggesting that I should take up Granny Brennan's offer of the old farmhouse and that Megan and I should go and live there. I looked at her a bit upset and said, 'Elisha, I am a little shocked; there are loads of things to think about. What about my three older children? I know they are young adults but I can't sell the house, and leave them homeless. I haven't even seen the old farmhouse in Johnstown for a bit. What sort of condition is it in?'

Elisha said, 'The house looks the same on the outside and it's a beautiful house. But I'm afraid the inside is in a bad condition. It's not liveable in and it will need new plumbing and wiring – everything will have to be replaced. There will be an awful lot of work.' Elisha smiled at me encouragingly. 'You have to ring Granny Brennan and tell her you will take the farmhouse. You won't move for a year or so – a lot will happen in the meantime.'

I laughed when Angel Elisha said this, and she laughed with me. Her laughter sounded like the sound of water flowing gently over pebbles. Elisha and I walked up the road talking about other things for a little while, and then she disappeared. But I didn't call the Brennans! The following Saturday morning Megan was holding my hand as we walked through the town of Maynooth on our way to the tea-rooms to have cream doughnuts. Suddenly I saw white angels walking towards us. White angels are everywhere in abundance. Wherever there are people there are hundreds of them. They are there and available to help us at all times in all ways. Unlike teacher angels, who are experts in a particular subject – such as medicine or passing exams, you name a skill or an ability and there is a teacher angel for it – white angels are not specialists but they are of enormous assistance in many ways. They are very bright in appearance, which is why I call them white angels. They vary in size, sometimes they seem extremely tall and other times they are the same size as the people they are around. The smallest I have ever seen have been the same size as the children they were with.

The white angels startled me because there were so many. The street was packed with thousands of them, and as I looked around me they seemed to be coming from everywhere. Things seemed to almost stand still. A light-coloured car was barely moving. There was a man in the driving seat but he looked frozen stiff. There were a man and woman on the far side of the street. It looked as if they were striding forward, one foot in mid-air, but not moving at all. I was standing with Megan. The light of Megan's guardian angel opened up, glowing so brightly that I was unable to see her. I knew straight away what was going to happen.

Megan started to sob uncontrollably. I knelt down beside Megan, consoling her with all the loving words I could think of, hugging her and telling her not to cry. Megan's wailing cry seemed to be soft for a second but then became louder and louder until it became ear piercing. I felt it could be heard miles away. I knew all my love was not going to work.

It was not going to stop this. I called God and the angels, and from the depths of my heart and soul begged, 'Please help her!'

The white angels surrounding us started to sing. It was a very high-pitched, sweet and mellow sound, almost hypnotic. Their singing soothed Megan and her wailing cry became a little softer and then slowly started to die away. Hugging her tightly with relief, I thanked God and the angels. The silence surrounding Megan's wailing was broken. Then I heard a screech of brakes, a car door slamming and a man shouting, 'Is she OK?'

I heard the footsteps of the man and woman I'd seen earlier, they were running towards us from the far side of the road.

'Is she OK?' the man from the car asked again. 'Can I help in any way?'

Then everything became still again. Those three good people became still as if in a trance. I watched the white angels touch them. It only lasted a few seconds and then everything came back to normal and I watched the man and woman cross the road. The angels with them turned around and smiled at me. It seemed the angels had made them forget what they had heard. I thanked God and the angels that there were so few people around that morning. The town looked quite deserted. Megan and I walked on to the tea-rooms. Angel Hosus was standing at the door and he touched Megan's head as we went through the door.

What happened that day made up my mind about Johnstown. I knew I had to take Megan away from Maynooth – the memories there were all too much for her. She needed a new beginning.

A few evenings later Granny Brennan called, saying that

the old farmhouse in Johnstown was now empty, the old man had died, and it was mine if I wanted it. I told her I did, and thanked her very much. She was delighted at my decision and so was I, even if I was nervous about all that was involved. I explained I needed a little time. We talked for a while and then said goodbye.

Chapter Four

The kindness of angels

I have always kept my private life separate from the work that God and the angels ask me to do. People who came to see me around the time Joe died were not aware of my loss. One evening, a few weeks after Joe had died, I was alone in the house except for Megan who was asleep, when there was a knock on the door. A man stood on the doorstep. I invited him into the hall and, as I did so, an angel whispered in my ear, telling me I was to say yes to what he would ask. I recognised the angel's voice – it was Hosus. The man told me that he had been driving past Maynooth on his way back to Dublin when he thought of me and that he wanted to thank me for the help I had given to him and his family. He said I had been a great help. He also asked if I could see a friend of his who was very stressed, and, if possible, he wanted me to see him over the next few days.

I was hesitant, but Angel Hosus had told me to say yes, so I did. We arranged that he would call me the following day to arrange a time. He thanked me and said goodbye.

As he walked towards the gates two angels appeared, one on his left and the other on his right. They spoke to me without words, telling me that this man had great faith in God and the angels and that he was a good listener. As he opened his car door he turned to me and waved. But I felt very heavy-hearted. When I turned back inside and opened the kitchen door, sitting at the table was Angel Hosus. I collapsed onto a chair beside him with tears running down my face, saying, 'I don't know if I can do this. Isn't it too soon for me to see people?'

Hosus reached out and took my hand and filled me with peace and courage, saying, 'Lorna, this is your life – to do God's work. You have God's legions of angels helping you and because of that you can do it.' Hosus reached up and wiped my tears away, and then disappeared.

The next day, the man rang and I saw his friend the following evening.

The weather improved and it was getting warmer, so one day I decided to take Megan to Dublin Zoo. We drove to the Phoenix Park and eventually found a parking spot about ten minutes' walk from the zoo. Megan didn't mind the walk at all, she was so excited, and I was so pleased to be walking through the park, watching the trees and birds and the children playing. I was also seeing angels playing with the children, unknown to them. As we approached the zoo there were a few stalls with women selling sweets and fruit. Just behind them there was a grassy glen with lots of children playing in it. I stopped because I thought I saw someone I knew standing beside one of the trees. Megan was laughing at the children rolling down the hill. She wanted to go and play with them. As I stood there looking down into the glen I realised that the familiar person wasn't a person but was an angel. It had its light dimmed so low and such a strong human appearance that it could have passed for a human being. It looked familiar but I couldn't really work it out. I kept saying to myself, 'No, it can't be.'

The angel with its very human appearance stepped away from the tree and walked over and sat on a bench. A few young children ran over to him and after a few minutes I watched him get up and go over to play ball with them. Other children and a woman and a man joined in. Children are very open to seeing angels, but it seemed that both adults and children were seeing this angel. They didn't realise it was an angel of course. They were having great fun. I really enjoyed watching it, as I had never seen an angel kicking a football before.

I still didn't know who the angel was but his familiarity was nagging away at me. Then the angel turned to me and waved and in that instant I recognised the Angel Michael. I smiled and waved back. He finished playing football and walked in the direction of the trees and disappeared.

The angels did so much to console me and cheer me up over that period and Megan and I had a great visit to the zoo.

At times, I was amazed how people managed to find me. It was all word of mouth. I didn't give out the phone number much, but somehow people managed to get it or they just arrived at the door. I might be hanging washing out on the line or be ready to leave for the shops. Sometimes they would want to talk then. Other times they'd ask would it be possible for them to come another day or to bring someone with them – maybe a sick member of their family or a friend with some kind of problem.

One afternoon there was a knock on the door. I opened

it to see three women standing outside. They were all dressed in skirts and cardigans of navy and white. They had no veils, but I knew instantly they were Catholic nuns. One was very elderly and had a walking stick and there was a young nun standing beside her smiling. On her other side was a nun of about fifty. There were lots of angels around them. I spoke to them without words, asking, 'What are you doing leading these women here? You know I'm still finding it really hard to see people.'

An angel standing beside the young nun looked at me pleadingly, joining its hands as if in prayer, saying, 'Lorna, please, they need to talk to you.'

I thawed. 'How could I say no, when you angels ask so lovingly on their behalf.'

'We apologise for intruding,' the nun who was about fifty said. 'I hope you don't mind us coming to see you, but we have heard so much about you, and Sister Catherine', she smiled at her elderly colleague, 'has wanted to see you for such a long time.' I smiled at them, opening the door wide.

'No problem. I'm delighted to see you all.' The youngest nun helped Sister Catherine up the steps. We went into the kitchen and the youngest nun introduced herself as Ann. The third was Mary. I asked them whether they would like to see me together, and straight away Sister Mary said, 'Sister Catherine would definitely like to see you on her own and we would prefer that also.' I suggested that Sister Catherine stay with me in the kitchen and showed Mary and Ann into the front room.

As soon as I came back into the kitchen, the light of Sister Catherine's guardian angel opened up. He was male and very beautiful, dressed in what looked like delicate, silver armour.

He told me to pull my chair over next to her, which I did. Sister Catherine reached out and took hold of my hands and started to cry. Her guardian angel glowed even more strongly. He had such compassion and love for her. A light slowly descended around us. Her guardian angel smiled at me. I knew he had asked the healing angels to come and help us.

There were four healing angels surrounding us. They were very tall and slender, dwarfing Sister Catherine and myself sitting there at the kitchen table. They were very, very bright and their brightness made them appear more translucent. They were an opalescent colour. White is the nearest colour I can think of but it is inadequate for the beauty of what I was seeing.

I see healing angels regularly – most weeks probably. I have never seen their wings clearly, though, and I didn't this time, but I know they have wings. Their appearance is such that they look almost identical to each other, but I can see subtle differences in their faces, like the shape of the face or their expressions. They almost always come in groups and always seem to work in circles, surrounding the person in need of healing. Healing angels are, of course, a gift from God and your guardian angel can allow them in. If your guardian angel says no to any angel (or to any spirit – a soul who has gone to Heaven), then it has no access. As I have said many times, your guardian angel is the gatekeeper of your soul. God pours His grace down through healing angels on to us. Healing angels can help us with all forms of healing. Physically they can help a body to resist a virus or heal our bodies more quickly; sometimes they heal us emotionally – for example, helping a depressed person to see more light in their life. And spiritually they can help us, for example by lessening our spiritual blindness, helping us to open our eyes more to God and His angels' existence and to the wonders of life around us.

Now the four healing angels stood very close to Sister Catherine and myself. I could feel great love and lightness. It felt as if God's grace was being poured into both of us. In between her tears she told me of her fears of dying, and that she knew her time was near. She told me she was ashamed of her fear, that as a nun she felt that she shouldn't have any fears, that Jesus would be angry with her for having this fear, for lacking faith.

Her guardian angel told me to hug her. 'Let her feel your love. It's a comfort she doesn't get often.' I hugged her. She was so frail, but she held on to me tightly. I whispered in her ear that there was no need for any fear, that God would take her gently. I assured her that there was no reason to be afraid of dying.

'When your soul has left your body, you won't want to come back. Why would you want to go back into a crock of an old broken-down body?' I said to lighten the atmosphere. We both laughed.

After a few minutes, Sister Catherine's grip loosened, and I moved back upright into my chair, still holding her hand. She said she had been lonely all her life – even with all the nuns around her. I told her about her guardian angel. She asked me to pray with her. As we prayed the healing angels touched her closed eyes. Then I was told to close my eyes as well and as we prayed I felt her fear leave her and a deep peace come over her.

I must have spent about an hour on my own with Sister Catherine. As we walked to the front room she thanked me.

'I'm not afraid of dying any more. I knew Jesus was telling me to come and see you. I had to come and now I know why.'

Leaving Sister Catherine with Sister Mary, I talked with Ann on her own in the kitchen. She explained that she was a novice, that she loved being a nun and was due to take her final vows the next year, but that every so often she had doubts about whether this was what God wanted her to do. I could see there were two teacher angels with her. One was to help her learn and the other to teach her how to pray. I smiled at her and asked, 'What do you feel in your heart?'

She answered quickly, 'God's love.'

I smiled at her. 'You have your answer, Sister Ann.' We prayed together and then I blessed her. She went to get Sister Mary with a big smile on her face. She was happy.

As Sister Mary and I talked the light of her guardian angel opened up for a brief moment, giving a female appearance of great strength of character. I can't remember what we talked about, but she asked me could I pray with her and give her a blessing. And of course I did.

I walked out to the car with the three of them, Sister Catherine holding on to my hand tightly and saying repeatedly, 'Thank you Lorna, thank God for me.' We said our goodbyes and I waved as they drove off. I walked back into the kitchen. Angel Michael was standing near the window. I was delighted to see him. He took my hand saying, 'You did well.' He filled me with strength and a moment later he disappeared.

I got a phone call asking would I see a young man who had been in a car accident. On the agreed morning I heard a car pull up at the gate and straight away I went and opened the door. I watched as a young man in his early twenties was pushed in a wheelchair up to the door by two people whom I presumed were his parents. We introduced ourselves and then started trying to manoeuvre the wheelchair up the steps into the cottage.

We sat around the kitchen table. I looked at the young man, whose name was Conor; the light of the energy around him was so dim. He couldn't speak and just sat there motionless, slouched in the wheelchair. His mother cried as his parents described Conor's state. He was severely brain-damaged and his legs were paralysed. He didn't seem to have much movement elsewhere. He didn't seem to understand or hear anything. There was no response and there was no way of communicating with him. The doctors had said there was no hope for him at all, that he would remain in a vegetable-like state for the rest of his life.

I looked at their son. There were healing angels around him but yet no light of energy around his body. The light of his guardian angel opened up, showing a great masculine strength and he said to me forcefully, 'He is not a vegetable, Lorna! Talk to him, he will hear you. He needs a reason to live. He needs courage to fight to get up out of that wheel-chair, to walk and live his life.'

Then the light of his guardian angel closed. I stood up and walked over to Conor and, praying silently, touched his legs, his hands, his arms and his chest. As I felt his heart-beat I put my hand on his head and looked into his eyes. 'I know you can hear me,' I said. 'I know you will get well, but you have to fight for it. You have to struggle to walk and talk. You have to do it. You must want to get better. I am being shown that you can get well, have a job, marry and have children, but you mustn't give up on yourself. You must fight to get better. I will pray to God every day for you – I won't give up on you. No matter what the doctors or anyone else says, you can do it. You can get your life back. But you have to fight for it.'

I stopped talking for a little while, praying over him. Six healing angels surrounded him. Their arms were outstretched, touching every part of his body. 'I know you can hear me,' I said to him. 'I know you have heard what I have said even if you can't show it. You can do it, but you have to fight.'

His parents were praying beside me with tears falling down their faces. They had believed what the doctors had said and they were fearful of getting their hopes up. They desperately wanted to believe there was a possibility that their son could get well. I saw them out to the car, still praying that Conor would get well.

Some time later – it could have been months, perhaps a year – his parents rang saying they wanted to bring Conor to see me again. He was a completely different person. He was still in the wheelchair, but he could move his arms and his head. And he could talk in a faltering voice, a little hard to understand perhaps, but I could understand him clearly. He said, 'Lorna, I heard you that day. I was crying out inside of me. You were the only one who seemed able to see I wasn't a vegetable. You gave me hope.'

Speaking was an effort for him, so he took a little break. I smiled at him as he continued. 'You gave me belief and courage to force my body to respond. Thank you. I know I will get better. Will you keep praying for me?' I prayed over him again, as healing angels descended. I blessed him.

I have seen Conor a couple of times since then – each time he had improved. The last time I saw him was about a year ago on Dublin's Grafton Street. He was walking down the street, laughing, hand in hand with a girl. He seemed to be walking perfectly. There was no sign of the horrific accident he had had. He didn't see me. His guardian angel opened up and gave me a big smile. I don't know if I'm ever going to see this young man again. I still pray and ask for healing for him and for everything he needs in his life.

Chapter Five

I decide to move

It was less than a year after Joe's death. Christopher and Owen had both finished college and were working near our home in Maynooth. Ruth was in her last year in school and was due to do her final exam the following June. There was a lot going on in their lives and for the while they were all living at home with me.

As I came in from hanging up washing on the clothes line one day, Angel Hosus appeared by the phone in the kitchen. I was glad to see him.

'Lorna, the phone will ring in a few minutes,' he said. 'It will be Granny Brennan. Tell her you would love to go down next Sunday to visit.' No sooner had Hosus said this than the phone rang. Of course it was Granny Brennan. We talked for a few minutes and then hung up. Hosus was still there, this time sitting at the kitchen table. I sat down beside him. 'Hosus, the whole family have been invited to Johnstown for dinner, and to go and have a look at the old farmhouse.'

'Lorna, when the boys and Ruth come home from work this evening, talk with them about your plans to move down to Johnstown,' Hosus said. 'Insist that they go down with you so they can visit the farmhouse and see what condition it's in. Everything will work out, no matter how difficult and impossible it may seem at times.' Then Hosus disappeared.

Most days the older children would arrive home at different times but that particular night they all arrived in the door one after the other. We sat down around the table to eat the stew I had made. Megan had already had her dinner and was in the front room watching cartoons.

As they sat around the table, the light of my three children's guardian angels opened up. For a moment it was as if time stood still – the whole kitchen seemed to glow with their light. Their guardian angels were, unknown to my children, giving me support, acknowledging me. As the mother of these three young adults, I was deeply touched that their guardian angels were supporting me in every way possible. I was moved by their compassion, love and beauty. Angels really are such fabulous creatures. Then the light of the guardian angels closed behind my children and I could feel my hair being ruffled, so I knew then that my own guardian angel was giving me support as well.

I told them about my concern about Megan, that it was too much for her being here in this house with so many memories, that it would be better for her if I took up Granny Brennan's offer of the farmhouse, and we moved down to Johnstown as soon as Ruth had left school in June.

They stopped eating in shock! After they got over their shock, though, they were clear that I must do whatever was right for Megan, even if they were sad at the idea of not being able to see her – and me – every day.

'Mum, that farmhouse was in a terrible condition when Dad was still alive,' Christopher said. 'It will be in even worse condition now.'

'I know it won't be easy, and it will take a lot of work,' I said. 'I can't leave you children homeless. So maybe you two boys could consider getting a mortgage, and buying this house from me? That way I would have some money to do up the old farmhouse.'

They all seemed to speak at once. 'Mum, can we think about this?' 'Can we talk more about it before you make the decision?'

I calmed them, saying, 'Of course we can talk more. You must remember I love you all and I wouldn't leave you homeless, but I do think Megan and I need to leave Maynooth.'

I couldn't tell my children that Angel Elisha had told me that God said I must move down to Johnstown. I would have loved to have been able to tell them. To help them to understand that I wasn't leaving them – but I wasn't allowed to share my secret with them.

I continued, 'I want you all to come down to Johnstown with Megan and me to see the old farmhouse this weekend. That way we will be able to see what condition it is in.' Ruth was very upset, crying, 'Mum I will miss you so much. How can I live without my mum and my little sister?' My heart went out to my children. I threw my arms around Ruth, giving her a big hug.

On Sunday we all headed down to Johnstown, and after a welcome cup of tea, Granny Brennan and her daughter Maura got into our car to drive with us the short distance to the farmhouse. We drove up a lane, then we parked the car outside the yard as the gate was locked. Just a little further up the road was a little gate into the front garden. Overgrown and wild, it brought back memories of the garden in the cottage in Maynooth in the early days of my marriage. These memories reassured me – I knew I would grow to love this garden too.

When Granny Brennan turned the key in the door we all had to push because the door was stuck. The door opened and we went in. The farmhouse was damp and cold. Angel Elisha was right, it was unliveable in. Granny Brennan commented, 'There is an awful lot of rubble to be thrown out. The old man had a habit of collecting things, and you'll need to get a skip.' Christopher told me he thought from the look of things that the whole farmhouse would have to be stripped. I felt Joe's presence even though I wasn't allowed to see him. I thought to myself, 'Yes, I could love this farmhouse. Megan and I could be happy here.'

Later, back in Granny Brennan's house, we discussed starting legal proceedings to transfer the ownership of the farmhouse to me.

Chapter Six

God's library

The angels had always said I would write books and I used to laugh at them saying I could hardly write my name, how could I write a book? Then, when I was fourteen I was given a wonderful vision of God's library, which made me realise how important books are and that perhaps I had an important role to play.

As a young child and teenager I often used to go fishing with my da and Arthur, his best friend. Arthur loved children and always had time for me. He was always full of chat. He looked a bit older than Da – he had lots of lines on his face – but I think he was about the same age as Da. Sometimes I would fish next to Arthur and Da. But most of the time I would leave them and find somewhere to sit, maybe behind them. There I could watch them fishing, but more importantly I could watch their guardian angels and the other Angels that would be with them and the things that would be going on around them.

Fishing did not always go smoothly. The fishing line might get caught on a branch or bush or even under a big stone in the riverbed. One day I watched my da doing everything possible to release a trapped lure, hearing him mutter under his breath that this was his best bait, that he didn't want to lose it, only to see an angel touch the fishing line and allow it to break free.

Another day I walked on up the river beyond them. When I got to a bend in the river I stopped and called out to my da that I was going further on. He called back that it was OK. When I turned around an angel was walking towards me. I had met this angel when I was about four years old; she had taught me lessons on how to pray.

'Lorna, come,' she said. I ran up to her and as I did lots of angels appeared behind her. We walked up a bit further where there were some trees. I sat down with my back to a tree.

'I never told you my name all those years ago,' she said, 'and you never asked.'

'I always call you the special angel of prayer,' I said.

She took my hands and said, 'Call me "Amen".'

I smiled at her and said, 'That's what you say at the end of prayers?'

'Lorna, I'm at the end of every prayer,' she said. 'God hears the prayers of every man, woman and child regardless of religion. There are angels present at the end of every prayer. With the last word, "Amen", angels enhance and glorify that prayer, imploring God for the prayer to be granted.'

'Angel Amen,' I asked, 'is that why there are loads of angels with you? Are you their boss?'

'There are lots of angels here to make sure that not one amen at the end of prayer is missed – even if the person doesn't use or forgets the word "Amen".'

'Angels work very hard!' I observed. Angel Amen smiled, but never answered my question about being the boss.

'Lorna, close your eyes now,' Angel Amen said. All the other angels gathered around and we started to pray. I was praying with every particle of my body and soul. Slowly the atmosphere started to change; I felt weightless, like a feather, floating not touching the ground, and yet I knew I was sitting on the ground. I was in a meditative state, wrapped up in God's angels. I was told to open my eyes. The Angel Amen was now standing directly in front of me. She seemed taller than she had been before, and even more beautiful. She stepped forward, as if in slow motion, and knelt down on one knee and raised her right hand and reached into my chest, saying, 'Lorna, God wants you. I'm going to take your soul. Don't be afraid.' It literally took my breath away and for one split second it was very frightening. I couldn't breathe.

Suddenly I found myself in an enormous corridor. It didn't seem to have any walls or doors and there was no sense of where it began or ended. I was surrounded by what looked like a mist – it was snow white but not blinding. Angel Amen was holding my hand as we walked along this corridor. Angels and souls walked past us in both directions, but I didn't take much notice. We walked a long way and yet it didn't seem to take any effort.

We stopped. The mist seemed to be evaporating. 'Lorna, we are here,' said Angel Amen, turning to me. I had no idea where 'here' was. There was a fine curtain, like silk, in front of me. This curtain seemed to have no beginning and no end. I reached out to touch it but Angel Amen stopped me. The curtain slowly started to fade and disappear, and as it did Angel Amen vanished from my side.

I found myself alone, standing in a gigantic library. There were rows and rows of shelves stacked high with books. I couldn't see the top shelves as they disappeared into a mist that lingered high up. Each shelf had elaborate wood carvings. These carvings matched those on the legs of the long tables in the room. The tables were enormous. In fact, I couldn't even reach to the top of the tables, and they also each seemed to be about as long as a barn. Around each table were three to five chairs placed unevenly. The chairs had carvings on the arms and legs and the backs were clear and undecorated. The tables were covered in books, both stacks of books and individual books that were open as if someone were in the middle of reading them.

Everything in this library was enormous – books, tables, chairs and shelves. In between the tables were enormous pulpit-like structures. These were the size of a small house. Up the side of each was a staircase leading to a large platform. Each pulpit was different and seemed to sparkle in its newness. I had never seen anything like them before. But the most incredible thing of all in this massive library was the enormous spiral staircase that was on my right and some distance away. Like the shelves, it seemed unending, curving up and getting lost in the mist that lay above the library. It also seemed to go down through the floor. It was very different to any spiral staircase I've ever seen. The stairs glinted with a white gold bright light.

Suddenly these stairs were very busy, with angels and souls going up and down. They seemed to come through the floor, some travelling up and others passing them on their way down the stairs. I looked at the floor closely for the first time. Initially I'd had the impression it was made of marble, but now I looked closer I realised it wasn't marble as we know it. I could see light and movement through the floor. It was translucent. I was astonished. Now I looked even more closely, I could see right through it, see the grand spiral staircase curving away below and see souls and angels moving on a floor below. I wanted to get a closer look and to touch the surface of the floor. I went down on my hunkers.

A beautiful angel touched me on the shoulder, saying, 'No, Lorna! You can go anywhere in the library you wish, but don't touch anything.' The angel disappeared. I was disappointed but instinctively I knew not to ask any questions.

The library was extremely busy. Part of me felt I should not be there, that I was intruding. It looked like a place that I, given my young age, would never be allowed into in the normal world. Yet the angels and souls who were there acknowledged my presence, nodding at me as if they had been expecting me. The spiral staircase was still extremely busy. Among the souls on it were three that I was told were those of Apostles. All the souls were much bigger than me – the right size for the library – but the angels all around them were taller still.

The Apostle Peter reached the end of the stairs and came in my general direction, followed by four angels. He had the appearance of a well-built, mature man with dark tousled hair. He had eyes that sparkled but the expression on his face was serious and preoccupied. The angels around him stopped at a table and started to search through the books scattered on it, making notes. Peter went up and into one of the pulpits. He gave no sign of having noticed me. Another two Apostles came down into the library – Mark and Simon. Mark, like Peter, was quite a blocky man – and also about forty. Simon on the other hand looked younger, rather boyish with a slight frame and hair that looked as if it had been bleached by the sun.[1]

---

[1] Editor's note: In some traditions known as Simon the Zealot.

Mark and Simon went up and into separate pulpits and started to search through books and they too started to take notes. Other holy souls from different religious traditions also came into the library, all followed by angels. I realise now that the religious leaders my attention was being brought to were leaders that I could recognise – in other words leaders of the Christian religious tradition in which I had been brought up. It is not that one religion is superior to another. If I had been a young Jew or Muslim, or any other religion, I would have been shown different spiritual leaders. Whatever these Apostles were searching for, it seemed to be very important to them and there seemed to be a great urgency about finding it. Peter, Simon and Mark went from one pulpit to another. I could only hear whispers of conversation. At that time I had no idea what they were looking for.

As I walked through the library among the enormous tables and pulpits angels continued to acknowledge me and the Apostles in the pulpits also seemed to keep an eye on where I was going. Once I saw Peter stop work in his pulpit, and look around anxiously, searching for me. When he spotted where I was, he turned back to his work. I watched angels taking books from the shelves and carrying them to the tables, which were by now full. Sometimes they stacked the books on the floor. Other angels were carrying books up into the pulpits. They were all searching very hard, and what they were searching for seemed to be of great importance, because the sense of urgency was incredible.

All of a sudden I understood. I was told, without hearing a voice, that this was something God had asked them to do. It was like a test and they only had certain amount of time to accomplish it. Somewhere in the library in one of the books was the answer they were seeking. I also realised that I knew which book it was in and where that book was, though I still didn't really know *what* it was. I found myself standing right in front of the incredible spiral staircase and for the first time I could see it close up. As I stood there, I realised it was full of the light of angels and souls who were going up and down. That was the glint of bright white gold that I had been seeing from across the library. The enormous steps of the spiral staircase were made of the same material as the floor. I could see right into the steps, right through.

Without words again, I was told to move away from the spiral staircase. As I turned around, I saw and felt a mounting sense of excitement in the library. I knew God was coming. The urgency increased. They had not found what God had asked them for! I felt sorry for Peter and the others. I wanted to tell them where the answer was but I wasn't allowed.

I looked up and could see Peter turning pages in a book. Mark left his pulpit, and hurried up the steps of Peter's pulpit, two steps at a time. I could not see Simon. His pulpit was the furthest away from me, and even standing on my toes I could not see where he was. I walked back in among angels and among the holy souls searching at the tables. Now I could see Simon moving briskly from one table to another, speaking to holy souls of different religions and angels. I watched the angels showing him notes they had taken from books. Two angels came over to Simon. They were carrying big books and gave some of them to Simon. He hurried off, carrying these books over to Peter's pulpit, followed by the angels carrying even more books. He was in such a hurry he nearly dropped the books and Mark hurried down to help him. So Simon, Mark and the two angels – all carrying books – hurried up the steps of the pulpit to join Peter. Together they all searched through the books, turning pages and going from one book to another.

I so wanted to help. I knew where the answer was! But I still wasn't being allowed to help them. I could feel God coming down the spiral staircase into the library. I ran! I ran as fast as I could and hid behind a book over in the corner. This book, upright and open, was enormous – so I was fully hidden. Then I peeped out from behind it to see what was going on. God descended the spiral staircase with tremendous power. It was incredible, and is very difficult to describe. The power was greater than the biggest storm you could imagine – roaring wind, rumbling thunder, flashing lightning. The feeling of anticipation was overwhelming. My soul was shaking with excitement. I was deeply afraid but on another level, not afraid.

I feel I am not doing justice at all to this moment with my description and, as I write, I am giving out to the angels and asking them for help. Archangel Michael has just put his hand on my shoulder and told me, 'You're doing fine, Lorna. God lets you know what you need to write, and we are here with you helping you.' This at least is some consolation to me as I write, even if I am still fretting about the lack of words to describe what I experienced adequately.

God was in the centre of the library now. Peter spoke first, admitting they had not achieved the task God had given them. God, of course, already knew this. God seemed to be annoyed with them.

God spoke. His voice was like roaring thunder. Not an angel or soul moved. If there was such a thing as a pin in Heaven, it would have been heard if it was dropped! 'Peter, such a small thing I asked of you,' God thundered. 'To find an answer in one of the books in the library. I gave you help and even with my help you couldn't do it.' With a rather human gesture of exasperation, God threw up His right arm as if to say, 'Be gone, get out of my sight all of you.'

Every angel and every soul disappeared except Peter and me. I was shocked to feel the astonishing, incredible power of God. With just that one gesture everyone else had gone. I moved in another little bit behind the book. I was afraid God would see me. I was deeply shocked at the thought that God had banished all these angels and souls. I was told, without words, not to worry, that God had only sent them away temporarily. I should have known better than to be fearful, as alongside his power I could feel God's incredible love. I could feel this love and I wanted to run to Him, but I had been so overwhelmed by this power that I stayed hidden.

Then God called my name. 'Lorna,' He called, 'why are you always hiding from me when you know I can always see you no matter where you are?'

I kept hiding, crouched behind the book and whispered, 'I'm afraid.' God looked down at me behind the book where I was hiding and smiled. I felt so tiny, so little.

At the same moment God and I reached out our arms to each other, and God took my hand. God's hand was so big, yet our hands fitted into each other. I felt safe and happy; I wanted to hold onto His hand forever.

'Lorna, there is no need to be afraid,' God said.

'I know,' I said in a whisper, 'but God, you are so big and powerful and I am so little.' Hand in hand, God and I walked over to the pulpit where Peter was standing. The steps going up into the centre of the pulpit were too big for me and without hesitation God bent down and picked me up in His arms like a father would. It was then I realised that we are all only children in God's eyes.

The platform of the pulpit was like a large room with shelves and a big oval desk in the middle. There was a wide shelf laden with books going all the way around the pulpit. Halfway around this shelf, it became a desk that was slightly tilted like a lectern. There were books stacked on top of each other on every surface. Many of the books were open as if someone had been desperately searching through them – which they had indeed.

'Lorna, show Peter where to find the answer,' God commanded, putting me down. I pointed to the desk. Now Peter took my hand. As we walked over to it I realised that there was no way I could look at any of the books on the desk – it was just too high. I stopped and looked back at God, then back to the desk. Some steps appeared, going up to the desk, high enough for me to look at the books on it. I smiled and said, 'Thank you.' I knew God heard me. He always does, just as He can always see me.

The top of the desk had books scattered everywhere, but there was one open book that was bigger than the others. I turned its pages, saying to Peter as I did, 'The answer is in this book.'

'I have gone through each page of it a hundred times,' said Peter, reaching out to help me.

'It is in this book,' I replied. 'I know it is!' I didn't really understand or know what I was looking for but I knew I would recognise it as soon as I saw it. The writing in the book was not familiar to me in any way. The letters weren't like any letters I had ever seen. It was a completely foreign language, yet I could read it. I could read names among the words. Sometimes there were several sentences linked to a name. Sometimes there was just a name on its own. Then I turned a page with Peter and saw my own name. I was so surprised and laughingly pointed it out to Peter. Peter gave me a big smile.

I felt God touching my hair and on the far side of the page I saw my name again and underneath it was what God had been looking for. The passage was only about three or four sentences long. Above it was my name and underneath it were many other names. I pointed to it, saying to Peter, 'There's what you have been looking for!' Suddenly the library was full of life once more. Lots of angels, many holy souls and the Apostles Mark and Simon were back. There was great joy, celebration and singing.

I read out the answer to Peter. I understood the answer at the time. It was very clear to me, but now I find it impossible to remember. I know the angels are blocking me from remembering what the words were for some reason. Ten years ago I could remember it. Perhaps in the future I will again.

Peter's face lit up. He was so relieved. He put his finger down beside mine and read it out a second time. He turned to God in joy. The task was complete. Suddenly Angel Amen appeared in the pulpit beside God and Peter. I knew it was time for me to go, but I looked at God and asked, like a little child, a toddler, 'Do I have to?' God told me yes.

Amen took my hand and suddenly I was back at the riverbank, wrapped in an angel blanket. As so often when my soul is taken the angels wrapped me in what felt like an enormous snow-white blanket. It felt so soft around me, like feathers, with what I would call an electrical charge running through it, sparking all the time. Amen was holding my hand and gently and lovingly putting my soul back into my human body.

'Lorna, open your eyes,' said Angel Amen. I did and she disappeared. I lay there feeling very tired and stiff. After a little while I walked back to Da and Arthur. I felt as if I had been gone for hours, but they acted as if I had only been gone for a few minutes.

I always remember the stairway in that library. It was so grand and impressive. Over the years I have been shown quite a number of different stairways, perhaps a dozen, both to Heaven and within Heaven. Each has looked unique but the one thing they have in common is that they all curve, they are never dead straight. You could call them spiral staircases. One reason I believe I am shown them is so that I can write about them in order to help to give people an understanding that Heaven does exist and that Heaven is never-ending.

The occasions when I have seen stairways have varied. Sometimes it has happened when I am in meditative prayer. On occasions I have been shown them as a person dies or when I have had near-death experiences. Obviously, though, I wasn't allowed to get to the top. I was sent back – or else I wouldn't be sitting here writing this today.

I love it when I am climbing a stairway to Heaven as I feel closer to God. Angel Amen normally accompanies me.

Chapter Seven

The rain touches me

Even though neither Christopher nor Owen had succeeded in getting a mortgage to buy the cottage in Maynooth from me, I continued working to sort everything with Granny Brennan, so the old farmhouse would become legally mine. But I knew that without the money that the boys would give me by buying the cottage, I wouldn't be in a position to do the farmhouse up, and it was completely unliveable in as it was. One day, Owen told his boss about the difficulties he was having getting a mortgage, and his boss offered to help. When Owen told me this, full of excitement, I had to smile. His boss was listening to his angel.

Owen's boss helped with the approach to the bank. Even with this help it took months, as Owen was only about nineteen and the bank kept reducing the mortgage they were prepared to give him. But eventually the mortgage was granted. I still remember the day Owen got word that it was fully approved. I heaved a big sigh of relief.

One morning a few days later, a truck with a small crane arrived outside the house in Maynooth. It delivered a small metal shed into the garden. This was for packing for the move. From that day on I started moving my and Megan's belongings into this shed. Megan enjoyed all the excitement.

When I became worried, Angel Hosus would come and

reassure me. 'Lorna, lots of guardian angels are whispering to different people to give you a helping hand. You don't even know some of these people, but don't worry, lots of miracles will happen.'

One evening, a neighbour knocked on the door. He said he had heard from Owen that I was moving and offered to help. When I told him about the farmhouse, he offered to send an architect friend of his, Tony, down to have a look at it to give me an idea of all the work that would need to be done. I accepted the offer gratefully and a few Sundays later met Tony down at the old farmhouse. He had a good look round and confirmed what my sons had said. It was in terrible condition and was going to need to be stripped completely. I explained that I was on a very tight budget. He looked around, asking himself how the list of things that needed to be done could be reduced. The list included rewiring, replumbing and putting in a new septic tank, replacing all the floors and window frames which were riddled with woodworm and spraying the place to make sure the woodworm was completely killed. There was very little that could be taken off the list.

On Tony's advice, after talking with the boys, I put an ad in the local newspaper looking for a builder. We got a few replies from builders but they were very expensive and there was no way I could afford the money they were asking. One day a carpenter called Eddie replied to the ad – he seemed more affordable, so Tony and I agreed to meet him at the house on a Saturday afternoon.

Megan and I arrived first, followed shortly by Eddie and Tony. I kept out of the way as they went through the farmhouse room by room and examined everything. After their chat Tony talked to me on my own and told me he thought Eddie was a good option, that his price was reasonable and he could do much of the work, even though I would have to get a plumber and an electrician later. I was thrilled. Finally things were moving. I had someone who could do the work on the house!

Eddie wasn't able to start for a few weeks as he had another job to finish first. This was fine as it gave us time to clear out the house before he started. I wanted to see if I could salvage any of the old furniture in the farmhouse. I love old things. I went down the next weekend with Megan and Christopher and we stayed in a bed and breakfast nearby. I salvaged a fair bit – a wardrobe, a couple of chests of drawers, two marble washstands. I even converted a wooden potty holder into a little stool. I would have liked to have been able to save more, but a lot of it was so badly riddled with woodworm that it fell apart. We moved what we could save into one of the big sheds beside the house and I started treating it immediately for woodworm.

Whenever he could, Christopher spent his weekends working there. One of the big jobs was replacing the wooden lintels that went across the top of each window. The first day we started on this task Christopher told me to take a hunk out of the wooden lintel as if it were a loaf of bread. I looked at him wondering how on earth he could do that with wood. I took a chunk out, just as I would soft bread, and to my surprise it crumbled in my hands. Apparently all the wooden lintels were as rotten and we had to remove them and replace them with cement ones. This was a very tough task as the cement lintels were ten foot or more in length and extremely heavy. Christopher had a friend helping but it was a slow process. I noticed that when these cement lintels were being put into place the angels were more attentive than usual and they told me to be very alert. I would see five angels around the lads helping to lift a lintel. It was scary watching, but comforting to know that the angels were there keeping a watchful eye too.

One day, while the new lintels were being put in and I was watching, an angel said to me, 'Lorna, go round to the back of the house; Angel Hosus is waiting for you there.' I climbed out of one of the windows and made my way across mountains of rubble. As I climbed I saw Hosus standing at the side of the house. As usual he looked like an old-fashioned schoolteacher and his cloak was blowing in the wind. He was smiling and laughed at me – I was covered in dust – saying, 'Lorna, those boots look too big for you.'

Just then I lost my balance and started to slip. Hosus reached out and caught me. 'Thanks, Hosus, I could do without bruises and scratches on top of everything else,' I said. We sat down on the rubble and talked for a little and I told him about my concerns. 'Hosus, when Christopher and his friend are working upstairs it's going to be very dangerous. There is no floor for them to stand on. They will be standing on planks lying across the rafters.'

Angel Hosus held my hand. 'Don't worry, Lorna. We will do everything we can to make sure nothing goes wrong.' Hosus filled me with calmness. I heard a car coming up the lane and Hosus disappeared. Only once when the lads were working upstairs did they lose their grip but they managed to hang on. I know it was with the angels' help. I was so glad when all the cement lintels were in place and that particular job was finished.

As for the barn – which would become the big main room of the house – taking out the floor there was a horrendous job. They had to go down three feet. The first foot wasn't too bad, mainly dirt and small stones, but after that they came across enormous boulders. They had to hire equipment to break these boulders into pieces. So the yards at the front and the back of the house filled up with rubble. At times Christopher would have to clear a path big enough just for the wheelbarrow to get through. This job also took months as Christopher could only do it at weekends. I felt like it was taking forever to get the old farmhouse habitable.

I didn't always bring Megan down to the farmhouse, because at times it was just too dangerous. She pestered Christopher, telling him she wanted to show one of her dolls and her teddy the new house. When she was there she would play in the corner with bits of wood. She would make a table or bed for her doll and a stool for her teddy to sit on. One day I listened to her telling her teddy not to fall on the floor because he would get all dirty. She loved watching what was going on and was fascinated by everything. Megan was very happy when she was down at the farmhouse. She would become more relaxed. Watching her I knew I had made the right decision to move – despite how slow and difficult all the work was.

At times I would look over and see Megan's guardian angel sitting on the floor playing with her. Her guardian angel looked about eight years old – a little older than Megan, who was five at this time. But they looked similar in many ways. They looked like two normal children playing together, except for the fact that her guardian angel didn't get covered in dust like Megan did. Sometimes her guardian angel would turn and look at me. She had big brown eyes – like saucers – and was so beautiful and bright. Her hair was long and dark, plaited and fastened with leather cords of different colours. I don't see Megan's guardian angel all the time and I feel privileged when I do. In fact I feel privileged when I see any guardian angel. As I say, I see the bright light of their guardian angel behind everyone. I have never seen a human being, man, woman or child, without the light of their guardian angel. But when a person's guardian angel opens up, I feel so privileged. This happens for various reasons. Sometimes the guardian angel tells me that something is wrong and asks me to pray for that person. Sometimes the guardian angel makes a spiritual connection between that person's soul and my soul. I may never see that person again and never know their name. That's not important. That person's guardian angel and my guardian angel would be doing what God has asked them to do – to make that spiritual connection between that person's soul and mine. For as long as that person's soul needs that spiritual connection I see their face. Each and every day of my life I see many faces in front of mine and I pray for healing within their lives.

Remember, everyone has a guardian angel. You are never alone; your guardian angel never ever leaves you. Other angels may come and go, and spirits of your loved ones may come and go. But your guardian angel can never leave you. Your guardian angel is a gift from God to you. Don't be afraid to ask your guardian angel to help you in all the things of your life. Your guardian angel is the gatekeeper of your soul. He is there to help you, just ask! It's as simple as that.

* * *

One Saturday, I walked down to the shops on my own to buy us some food for lunch. I walked down the small, rather overgrown lane that ran by the house. The lane was mostly used by tractors and for herding cattle from one farm to another. It had been raining a lot that week so it was quite muddy. I don't remember the walk to the shops. Sometimes when I am walking I am in a meditative state of prayer and in this state I'm unable to remember how I get from one place to another.

On the way back, though, it was different. As soon as I reached the back lanes the Angel Michael began to stroll beside me. He was as tall as ever, this time with dark flowing hair tied back untidily. He was wearing a heavy coat and wellington boots and he could have easily been mistaken for a farmer working out in the fields. I was delighted to see him. He took my hand. I find it very hard to describe what it is like when an angel takes your hand, but there is incredible peace and love. I turned and looked at him. 'Michael, I wish you could hold my hand forever,' I said.

Michael didn't reply to this. Instead he said, 'Lorna, I think it's time for you and Megan to move down to Johnstown.'

I looked at him, horrified. 'There is no upstairs, no electricity, and no windows. There is not even a toilet. We have to use the fields! It's freezing cold! How would I manage with a young child on my own?'

Michael gave me a big smile as he said, 'Lorna, I want you to talk to the builder in a few days. Ask him to get one room ready for you upstairs. He will have to use extra planks across the rafters to make it safe and put temporary windows in. He should also put in a door that you can lock. I'm afraid he won't be able to make stairs yet, so you will have to use a ladder. This way the work that needs to be done on the farmhouse will move much faster, because you will be there every day.'

As we stopped on the railway bridge the sun shone through the clouds. I turned and looked up at Michael, who was still holding my hand. 'Michael, I am scared! There is no electricity and no lights. There is no other house on the lane and so there are no streetlights. When it's dark here, it is pitch black.'

'Lorna, don't be afraid. Remember the angels will be with you. Whenever you feel afraid just call me and I'll be right there by your side. Come on, let's get you home before it rains again.'

I thought about it. 'I can't move house until Ruth has finished her exams.'

'Don't worry,' he smiled, 'she will be finished in a few weeks and it will take Eddie that long to do the preparation work he needs to do.'

As we walked he also explained that my friends, the Brennans, had things that would be of help to me. I asked what.

'Lorna, things like a tent, and an inflatable mattress,' Michael answered. 'You will live in a tent in that room upstairs.'

I looked at him in surprise. 'In a tent?' It started to rain heavily as the farmhouse came into view and Michael disappeared. I ran up the path and I was glad to get in out of the rain and cold. Christopher had water boiling on the little camping stove that we had, and we enjoyed a cup of tea and some bread.

On Monday morning I rang Eddie, the builder, and told

him what I wanted and a few days later Megan and I headed down to Johnstown to meet him to discuss the plans for making it habitable. Eddie had his doubts. 'Are you sure you want to move down before the house is finished? There are rats. Aren't you afraid of them?' I knew there were rats – I had seen them. One day Christopher and I were sitting on a plank having our sandwiches and three rats came up and stood on their hind legs looking for food! The old man who had lived there used to feed the rats; I guess he had made pets of them. Eddie offered to poison them, but I was reluctant to do this. I told him just to make the top room secure and that I'd chase the rats away and hopefully they'd get the message.

As he left at the end of that day Eddie said, 'You're a brave woman!'

Later, I carried Megan out to the car, I strapped her into her car seat, gave her a colouring book and some pencils. I told her I was just going to check we had left nothing in the house. There was no way to actually lock up the old farmhouse. There were just boards over the windows and a lightweight board over the entrance. I called Michael. Immediately he appeared in the open doorway. He had a bright yellow builder's helmet on his head and a shovel in his hand. He looked as radiant as ever, his eyes gleaming with life and light like the sun. He lit up the old farmhouse. He walked into the room and touched my shoulder. The shovel he had been holding disappeared.

'Lorna, you called me.'

I looked at him. 'Michael, your shovel disappeared but you still have a helmet on!' We both laughed. 'Thank you, Michael, you are filling me with peace,' I said. I had been very anxious since he'd told me I should move to the old farmhouse and live in a tent. I found the idea of living on a building site without another adult very scary. Now Michael's presence calmed me.

'Lorna,' Michael said, 'you will manage. Remember the angels will be with you. God knows all your fears and anxieties. God has said to tell you to try and put them to one side.' He became practical again. 'Now you should go and call on the Brennans and ask for a loan of that tent and inflatable mattress.' Michael touched the top of my head and disappeared. I pulled the makeshift door behind me and walked slowly across to Megan and the car.

As we pulled in at the gate of the Brennans' house, the hall door opened and Maura stood in the doorway with some of the younger children hiding behind her. They seemed delighted to see us and we sat talking over tea and sandwiches. I told Maura and Granny Brennan my plans to move into the house despite its very basic state. They offered to turn their front room into a bedroom for Megan and myself, which was very kind of them, but I was adamant about staying in the old farmhouse. They insisted that in that case at least, we could come and have a hot shower in their house and have dinner with them in the evenings. Of course, without my even asking they also offered me a tent and inflatable bed just as Michael had promised.

A few weeks passed while I sorted out the essentials we would need. I prayed that the angels would tell me the right time to move down to the house.

It was a wet day in Maynooth in June 2002. Ruth had finished her final school exams the day before. I delayed going to the shops in the hope that the rain would ease off. By the afternoon the sun started to peep in and out between the clouds. Megan and I put raincoats and wellingtons on and off we went. It was cold but the rain had stopped. Megan played in the puddles as we walked down to the village. We did the shopping, but as we reached the beginning of the road to the house, it got dark again and started to lash rain.

'Let's play a game called the rain touching me,' I suggested.

Megan was all for it. As we walked I held one of her hands and told her to put the other hand out and feel the rain touching her. Megan did so and turned to me excitedly. 'Mum, I can feel the rain touching my face too,' and she laughed. She stuck out her tongue trying to catch drops of rain. We ran a little and then walked again and in no time at all we reached the cottage. We were soaked to the skin. Megan ran around the garden in circles with her arms outstretched. I couldn't get inside fast enough but she begged to be allowed to stay out in the rain.

As I turned the key in the door, desperate to get in out of the rain, I got a shock! Angel Kaphas stood there, just inside the door. He startled me! He had not changed in those many years since I had last met him when he came to tell me that something special would happen for Joe. Now, as then, he was a sight to see – striking and magnificent. He seemed to be made of jagged glass splinters, identical in size. All his features were very sharp and the glass splinters reflected light onto his face. Kaphas is extremely tall – the ceiling in the hall seemed to disappear. From him came this beautiful soft enchanting music. It was spellbinding

'Hello, Lorna,' said Angel Kaphas in his gentle soft voice. 'Are you ready? Have you your packing done? This weekend you and Megan will move down to Johnstown. No buts or questions, Lorna.' He smiled, as if to say as far as he was concerned it was settled. We were to move that weekend. He looked out at Megan still turning around in circles, arms outstretched in the pouring rain. 'Go and show Megan some more about enjoying life. Remember how we taught you when you were a child to enjoy the light and energy of the rain.'

Without hesitation, I put the shopping bags down in the hallway and ran back out into the rain to Megan. 'Let's play another game.' I reached out and took her right hand and just touched her fingertips. 'Turn your head up to the sky and keep your eyes wide open.' She was all excited. She was enjoying the rain touching her face and her eyes started to sparkle. Angel Kaphas came and took my right hand and Megan's left; we were in a circle as if we were playing ring-a-ring-a-roses. Life spun around us – the light and life of the rain, energy falling from the heavens. I could see individual raindrops moving slowly towards my eyes. The light and the life of the rain touched us as the energy of life spun around us. It was incredible.

As I spun with my eyes wide open, looking up into the rain, I felt a jolt and I lost my breath. My soul moved forward from my body. Mine and everyone else's soul is normally located in the body – filling the shape of the entire body. When it moves forward something spiritual is happening. When this moving forward happens to me I can see my own soul in front of me. When I see this it fills me full of enormous joy and peace – a certainty of knowing that God is taking care of everything. I have no idea whether anyone else can do this and see their own soul.

When I am privileged enough to see another person's soul

move forward, I only see it come marginally forward, it remains within the body. One exception to this I can remember is what I was shown just before my father died, when I was shown his full soul rise above his body, anchored to his body by a gold chain.

I'm still not entirely sure why my soul came forward that day. I can only presume that the angels were trying to reconnect me to life, to help to heal me and feel the joys of life once more. As suddenly as the rain came, it stopped! The sun came out just as suddenly. We stopped moving and stood for a moment. Megan stood still, not moving at all, as if in a trance, her eyes like saucers. I saw Angel Kaphas standing behind Megan. He touched her head and everything came back to normal.

'Mum, did you see the light shining in the raindrops, all the colours? The raindrops were enormous!' she said with such enthusiasm.

I smiled. 'Megan,' I said, 'that was the light of the life of the energy of the rain touching you.' Megan, of course, had noticed nothing strange about me. She begged to play the game again, but I said it was time to go in and get dry. She ran into the house. I turned to Kaphas. 'Thank you so much,' I said in a voice full of gratitude. Kaphas did something that angels don't do often. He walked towards me, slowly fading from my sight. I could hear music as he started to ascend up into the clouds. I could hear the music until he completely disappeared. I know he did that for me, and I thanked him with all my heart. When I turned around I saw Megan standing at the hall door. I never asked Angel Kaphas if he allowed Megan to see even a glimpse of him or to hear his music – maybe someday I will.

Chapter Eight

An angel's feet light the way

That evening after dinner, I told Megan to go to her room and play. I needed to talk to her big brothers and sister. As we sat at the table, talking over tea, I told them that the time for Megan and me to move down to Johnstown had finally arrived. We were going that Saturday morning. Christopher said, 'Mum, one of us will need to go down with you.'

'No,' I said, 'I need to do this myself with Megan. It all has been arranged with Maura Brennan and her family. We will be calling at their house first and having lunch. Then up to the farmhouse with the tent and the blow-up mattress.'

Ruth laughingly said she wanted to come down the first chance possible to see what it was like living in a tent in the bedroom. Owen fretted. 'You only have a little gas cooker – what about food?' I reassured him, saying the Brennans had told us we could have lunch with them anytime. We talked about how lucky I was to have such good friends who were also really good people nearby.

A little while later I told Megan we were moving that weekend. She jumped up and down with excitement. She couldn't wait for Saturday and the idea of sleeping in a tent. She ran into her brothers and sister to tell them. As for myself, I was looking forward to the move as well. I knew it would do me good just as much as it would Megan.

The week went quickly. Friday night we had everything in the hall ready to pack into the car for Saturday morning. I didn't sleep very well because my heart was aching. Already I was missing Christopher, Owen and Ruth. And I was worried at the thought of them having to stand on their own two feet as young adults without a parent. I was twisting and turning in the bed, praying every now and then. In my frustration I called out, 'Angels please put me asleep.' I felt an angel sitting on my bed and I turned around and it was Angel Amen. 'Lorna, stop worrying,' she said, as she reached out and touched my eyes. 'Close your eyes now; you need to sleep.' I did. The next thing I knew it was eight o'clock and the first thing I did after opening my eyes was to thank Angel Amen. During breakfast Christopher said, 'I don't care what you think. I'm going to follow you on my motorbike. I'll meet you in the Brennans' house.' I didn't argue. To be honest I was kind of relieved.

By ten o'clock the car was packed. There were lots of hugs. I could see the tears in Ruth's, Owen's and Christopher's eyes. They were holding them back in order not to upset Megan. Megan was delighted Christopher was coming too. 'You can sleep in the tent as well,' she offered. I nodded to Christopher to say nothing. Owen lifted Megan up into the air and gave her a swing and all was forgotten. Then Owen put Megan into the car and strapped her into her seat. Ruth opened the gates and as we drove off I glanced in the car mirror and saw the three of them waving from the gate. At that moment the light of their guardian angels opened up. It was a wonderful sight and filled me with confidence that they would all be OK.

We were about an hour into the journey when Christopher overtook us on his motorbike. When we arrived at the Brennans the children were playing in the garden waiting for us. Christopher's motorbike was already in the driveway. We were given a great welcome. After lunch Maura and the children carried the blow-up mattress to the old farmhouse, cutting across the field at the back of their house. I watched as Christopher somehow managed to get the tent into my car. It was a tight squeeze but he had plenty of angels helping him. When I arrived at the farmhouse Maura and the children were there waiting. I stepped through the makeshift door into the room that we still call the barn. Eddie had done his best to clear it up – but it was still full of building material. The timber was piled high, there were pipes of all shapes and sizes, bags of plaster, buckets of nails and lots of tools. I smiled. The Angel Michael had been right. Eddie had done a brilliant job on the wooden ladder we would be using to get upstairs. It looked strong, but all the same it was only a ladder and it was a long way up to the landing.

Maura went up the ladder first, followed by Christopher then Megan. She was very nervous and I encouraged her up the ladder with me behind her. 'Mummy I'm afraid I will fall,' she sobbed. I assured her I was holding on to her tight. Christopher was also reassuring her from above. When she got to the top of the ladder, he took hold of her and lifted her on to the planks. There were two planks leading from the top of the ladder to the bedroom with a sheer drop on each side. It was quite a distance to the bedroom – about twenty-five steps. Christopher warned Megan to be very careful and never to walk across on her own. The rest of the Brennan children followed us up the ladder, without hesitation, as if it was an everyday task. When I reached the bedroom I was surprised to see just how big the room was. The builder had done a fine job. The temporary windows were great, even if they were a little draughty around the edges. The children ran around the room playing. Maura told her girls to mind Megan while we went down to unpack the car. As we went out the door I glanced back. Megan and the Brennan children sat on the floor playing a clapping game. A circle of angels appeared around them. I smiled as I closed the door behind me.

Getting the tent and all the other things upstairs was difficult and scary. I never stopped talking to the angels and asking them for help. Eventually we had everything up. There was great excitement among the children erecting the tent. By now it was starting to get dark and the mattress was put inside the tent with pillows and blankets. Everything looked cosy. Maura decided to take her children home before it got too dark for getting across the planks and down the ladder. I took one of the torches out of a box. As we left the room I heard Megan asking Christopher whereabouts in the tent he wanted to sleep. As I closed the door Christopher winked at me.

I drove Maura and the children home. Then driving back to the old farmhouse I stopped in the lane for a few minutes. By now it was pitch black except for the dim light coming from the window of the bedroom. It looked so welcoming. I was happy. I turned on the torch as I got out of the car and made my way back up the ladder. I peeked in at Megan. She had fallen asleep. Christopher whispered, 'Mum, there was no problem when I explained to Megan that I wasn't staying. She understood that I have to go back to Maynooth because of work in the morning. I'll come down to visit as often as I can.' He gave me a hug and picked up his helmet, telling me to lock the door as he went. I could hear him walking along the planks and going down the ladder. I looked out the window and waved him goodbye. I watched the light of the motorbike disappear. I felt an angel touch my shoulder. I turned around and it was Angel Hosus. With a big smile he said, 'Living in a nice and homely tent in a bedroom. All as you need now, Lorna, is a campfire with a boiling billy-can for tea.'

'Good idea,' I said, as I put on the small stove and filled the billycan from a bottle of water. My first cup of tea in my new home! 'Hosus, I really like it here, I feel at home,' I told him and we talked for a while. Then Hosus peeped in at Megan. He told me I needed to get some sleep and disappeared. I moved slowly into the tent, trying not to disturb Megan. I must have fallen asleep in seconds.

The work of the farmhouse definitely moved quicker with me there. One stormy night in July, the wind was howling around the house. There were lots of nooks and crannies in the old farmhouse and the wind made a terrible noise. An angel woke me saying, 'Lorna, Megan is not well. She has a high temperature. You need to take her down to Maura's house.' The angel continued, 'Pick her up and put her across your shoulders.' I was terrified. How I was going to get across the planks and down the ladder with a sick child? The angel disappeared. I turned Megan over on her back. She was very hot and soaking wet from a fever. I grabbed the torch and the car keys. As I opened the bedroom door, I could see nothing. It was pitch black. There was no moonlight. I stopped, allowing my eyes to adjust to the darkness.

The angel who had woken me appeared in front of me saying, 'I will walk ahead of you. Don't be afraid, Lorna. Megan will be OK.'

'I am frightened,' I told the angel. 'Megan is so heavy, and she seems to be on fire.' We were surrounded by darkness. The beam from the torch seemed to give little light. I could see nothing else, only the plank and the angel ahead of me and the subtle light that came from the angel did not reflect anywhere else. But then suddenly the planks became filled with a light emanating from the angel's feet. The angels were helping me.

'This is really scary,' I said to the angel walking ahead of me. I was afraid I would lose my balance, that we would fall from the planks down to the floor below.

The angel turned around and said, 'Follow me.' I walked slowly across the planks. I could hear the voice of the angel saying, 'You won't fall, Lorna. Take one step at a time.'

When I reached the top of the ladder, I said to the angel, 'Now how am I going to get down this?'

The angel said, 'Put Megan lying down on the two planks and go down on your hands and knees.' I laid Megan on the planks as close to the ladder as possible and took a deep breath as I went down on my hands and knees. I felt the angel take the torch from my hands. I then put one foot on the ladder. 'Now put Megan across your left shoulder,' the angel said. As I moved Megan into position I was shaking. I was so scared we would fall.

Angel Hosus appeared beside me. 'Lorna, don't hold your breath so much. You're doing very well.' With Hosus there

I became calmer and positioned myself on the ladder. As I inched my way down slowly, one step at a time, Angel Hosus moved with me. During all of this Megan never fully woke. I know she was hallucinating; I could hear her talking to herself in a nonsensical way.

I was so relieved when we reached the bottom of the ladder. I walked through the other rooms and then into the barn, the angel walking ahead of me all the time lighting the way. Hosus was standing at the makeshift door and he had it open. As I walked out the door, still carrying Megan, I turned and thanked the angel with the beautiful light. He smiled, saying, 'My name is Avajil,' and disappeared.

I crossed the yard and put Megan on to the back seat of the car. As I turned the ignition I saw the light of Megan's guardian angel open for one second in the mirror. I saw her wiping Megan's brow with such love and care. 'Lorna, get a move on,' said Hosus from the passenger seat. As I pulled into the drive there was a light on in Maura's house. I felt relieved when I saw the hall door opening. Maura helped me carry Megan into the house. We put Megan into a bath of cool water and sponged her down. Then we gave her a spoonful of medicine and put her into a bed. Megan smiled at us and quickly went to sleep. I called the doctor and he said he would call early in the morning. The next morning he checked out Megan. Her glands were up, he said, and she had a sore throat, but he assured me that in a few days she would recover. We spent those few days in Maura's house.

Word was spreading and people were starting to find out where I was living. Sometimes people couldn't even get into the yard, because of the rubble and the mud, but by and large they didn't seem to mind. At times someone would pull up and get a shock, landing in the mud as they stepped out of the car. I started to tell people who rang me that that they had to bring their wellies. I'd tell them there was no toilet and that I was afraid they would have to use the fields, just like me. Mostly they would laugh and disappear into the field for a few minutes.

One sunny day, Megan and I had just left the farmhouse and started to walk down the lane. I watched a car turning into the lane and driving towards us. I knew whoever was in the car was looking for me because I could see angels ahead of the car, guiding it along the lane and around the potholes. I also saw an angel moving along the driver's side. The car stopped and a woman wound down the window and asked me if I knew where Lorna lived. I introduced myself. She told me that her name was Margaret and that this was her second time driving to Johnstown looking for me. She said she was desperate to see me because of some health problems her children had. 'I was determined to find you. I kept saying your name to the angels. I have never prayed so much, and thanks be to God and the angels I have found you.' We chatted for a few minutes more and I agreed to see Margaret and her children – four boys, I learnt – a few days later. I explained to her that I would have to see her and her children in her car instead of the house as everything was still in such a mess with the builders, and I told her about there being no loo.

'Lorna, If you lived in a shack in the middle of a swamp it wouldn't matter,' Margaret said. 'I just want you to see my children.'

A few days later a car pulled in as close as possible to the door of the old farmhouse. I had taken Megan down to Maura's so I wouldn't be disturbed. I ran out to the car with a coat over my head to protect me from the pouring rain and opened the car door. Inside, the car was packed with Margaret, her four beautiful sons, everything the children could want – toys, food and drinks, clean clothes – and angels. The car was packed with angels!

The children weren't shy in any way and started to talk to me immediately – all at the same time. Margaret was speaking to me at the same time too. It was so warm and cosy in the car, so full of love. An angel sitting beside one of the boys told me he wasn't well, that he had severe asthma. He was maybe five years old, and looked very pale. I reached my hand into the back of the car, touching him. His mother told me his name was Tony. Holding back the tears as she looked at him playing happily in the back of the car, she said that the doctors didn't know what more they could do for him. They kept changing his medication, but it didn't help. As I listened to Margaret I talked without words to the angels, with my hand on Tony's knee. Having listened to them I told Margaret to go back to her doctor and ask for a second opinion.

I prayed over Tony and blessed him, asking God for healing angels to be around him constantly, for healing to be granted so that this young boy could grow strong and healthy. I blessed and prayed over the other three little boys and asked their guardian angels to help them to be as good as possible for their mum and dad. The children told their mum that she needed to be blessed too. She told them to be quiet and play with their toys as she turned to me. I saw the angels putting a shield around the children, not allowing them to hear the sound of our voices.

Margaret spoke about the relationship between her husband and herself. How she felt they were growing apart, and how she couldn't cope any more. She was scared her marriage would fall apart. Her husband worked all day and when he got home she was exhausted too and there was no peace with the children. Tony needed a lot of attention and at times this affected his three brothers too. They could be very bold and difficult to control and their dad would shout at them. And then all the children would end up in tears. It was very stressful, Margaret told me. I looked at her. 'Margaret, I have asked the children's guardian angels to help them to be good,' I said. 'And I'm asking your and your husband's guardian angels to bind both of you together in love and to find time for each other.' I blessed Margaret and prayed over her.

Margaret asked whether she could come back in a few weeks and I agreed. When she did, she looked like a different woman, much of the stress was gone from her face, and she was smiling. Margaret came to visit me a few times and each time I could see the change in her. Tony had been referred to see a specialist and was doing much better.

Eventually she no longer needed to see me at all. Some time later, when I hadn't heard from her for a year, she rang and asked could she come and visit. This time for the first time she brought her husband as well as the boys. He thanked me for all I had done – for being there for Margaret and their sons. He told me how much better Tony was. Margaret stood beside him with her husband's arm around her and told me she was happy. Her husband had told her he loved her. The fear she had of their marriage falling apart had gone. She thanked God and the angels for binding them together in love. I was so pleased to see this. I blessed and prayed over all of them including little Tony.

One afternoon I heard a noise and, looking out the window, I saw a well-dressed man getting out of his car. He started climbing over the rubble in his shiny shoes and, despite his best endeavours, stepped in the mud. I burst out laughing as I watched him from the window upstairs. He was surrounded by angels who were mimicking him.

Taking Megan's hands I walked along the planks – by now we were used to this and it was no problem – and down the ladder. As we reached the barn the man was already stepping through the makeshift door. His shoes and trousers were completely covered in mud and he looked a bit miserable. The angel standing beside him told me that he had wanted to make a big impression on me and was disappointed. The man apologised for coming unannounced, and introduced himself as Robert. He asked for five minutes of my time and for a blessing. I told him that I would give him the time but that it had to be in my or his car, and that I would have my daughter with me. Robert seemed a little hesitant and the angel standing beside him shook his head, saying, 'No, you need to see him on your own, Lorna.'

Just then Eddie came into the barn and I asked him to mind Megan for a little while. I could see the look of relief on Robert's face. Robert suggested we used his car as he didn't want mud all over mine. I told him mine was already covered in mud. As I opened the passenger door of his big flashy car I could smell the newness. It was spotless. I suggested we used mine so as not to spoil his, which was obviously new and very expensive, but he insisted we stayed there. He told me he had a lot of health problems and a lot of problems with his family. As he talked I prayed, without him realising I was doing so. The light of his guardian angel opened for just one second and then seemed to close again. Then I saw healing angels coming one at a time all around Robert, the first angel touching his head, another angel his chest and another his lower back. As they did this a fourth angel seemed to be moving the life force around his body. These angels were radiant and beautiful, huge and very slender. It was as if they were made of clear crystal. Each was unique, and I could see the grace of God, a beam of light entering each angel. These were the healing angels. I could see Robert become translucent. As he spoke and told me about his problems, I could see every organ and all the arteries and veins. I could see the angel running his finger along all the veins and arteries, as if moving a life force through Robert's body. Robert, of course, was oblivious to this. Then he stopped talking and asked me to bless him and, as I did, the healing angels seemed to become one. When I said 'Amen' at the end of the blessing, they were gone.

Robert looked at me. 'I feel much better already. Would it be all right to come to see you again?' I told him it would be, on the condition that he went to a doctor and got blood tests done. I gave him my mobile number so he could call in advance the next time. About four weeks later, Robert came again. The doctors had diagnosed a health problem, but were treating it. He would be well soon. He came back to me on many occasions over a few years. During that time I saw him change into a much brighter and more caring young man, who was able to live life to its full. He also learnt to become more relaxed and informal and no longer dressed up for coming to see me.

In September 2002 Megan started in the local school in Johnstown. I very much hoped she would make new friends. The first school morning she didn't want to go. I persuaded her to try on the new school uniform and eventually she agreed, but on one condition. 'Mum, will you come in to the class with me to meet my new teacher?'

I smiled at her. 'Did you think I was going to leave you at the door?' She threw her arms around me and we hugged each other.

It took her little while to settle into her new school, to get used to a new routine and to make new friends. Ruth came down to Johnstown as often as she could. She and Megan are so close.

Eventually, in November 2002, six months after we had moved in, the house became properly habitable and we were finally ready to pack up the tent and move in properly. There were now floorboards upstairs, and we were delighted not to have to walk along the planks any more. There was glass in the windows and we had outside doors. Mind you, there were still no stairs, just the ladder, but we didn't worry about that too much.

The night before the 'big move' Ruth had come down and Megan, as always, was delighted to see her. The following day that big container that we had packed many months before arrived and a truck. Christopher and Owen arrived too. The first thing we did was to go into the room that would become my bedroom and take down the tent that we had been sleeping in for six months. I was so pleased to finally have a normal bed and bedroom. We laughed when the inflatable mattress made a hissing noise as we squeezed all the air out of it. When everything was rolled up, we carried the little gas cooker and pots and pans downstairs to the room that would become the kitchen.

Getting the furniture out of the truck and into the rooms downstairs wasn't too much of a problem, but getting the bed bases, mattresses and other furniture up the ladder was a different story. Eventually all the furniture was in place and after a cup of tea, the boys and the truck headed back to Dublin.

I looked around the barn. We now had furniture – but it was still a real mess. There were still piles of building materials everywhere. Because the floorboards had still not been laid downstairs, we had cement floors, which meant dust everywhere. And there was still an awful lot of work to be done. Ruth suggested we started with my bedroom, but I felt it was important that Megan's was first. She had been so long without a bedroom of her own. Ruth and Megan held hands as they walked out into the hall and started to climb the ladder.

A few moments later Angel Hosus appeared, sitting on top of a pile of floorboards in the barn. Today his robe was purple, which was a bit different from any teacher's cloak I have ever seen. I walked over to him and Hosus moved to another pile of floorboards, inviting me to sit where he had been sitting. He took my hand, making me feel good.

'Lorna, you see how happy Megan is now?' he said. 'And your other children.'

'Yes,' I replied. 'I do and I'm starting to feel happy too.'

'Lorna, the angels are whispering to the builder continuously to get everything finished as quickly as possible. We know that to you everything seems to be going very slowly, but it's not really. It's giving you time to heal and to accept the changes in your life.'

Megan called me and Hosus disappeared. I hurried out into the hall and up the ladder. When I reached the top of the ladder Megan and Ruth were standing there all excited. Megan took my hand and, as we walked down towards her bedroom, she pointed out the other bedrooms. 'That's Ruth's.' Ruth smiled and said she loved the room. I was concerned that all my children would see the old farmhouse in Johnstown as their home too. Pointing to the left Megan continued, 'The two boys can share that room.' Her room was next to mine at the far end of the landing. Ruth helped Megan to make up her bed and arrange her toys, while I started making up my own bed.

Some time later Megan called me to come and see her room. It had no door yet. I saw Ruth and Megan curled up on the bed together and I could see the light of their angels covering them. Megan was as proud as punch. Her enormous collection of teddy bears was lined up at the end of her bed and on the wide windowsill. It looked fabulous and I was thrilled to see her so happy. Ruth suggested we all needed some food. We had a cooker, but only a temporary sink. There was a table and chairs, but no cupboard, so the room was full of boxes and bags of food and kitchen things. Ruth cooked us stir-fry chicken and, after I had cleaned the tables and chairs, we sat down and ate hungrily. We were all starving. We slept well that night. It was great to sleep in a proper bed. We had an early start the following morning as Ruth needed to get back to Maynooth for work. Megan cried as Ruth drove away.

Chapter Nine

Christmas in the barn

Christmas was about six weeks away. I really wanted us to celebrate a family Christmas in the farmhouse in Johnstown for the first time. The builder did as much as he could to make the house more liveable. He put floorboards in some rooms downstairs, a cupboard in the kitchen, and doors on our bedrooms.

The weekend before Christmas, Ruth, Christopher and Owen arrived down at Johnstown. I hadn't been expecting them, so I was doubly thrilled to see them. Since the children had been small we had always gone together to pick a Christmas tree and they had always loved it. They decided that this tradition should continue so we took off in the car looking for Christmas trees. We went to different places selling trees — a garden centre, a car park — but Megan said she didn't like any of the trees she saw. Owen groaned, 'This could take all day!' He agreed with Megan that she would choose one at the next place we stopped.

We drove on and pulled into a car park with loads of Christmas trees. I could see tens of angels going in and out among the trees checking them, deciding which one Megan should pick. I smiled to myself watching it. The angels found the Christmas tree they wanted and they lit it up so it seemed to stand out from all of the rest. I stood back and watched, and of course when Megan came to this tree, she turned to her brothers and sister and said, 'This is the one I want.' All the angels surrounding the tree cheered. We bought the tree and put it into the boot of the car, with one of the back seats down. I don't know how we all managed to squeeze in.

There was a place on the floor in the barn for the Christmas tree. The boys brought in the tree, while Megan went searching through boxes in the back to find the decorations. We suddenly heard a shout. Ruth and I ran in to find Megan trying to pull this enormous box, about twice her size, across the room. We laughed so much. We eventually got the box of decorations into the barn, with a little help from two angels whom I could see pushing. Then we all decorated the tree together.

The older children stayed overnight. The next day, as they were outside the house packing the car to go to Dublin, the light of Ruth's guardian angel opened up for a brief moment. Her guardian angel was beautiful and showed me a female appearance full of gentleness, kindness and strength. Her guardian angel was all blue, a beautiful radiant blue. She held a whip in one hand and in the other she carried a helmet. I spoke to her without words calling her by her name – which Ruth knows. 'Ruth is overflowing with the Christmas spirit,' her guardian angel told me.

Ruth was standing at the car looked at me strangely, saying, 'What's the big smile for?'

'I'm happy,' I answered her. Ruth's guardian angel disappeared. I gave them all a big hug. The biggest hug was for Owen. I wouldn't be seeing him at Christmas. He was going off on a long-planned holiday to Australia. I would miss him.

They took off, Ruth and Christopher promising to return as early as they could on Christmas Eve.

Megan had made a Christmas card and some decorations in school. She was very proud of her creations. She hung these on the main door so everyone could see them as soon as they came to the house. Ruth and Christopher arrived down on Christmas Eve about three o'clock. The first thing Ruth did was check the fridge to see had I made her favourite mousse for dessert on Christmas Day. I heard her murmur 'yummy' to herself.

The fire was lit in the little cosy room and we had a crib in the window. We went to the children's Mass in the church in Johnstown on Christmas Eve. It was packed and we nearly didn't get a seat. I love going to the children's Mass on Christmas Eve. I get enormous pleasure out of seeing and listening to children celebrating the birth of Jesus and, of course, watching all the angels around them. As the children went up to the altar for Holy Communion I was shown some of these children's souls. They were dancing in and out of their bodies, moving about four inches out and then moving back into the body again. These souls were so radiant.

At Christmas I am shown many children's souls. During the rest of the year I see souls of children, but not normally in the same abundance as at Christmas. The angels tell me it is because the children are so full of Christmas spirit, and of course they have come from Heaven quite recently. I thank God each time I am allowed to see someone's soul. The soul is more important and more beautiful than any angel. It is an enormous privilege to be shown a soul.

Outside the church everyone was wishing each other a

happy Christmas. When we got back to the old farmhouse the house was filled with the light of the angels. It felt warm and cosy. I could feel and see great joy and excitement as we all busied ourselves preparing for Christmas morning. As for the angels, how can I describe their excitement? There are no words really for the joy that I see from angels at Christmastime. They are bubbling with excitement, like excited children. I can see it in their faces and in every gesture they make. They too were preparing to celebrate the birth of Jesus.

Everyone helped to prepare vegetables and the turkey for Christmas dinner the following day. We set the table in the barn and the place looked fantastic. Megan couldn't wait for Santa Claus, so at about eight o'clock I brought her up to bed. She said her prayers, and I kissed her on the forehead and said goodnight. As I reached her bedroom door I looked back at her. Her Christmas stocking was hanging at the end of her bed. An angel touched her brow and she fell fast asleep immediately.

I went into my own bedroom and, as I opened the door, I saw Angel Michael, Hosus and Elijah and loads of other angels sitting on my bed. Michael came over to me and took my hands and said, 'Lorna, we don't want you to be missing Joe. God has sent his spirit to visit you for a few minutes.'

I looked at Michael, and burst out crying. 'I hope they are tears of happiness,' he smiled. All the angels disappeared, and I was in the room on my own. The next moment I saw a light within the bedroom by the window. Joe stood there and then slowly walked over to me. He looked as he had as a young man and in full health. He was glowing brightly. I was overjoyed. He reached out and took my hand and then put his arms around me. I felt so peaceful. I wanted to stay in his arms forever.

'Lorna,' Joe said, looking into my eyes, 'I expect you to be strong and to live the life God wants you to live. When you need me, your guardian angel will allow me to be by your side, but I will never be able to hold you again in my arms – not until we meet in Heaven.' He continued, 'Remember I love you. Tell the children I love them, I will always be with them spiritually.'

Then Joe took his arms from around me and, holding my two hands, he said, 'Let another man into your life and let him love you.' As he disappeared, Joe said, 'Happy Christmas, Lorna.'

'That's the best Christmas present anyone could get,' I said into the space left behind. I was so happy. I stood there for a few moments thinking about the gift of Joe's arms around me. I slowly walked down the landing. There I met Ruth who said she thought I must have fallen asleep. They were all wrapping presents downstairs. I joined them. An hour or so later we went to bed and as I was closing my eyes, I thanked God for a wonderful day.

I was woken on Christmas morning by an excited Megan with Santa's stocking full of sweets in hand. Megan then woke everyone else and we all went downstairs, well, down the ladder. Ruth had been up even earlier than Megan and had turned on the lights of the Christmas tree. The barn looked fantastic. The angels were sitting everywhere. I wished my family could see what I see.

Megan screamed with excitement when she saw Santa had left her a bike. Santa was wise and had also left stabilisers, a helmet and knee-pads. She cycled from one end of the barn to the other with her brother helping her. Ruth announced that it was time to open other presents. She was as excited as her little sister! We took turns opening one present at a time, giving whoever the present was from a big hug.

The morning passed with lots of laughter and fun and we played games. Owen rang to wish us a happy Christmas – we missed him but he was clearly having a great time. He teased us about the sunshine he was enjoying in comparison with our rather cold, dull weather.

At four o'clock we sat down at the big old table in the barn, which was beautifully decorated, and said grace. We also wished Joe a happy Christmas. We were all missing him, and even though I had been given the gift of being held by his spirit the night before I now felt his absence acutely. It felt wrong to be having our first family Christmas in a new home without him. But we had a gorgeous dinner which we all thoroughly enjoyed – and Ruth in particular enjoyed the raspberry and cream mousse I had made for dessert. The rest of that day and the following days passed very pleasantly, and Megan became quite good at cycling. She practised on the lane outside the house with her brother helping her.

After four days the older children returned home. It had been a wonderful Christmas. I always enjoy Christmas. For me it is a special time for family and friends to be together, but that first one in Johnstown had been very special. I finally felt like the old farmhouse in Johnstown was home.

Chapter Ten

Witnessing the Nativity

I am learning more and more about the angels and the way they work in the world all the time. For many years at Christmastime I'd seen angels flying over houses and dropping balls of light onto them. I used to wonder what it meant. What on earth were they doing? Then I had a vision, which made it much clearer.

I have visions on occasions. These are not at all like dreams. They take place when I am fully awake. When I experience them it's like a jolt to my whole being. My soul is separated from my body, and in truth I know I'm very close to death at those times. Even if the vision is beautiful – and some are not – the transition into the visionary state is always a painful and frightening one. It's uncertain too. The process is not always the same. I know that in these visions I'm being shown something very important, something about the whole world and not just my immediate surroundings. A message for the world if you like.

The vision that helped me to understand what the angels were doing at Christmas happened to me in the run-up to Christmas when Joe was still alive. He was in hospital and I wanted him home for Christmas. It was mid-afternoon and I went into the sitting room at home to pray. As I started to pray I could feel the angels gathering around me, wrapping themselves around me like a cloth, first softly then tighter and tighter. This is one of the signs of a vision. I know that if the angels didn't support me like this, my body would drop to the floor as soon as the soul left it.

Now my eyes are wide open but I'm drifting away from this world. It's fading. Then just for a split but very frightening second it's as if my breath has been taken away. I've stopped breathing. I'm somewhere else, in a different dimension. It's dark. I become aware of two shadowy beings, one on either side of me. They're leading me towards a vast stone wall, so high that it seems to reach up to the sky, and in the middle of this great wall there is a gateway. The stone, grey like granite, is sparkling with tiny dots of light in many different colours. There are carvings on the gate, but I don't focus on them long enough to make them out because my gaze is drawn, inevitably, to the two gigantic, golden angels, bigger than trees in the garden of Maynooth College near where I lived. Almost as tall as the wall even. They are standing guard on either side of the gate. As I approach these two angels turn and begin to push open the gate. The gate is like one gigantic block of stone cut down the middle, but with the two halves pressed together. It doesn't swing backwards or forwards, but must be pushed to the sides like a sliding door. I can see that it is immensely thick and heavy. But it begins to yield to these giant angels because they are immensely strong. As the two parts of the gate begin to slide back, I see that the crafted stone blocks that make up the gate are about three feet thick. Then I see a flicker of light in the opening crack. 'What's in there?' I ask myself. I'm trying to peer in . . .

Then as I continue to approach, the crack widens, the light

becomes brighter, until suddenly, once the gap is about a yard wide, there is an explosion of light and countless angels begin streaming out. They're everywhere, dazzling me at first. As I walk through the gap it seems as if there are millions of them and now I see that each one is carefully and lovingly holding, as if very precious, a ball of light like the ones I've seen angels dropping down into houses at Christmas. Some of them glance and smile at me but most just rush past as if they don't know I'm there. A great wind flows by, gentle yet strong and getting stronger as they pour out.

Then suddenly it is all over, and I find myself in the dark again. Above me only the starry night sky. I can feel that the ground beneath my feet is soft. Then somewhere ahead of me, a small distance away, as if at the bottom of the garden, I see a small flicker in the dark. Two angels appear by my side, and as I begin to move forward again, I begin to make out a small, rounded hillside and set into it there is a cave. I'm getting closer and closer. I wonder to myself, 'Am I moving towards it or is it moving towards me?' Then either I stop – or it stops – and suddenly I can see the cave more clearly. It's as if the angels have turned up the light to make this possible. There is a crowd of angels flying over and around the hillside and it is they who are creating the gentle, flickering light by which I am making my way. These angels aren't carrying the balls of light like the angels who rushed passed me earlier. These angels are here to light this cave, and to protect it from icy winds. There is a small, higgledy-piggledy man-made construction in front of the cave, about three feet deep, made up of large, smooth, rounded grey rocks, each about a foot cubed, with a roof or awning made with bits of dried wood, straw and moss, such as you might find on a compost heap. As I get nearer I can see that the cave is bigger than it first looked, perhaps about twenty feet wide and thirty feet deep. I sense life there, in the darkness at the back, a number of small animals. I can smell animal life. Some of the animals are maybe about the size of a goat, but it's not them that I focus on. The angels surrounding me tell me that this was the birthplace of Jesus.

I see the young woman, Mary, first. She's standing in the middle of the cave, her head bent slightly, her long dark hair tied with a white scarf that folds underneath it. She's attending to her baby – and the first thing that really strikes me is how young she is! She's a young teenager with a round, pretty, girlish face and right now she's concerned to make her baby more comfortable. The baby, I now see, is lying on something that looks like a stone feeding trough that has some loose clothes draped over it to make it softer for the baby, and the mother is sorting this out. She's folding some more cloth, some linen and then she kneels down to put it under the baby. There is so much love and care in this.

And now I see the father, taller and much older, maybe late twenties, even early thirties. He's coming over to her, so affectionate to her and the child. Joseph has a worn face and a dark beard, not black but dark brown, cut short and a little untidily. But it's a lovely face and you can see straight away that he is a good man. They're talking to each other, but I cannot understand what they are saying, and they are not aware of my presence either. I feel as if they might suddenly look up and see me, but for some reason God does not allow that.

The baby reaches up to catch her finger with a little turn

of the head and a smile. He is, I realise, about three months old. Not a baby with a huge head of hair, but what he has is a soft, light brown, and one of the first things I notice – it's the sort of thing a woman will always notice – is his lovely long eyelashes. His eyes are startling, the whites very white, the pupils dark, and twice he turns his head in my direction, and I'm sure he's seen me. A mother will know how I know! I want to go over and pick him up and hold him but something stops me. Everything about him is like any baby you might see any day of the week, except that he seems to me to emit a gentle golden glow.

I become aware that his attention has been caught by other things and then I begin to see the angels that he can see. There are about twenty of them in a circle all around Jesus, Mary and Joseph. They're facing inwards, of course. These angels are different from the ones I've passed at the gate and different from the ones protecting and lighting the cave over-head and keeping it safe and warm. They are tall and beautiful with wings that move gently and change colours and tone all the time, translucent, a yellowy gold. Their gowns seem to flow down them all the time like waterfalls. Some sing for a while, maybe four or five together. Then they stop and another four or five take over singing for a while, as if the song is being passed on between them. They are holding long white feathers, delicate and streaked with yellow and gold on the tips, and hanging on either side are lengths of string, about thirty of them on each feather. Most of these lengths of string are red, but about four are gold and silver. And attached to the bottom of each is a golden bell. The angels are ringing these bells to entertain the infant. It is these bells and feathers that are catching his attention.

At one point, the baby closes his eyes and falls asleep. Mary and Joseph are watching him closely, talking about him being asleep. I know this although I cannot make out the words. Then he opens his eyes as if to say, 'I fooled you, I wasn't sleeping really!' and all the angels laugh. I feel such love and happiness there.

Then the angels who have been standing by me, slightly in front, turn to face the other way and move back in the direction we have come from. I protest a bit, but really I know it is time to go . . . And with a jolt I find myself back in the cottage, looking out of the window.

I felt as if I'd been watching Jesus, Mary and Joseph and the angels for maybe twenty minutes, but when I returned to the cottage I could tell from the quality of the light that I'd only been away for a very short time – maybe just a couple of minutes. It gets dark very quickly at that time of year and now it was no darker than it had been when I'd first begun to slip away. Time is just for us, really.

When I began to think about the things I'd seen, some strands of meaning began to emerge. When we think about the Nativity, we generally think of people – the wise men and shepherds – bringing gifts to the child. What I had been shown, in the shape of the angels carrying away the balls of light, was the child giving gifts to the world – countless gifts. In a sense, all children give countless gifts. Because young children have recently come from Heaven, they are full of love and true spiritual feeling, and in this way they influence their parents and other adults around them.

In the presence of children we may sense their sense of wonder. The sad thing is that as we grow up, we tend to forget what Heaven was like. We may perhaps remember later in life if we work at our prayers, but for the most part most of us spend most of the year squarely in the material world. Then at Christmas we may be afforded a glimpse of something else. Something happens. Somewhere in the spirit world that gate which I saw in my vision opens. It opens at the turning of every year. We call it Christmas because we remember also that particular turning point in history some two thousand years ago. But people all over the world, in other religions, even people who lived before the events of two thousand years ago, have always known about this yearly opening of the gate. They have also known that in the depths of winter this great gate opens up and a special kind of spiritual being, a special kind of angel – as we call them in our tradition – streams into the world, millions of them streaming into our world to help lighten the darkness, and to fill every heart with hope.

And that I think is the explanation for what I'd been seeing, the angels flying over the house and dropping the balls of light down onto them. There would be an explosion of light that would fill every nook and cranny, lighting up the brickwork and the cement in between. What the angels are doing is helping adults to connect with their memories of Heaven, the spiritual feelings of love and hope that the children of the house carry inside them – or if there are no children, that all adults carry inside, though it may be hidden for most of the year.

If we feel prompted to invite someone round who we know is on their own, or prompted to give a gift – it really doesn't matter what it is in material terms – then that may well be the influence of the very special angels who carry gifts away from the baby Jesus at Christmastime.

Chapter Eleven

Megan's first Communion

Slowly but surely Megan and I settled into a normal life in Johnstown. Megan was getting on well at school. She came home all excited one day telling me she had been invited to a birthday party that Saturday. When I drove over to collect her from the party I was very pleased to be invited in to meet other parents, giving me a chance to meet new people too. Everyone seemed so supportive and welcoming.

My best friends in Johnstown were, of course, the Brennan family. They continued to be so kind and I would have been lost without them. I thanked God and the angels every day for their friendship. We saw quite a lot of each other. Sometimes Megan and I would call in when we were on our way home from school. Megan would play with the children while I drank tea and chatted with Maura or Granny Brennan. There were lots of birthday parties in that home too because there were so many children in the family and Megan really enjoyed those. Sometimes at the weekend, Megan and I would also go walking with the Brennans. There were so many beautiful places to go walking around Johnstown. I love walking and I love the air down there. Country life really suited Megan too and we were happy and healthier than we had been for years. I made other friends too. I would regularly meet a friend for coffee in a cafe in

Johnstown. When she and her husband were moving house, they very kindly offered us their beautiful old dark wood fireplace – and it worked wonderfully in the cosy room in the old farmhouse.

The old farmhouse had really become a wonderful home that we loved. The other children loved visiting it when they could. From the house we have the most beautiful sunrises. As the sun comes up it comes straight in through my bedroom window. Sometimes, early in the morning I'd look out into the front garden and into the field beyond and I would see foxes or rabbits, not to mention all kinds of birds.

Megan was seven now, and was preparing for her first Holy Communion. In Catholic schools in Ireland, first Holy Communions are big celebrations, and a very special time for the child involved. Ruth said she wanted to buy the Communion dress. A friend, an elderly woman in Johnstown, offered to knit a white cardigan for her, and her brothers said they would buy the shoes and other things she needed.

One Friday afternoon about six weeks before the Communion in May, I drove down to collect Megan from school. We were going to drive directly to Maynooth, so that we could spend Saturday shopping with Ruth for Megan's dress in nearby Dublin. I sat in the car watching school-children walking out through the school gates. The guardian angels of the children opened up and I was shown the guardian angels guiding each child to its parents. It was so beautiful to see.

Then Megan walked through the gate. The light of her guardian angel didn't open up, but there were two other angels walking beside her and to my surprise I saw the spirit of my grandmother walking beside Megan. It was the first time I had ever seen her spirit. She had the human appearance of the beautiful gentle grandmother I remembered as a child. When Megan reached the car my grandmother smiled hello at me through the car window and disappeared. I thanked her – forgetting that Megan was locked out of the car. She knocked on the window and I let her in. Traffic was heavy and it was after six when we got to Maynooth and the shops. Megan was very tired, but she was having difficulties sleeping. Ruth got into bed beside her and held her in her arms and Megan was asleep in no time.

I walked into the front room and sat down. The house was silent. I must have fallen asleep on the armchair next to the fire for a little while. When I woke Angel Hosus was sitting on the couch. He had his funny-shaped hat in his hand. I don't think I have ever told you about Angel Hosus' curly hair. He has lovely soft curls, a bit like those I had as a child, but fuller, and when he takes his hat off they fall loosely over his ears, reaching his ear lobes. I was startled to see him sitting there. I was still half asleep and stretched myself in the chair.

'I am here to keep you company for a little while,' he said, putting his hat on. 'How does it feel, Lorna, to be back here in the cottage?'

This was the first night I had spent in the cottage since moving to Johnstown a year earlier. I sighed as I said, 'It does feel strange, Hosus, being back here in the house without Joe, particularly now – with Megan's Communion.'

Hosus reached out and took my hand. I said, 'I'm sitting in Joe's chair you know. It was his favourite chair, but sometimes he used to insist that I sit here, and he would sit on the couch where you are. Looking at you sitting there, Hosus, I can't help thinking of Joe. It does feel very strange him not being here. You are sitting exactly where he sat the night before he died.'

'Lorna, I know it feels strange for you not having Joe around,' Hosus said. 'God has asked me to let you know that the spirit of Joe will be around for Megan's Communion.'

'Thanks, Hosus,' I said with a little smile. 'Thank God for me.'

'God already has his thanks,' Hosus said. 'Now I think you should go to bed.' With that Hosus disappeared. I got out of the chair feeling light-headed. I don't remember going to the bedroom, getting into bed or going to sleep, but I woke the next morning feeling refreshed and much better. As I got out of bed I remembered the message Hosus had given me and gave God thanks.

That same day in Dublin, Megan tried on so many white Communion dresses. But the dresses just didn't seem to suit her. After lunch we found a shop which specialised in Communion dresses down a little lane. Here Megan found a dress she loved. We found her gloves, shoes, a bag and a little crown that went with it. All dressed up she looked like a little princess.

She couldn't wait to get back to Maynooth to dress up for her brothers. They made a great fuss of her. Owen suggested that on the day of her first Holy Communion we should have a barbecue. He and Christopher worked out the logistics, bearing in mind that May in Ireland could be sunny, but could also be wet or cold. Megan was thrilled. Ruth arrived the evening before to do her hair.

As her brothers and Kiera – Owen's girlfriend – and Brendan – Ruth's boyfriend – arrived, I gave thanks to God and the angels. All the floorboards were finally down in the barn and it wasn't raining. It was cold, but the angels assured me that the sun would come out later.

A friend had given me a present for Megan, a beautiful prayer book and rosary beads, so I gave them to her just before it was time to go to the church. When we got to the church Megan led us to the pew that was for our family. I sat in the church, watching it filling slowly with the young boys and girls who were making their first Communion. The light of each child's guardian angel was beaming brighter than usual. I saw one angel take a child's prayer book and hold it in its hands, turning pages and saying prayers. I saw the pages turning, but I'm not sure the child or anyone else noticed. The church was crowded with people and packed tight with angels.

The priest walked out to the altar, followed by the altar servers. There were two enormous angels on each side of the priest as he welcomed everyone and especially the young children making Holy Communion. A multitude of angels descended onto the area of the altar with the tabernacle and altar table. The children making Holy Communion, all in white, walked up the aisle in pairs to join their families. The light of each of their guardian angels was wrapped around each boy and girl. And they were surrounded by a crowd of other angels singing in praise. Their song of praise was very high in pitch, and the sound travelled like waves to Heaven. I could have sat and listened to it all day. When an angel sings it puts me into a most beautiful state of prayer immediately.

When I opened my eyes I saw him. Joe's spirit was standing there to one side of the altar smiling at me. He was at Megan's Holy Communion. Without words I said thank you and a few moments later, Joe disappeared. I was a little sad, but glad he was there for those few moments.

When the time came for the young children to receive Holy Communion I watched as each child walked to the altar. When the priest reached out to give the child the host, or Communion bread, the two enormous angels standing at each side of him reached out with a host. These two hosts touched and infused the Communion bread the priest was giving in a synchronised move. These angels' movements were so gentle and loving. I believe these two spiritual Communion hosts were infusing the priest's Communion bread with extra grace and blessings for each child. Other angels touched each child on the head, and accompanied them back to their seats. All the time the light of each child's guardian angel was glowing.

Megan was excited and nervous when it was her turn to go to the altar. I prayed as I watched the angels assisting the priest giving her Holy Communion. Suddenly Joe's spirit appeared again, standing beside Megan. When she turned around to come back to her seat, Joe walked beside her. He looked as he had early in our early marriage – a handsome young man in his late twenties dressed in a fine suit. As he walked down the aisle he kept looking down with a proud smile at his little daughter Megan. Then he looked up and he spoke to me without words. 'Tell Christopher, Owen and Ruth that I love them and I will always be with them when they need me.' Then Joe's spirit disappeared. There were tears in my eyes as Megan came back into the pew and sat back down beside me.

Outside the church, the sun was shining as the angels had promised. People were chatting, complimenting the children and taking photographs. Christopher and Owen took photos of Megan and her friends, who kept giggling. We must have been almost an hour outside of the church before we slowly headed home. The barbecue was a great success – Megan even managed to eat it without getting her dress stained, a small miracle in itself.

Chapter Twelve

Kindling a light of hope

All my life, from the time I was a young child right up to today, I have been shown people – men, women, even children – who are thinking about committing suicide. I know that they are contemplating suicide from what I am shown and told by the angels. At times like these the guardian angel wraps itself around the person who is considering taking his or her own life, intertwining with the physical body to try and kindle a light there – to show the person that there is some hope. The wings of the guardian angel are open and wrapped protectively around the person. And another part of the guardian angel is plaited into the body, a bit like the strands of a rope. When I'm being shown this, the guardian angel will always say something to me. Sometimes they will just tell me that the person has been through a massive trauma. Sometimes this communication is as short as 'This person is in horrific emotional turmoil.' Sometimes they will tell me the details. There may be other angels around, and occasionally they will give me more details. Sometimes, but not always, I may see a spirit around them also.

It always shatters me when I encounter someone considering suicide. I find it deeply upsetting. It brings tears to my eyes.

* * *

One of the first times I came across this I was about ten years old and shopping on a Saturday with Mum in the centre of Dublin. Mum went into a shop called Hector Greys, where you could buy things very cheaply. I stood outside, holding the shopping bags and the trolley. Angel Hosus appeared beside me and took my hand. He was very bright that day. He told me to look across the road at a mother with a toddler. I did. The mother's guardian angel was intertwined with her physical body. I was upset. I didn't understand fully what I was seeing, but I knew it was something terrible. 'I want my mother,' I said and pulled away from Hosus. I picked up the bags and ran as fast as I could with them and the trolley into the shop to find Mum. I couldn't, of course, explain to Mum why I was upset.

After a bit more time shopping Mum suggested a cup of tea and we went to the self-service cafe in one of the big department stores. When we were sitting at a table with our tea I saw an angel appear beside Mum. I smiled at the angel. Mum was staring at her tea and didn't notice. As the angel whispered in her ear Mum looked up and asked me if I would like to go and buy myself a biscuit. I nodded. She gave me money and I went and rejoined the queue. While I was queuing Angel Hosus took my hand again. 'Look over there,' he said. And there was the same mother and child sitting at a table having something to eat. Again I saw that the mother's guardian angel was intertwined with her physical body. I felt very upset. I took a deep breath. Angel Hosus didn't say a word; he just squeezed my hand. Then the light of the mother's guardian angel opened up. Her guardian angel looked so beautiful. I was allowed to hear the thoughts of the woman. She was in a very dark place. She was extremely depressed. She felt unloved by her husband. Although her guardian angel told me he did love her, she felt she couldn't cope any more. She looked at her little daughter. I could hear the thoughts of her love for this little girl, but her feeling was that perhaps her daughter would be better off without her. There were tears in my eyes as I handed over the money for the biscuit at the cash register. The woman asked was I all right. I told her I had dust in my eyes.

Angel Hosus told me to walk the long way around back to Mum's table and to walk past the table with the mother and daughter. As I was passing the mother's table, I knew I had to touch her, even slightly. I had to make the connection that God was asking me to make. A connection that would help her guardian angel succeed in stopping this woman taking her own life, in giving that young mother enough light, love and hope to stop her doing the deed. Her guardian angel said to me, 'She is meant to live. She just needs help, not only from us, the angels, but also from family and friends. Lorna, pray for this wonderful mother.'

As I walked past her I nudged off her gently. It was so slight and she didn't even notice. I went back to Mum and sat down. She asked me if I had got lost. I pretended I had forgotten where she was sitting. While eating my biscuit I watched the mother and little girl. They were about six tables away from us. I watched the enormous love that her guardian angel had for her. My eyes teared up again and Mum asked, 'What's wrong? Why are your eyes red?' I told her I had dust in my eyes. Mum reached out to have a look. 'I can't see anything.' We got up and left and as we reached the stairs I stopped and looked back at the mother and young child and said a little prayer.

For about two years after that I kept on seeing the mother's face in front of me. I prayed constantly for her. Eventually the angels told me her life had turned for the better and she had stopped having thoughts of taking her life. I was so happy to know that she was OK and that her little daughter still had the mum she loved so much.

On a sunny autumn day shortly after we moved there, I went for a walk in the countryside around Johnstown. There weren't very many people around. I was very upset when I saw a young man of about twenty sitting on a tree trunk looking rather sad. His guardian angel was intertwined in his physical human body. His guardian angel told me that the young man felt inadequate, that he was no good at anything and that life wasn't worth living. I felt so heavy-hearted. I prayed and gave out because I felt so helpless. Shortly afterwards I reached a small pond that flowed into a stream. I sat there in tears. Just as I was about to get up and walk on, Angel Elijah appeared across the other side of the pond from me. It was a small ornamental pond – only about five feet wide. But with Elijah there, everything changed. The water became a large lake and Elijah walked across it. Despite the power and strength of his walk it took him quite a while to reach me. I greeted him. 'Come for a walk, Lorna,' he said, stretching out his hand.

We walked along a pathway and up some stone steps to where there were lots of large trees. I asked Angel Elijah where we were going but he didn't reply. We walked over to a big beautiful tree. I leant against it and Elijah took my hands. I knew the angels were taking my soul, and I lost my breath. I knew I was in Heaven. Everything around me was so bright, so luminous. God appeared beside me. It was as if we were sitting in the middle of the light of the sun, it was so bright and radiant, but yet not blinding. God's face was radiant and so full of love. I can't put it into words. As God allowed me to see His eyes I knew they could see everything. When I looked into God's eyes for a brief second it was as if I saw all life and creation, all love, all hope there. No matter how beautiful and radiant angels' eyes are, God's are beyond that. It is so far beyond our comprehension. God was dressed in robes that were more brilliantly white than any white that I had ever seen and a brilliant light shone from His fingertips and feet. When I looked around I saw we were surrounded by a multitude of angels. I couldn't count them.

'Why are you so upset, my little bird of love?' God asked in a very tender and gentle voice.

'I feel so alone and helpless around suicide,' I said.

'You are never alone,' God said. 'I'm always around you, Lorna.' He smiled at me. 'I see, you are trying not to hide from me as much.'

Nervously, and excited with joy at being in God's presence, I replied, 'I hide because you are so powerful and I am so overwhelmed by your presence. Even now I want to run and hide.'

God smiled at me with great love and compassion, and said, 'I know suicide upsets you greatly because you feel everything of that person's emotions and you feel their soul. Lorna, you are my little bird of love. The souls need your love, and so do I. Your prayers are so full of love and compassion.' God continued, 'I love all my children. I don't want any of them to commit suicide. I am always there with them and there is always hope. I and my angels do our best to help people to see this hope. I have given my children free will so I can't stop them taking their own lives, but when one of my children does so I wrap them in my blanket of love and bring them to Heaven.'

I felt tears come into my eyes again. Then God stretched out His arms in a welcoming gesture. As He did this we were surrounded by beautiful souls. They were all around us, and appeared as men, women and children of different ages. I knew without God saying a word that these were souls who had taken their own lives because they had found life unbearable. They had felt they were living in a pit of darkness. Within themselves they had felt unloved and uncared for, and had little self-confidence or self-belief. They had not been able to see the light and the love that was within them. They may have had families and friends who loved and cared for them deeply, but because they were in that pit of darkness they couldn't feel this. They couldn't see the light of this love. But now, all these souls were radiant, full of an indescribable joy and happiness.

I smiled watching them and God smiled back at me. Then everything disappeared. God, all the angels and souls, and all that beautiful light disappeared. Everything came back to normal. I was there standing under that beautiful big tree. I got up and walked back to my car and drove home, feeling comforted. Thinking about everything, I realised that love has to penetrate that pit of darkness.

People considering suicide don't realise that they are perfect, unique and very important. Each and every one of us has a unique role to play in this world – no one else can play this part. We all need each other. When someone commits suicide it diminishes everyone throughout the world. If someone of any or no religion in, say, Kenya, were to commit suicide today, that would diminish and affect every one of us, even if we have no knowledge or consciousness of it.

At various times, I have spoken with people who have tried to commit suicide. Very often they have told me how grateful they were that they didn't succeed. Sometimes, even with all the help and love they are given, the person may still never be able to climb out of that darkness. The pain is just too much and they cannot help themselves. They take their own lives. I know that then they are wrapped in that blanket of God's love and taken to Heaven.

One day, I was sitting on my own in Bewley's cafe on Grafton Street in Dublin. A woman came in with her teenage daughter. The daughter's guardian angel was intertwined in her physically. I was so upset. The girl was very attractive, about fourteen. Her guardian angel told me that she was in a mixed school and was being bullied physically and emotionally. The bullying was extreme and the bullies were making her life unbearable, stripping her of all her feelings of self-worth. If you only knew how I prayed. I still see that young girl's face so I know she hasn't committed suicide. But I know her angel is still intertwined with her physically so that there is still a risk she will.

Teenagers are most vulnerable to suicide because of their intense emotions and sensitivity. Teenagers are so fragile and tender, and yet all the time they are trying to show they are strong. They say that they don't care and that nothing hurts them, but underneath they are scared and afraid. Even the most charming and apparently confident teenager may be subject to these doubts. This apparent confidence is sometimes one of the reasons why people are especially shocked when a teenager does commit suicide.

Teenagers have a tough time as they are learning about relationships and sexuality, and measuring their worth by their success in these romantic relationships. Young teenage boys sometimes contemplate suicide because they become confused sexually. Sometimes a boy will have no interest in girls and become frightened when he sees his friends are attracted to girls. It is important that boys are told that some boys are just slower than others in their sexuality coming forward. I met an eighteen-year-old young man who told me he had contemplated suicide at sixteen because he was afraid he had no interest in girls. He thought he was gay and was being teased about it at school. He was so confused and terrified of what his family and friends might think if he was homosexual. He planned his suicide meticulously, but he kept putting it off. Then gradually he began to realise that he was interested in a girl down the road, that when he bumped into her he couldn't stop looking at her and he always felt really nervous around her. This confused him even more for a while. Now she is his girlfriend, and all thoughts of suicide are gone from his mind.

I am frequently asked about homosexuality. God tells me that this is a part of what He has created. He already knows which of His children will be lesbian or gay at conception. This is part of their life path and He loves them the same as everyone else. A young man came to visit me in Johnstown. When I saw him outside the door I could see his guardian angel intertwined in his physical body. He was a good-looking young man of about twenty-five. His angel told me what was going on, but it took the young man, who was very nervous, quite a while to get to the point. Eventually he told me that he was gay and was living in fear of his family, friends or work colleagues finding out. In particular, he was terrified his father would find out. He was the eldest son. He told me he had never told anyone, that I was the first person. He used to go out with girls to cover things up, but he felt this was wrong and unfair to the girls. He told me he had gone to the brink of committing suicide several times, but had always pulled back at the last moment. I was being told by his guardian angel that the young man remained determined, but that each time he had listened to his guardian angel, and so pulled back. But his guardian angel knew that if he tried again he wouldn't be able to stop him. My help was needed.

I talked to the young man for some time, trying to instil in him the courage he needed to talk to his father. He knew he had to do something, that he couldn't keep living a lie. I still see his face in front of me every day. I know he is still finding things tough, but I pray that he will find the courage and that his family will find the love and grace to accept him and that with time he will lose the thoughts of ending his life.

Chapter Thirteen

Bursting in through the door

One summer's day when I was in my early twenties and not yet married, I did something that was unusual for me. I decided to go for a long walk in Phoenix Park – a big, wild park quite near Old Kilmainham where I had lived as a young child. I took the bus from Leixlip and walked through the gates of the park. The angels told me to follow a particular path through a little valley. It was a beautiful sunny day, but there weren't many people around. An old man passed me. Ahead I saw a young boy running across the path. Behind him came a young man – I assumed it was his father – and a young woman. Suddenly the light changed as if it had become dusk all of a sudden. Michael was walking beside me and holding my hand, and suddenly I was surrounded by angels. I looked ahead; the path I was walking was becoming narrow and thorny and I could feel bushes brushing against my bare ankles.

Michael told me they were going to take my soul. For a moment I lost my breath. At the end of the path there was now a beautiful bright light. I felt myself being brought towards it, being transported. I couldn't feel my body. I was a young child running barefoot down a sandy street with little shops. I was carrying something in a muslin cloth and my dress had ridden up to my knees. I remember each step. I was running fast, but I was not out of breath. Then I was running up some steps and bursting in through a door, not very solid. Mary, mother of Jesus, was in the room sorting out things on a little table, old and well worn. She was preparing food, her hands covered in flour. The room was pretty empty. There was a small opening in the wall, with enough light coming through it for her to be able to work by. I understood that Joseph was away. Mary needed whatever I had been carrying in the cloth. She spoke to me, asking, 'What took you so long?' I knew I was late and had done wrong.

I remember climbing up onto an imperfect rough wooden stool. I knew she was good and that this was where I wanted to be. She was still very young, about ten years older than when I had seen her at the Nativity. She wore loose clothes of a golden brown colour, and her hair was tied back – I couldn't see with what. Then she said, 'Did you see Jesus?' I shook my head. I was watching her prepare the food. Then it was time for me to go. I climbed down off the stool. Mary wiped my face and dusted off my lap.

I left and was heading home. I could feel myself lifting up my child's legs as I ran again. Then I met Jesus in a group with three or four other boys. They were his friends and my friends too. They were playing a game with stones, throwing them to try to knock down a little pile of them. Jesus looked like the other boys. They were all about ten or eleven years old. I'm not sure whether I called him but he turned round and looked at me. His expression said, 'What are you doing here?' He was happy playing his game, doing what the other boys were doing. He said hello. He knew I had come from his mother. We were in a town or a village. There were other people all round, heading home.

Then the angels returned me to Phoenix Park and I was back on the path with the Angel Michael holding my hand.

On Mother's Day in March 2005 Megan and I drove to Tramore for the day. It's a lovely seaside town about an hour and a half from Johnstown. Ruth had given Megan money to take me out to lunch, and Megan had said she would like to be by the sea. It was a blustery spring day, cold but with sunshine and no rain. We took a long walk along the beach and then went to a pub that served food. We had a great lunch and enjoyed it enormously. Afterwards, we headed back through the town to the beach, which was now quite busy with lots of people walking and children playing. I was sat on a little wall while Megan played in the sand. To be honest I was feeling lonely sitting there. I spoke to God, telling him I needed some more joy in my life. I looked out towards the sea, glancing back and forth at Megan, making sure she was OK. Then I saw the energy of the sea rise up from the sea. It was like a glittering mist of sea colours, emerald greens and sapphire blues, and gold. It rose up from the sea and very slowly moved in like waves of energy. It took about five minutes to reach the beach, and then another five minutes to engulf the beach and the people on it. It was so beautiful.

Suddenly, within the mist a light appeared, then another, then another. Suddenly I could see loads of lights floating around the people. Then they burst open and I could see angels. Now there were more angels than people on the beach. These weren't guardian angels. They were very bright and because of that I couldn't see them clearly. They were different colours but each angel was one individual colour. They were much taller than the people on the beach and some of them had wings, but none of them had open wings. They were dancing; I couldn't hear music but they all seemed to be dancing to the same music, weaving in and out between the people. They didn't seem to be dancing with each other, as we might, but were each dancing their own dance. Four of these dancing angels came up to me as I was sitting there on the wall and danced in front of me, between myself and Megan, who was about five feet away from me. They made me laugh. It was wonderful to see, and then they danced around Megan. After a while these four angels danced off among the people, still engulfed in the glittering mist.

Tramore has a lovely beach. Where Megan and I were sitting it was sandy but over to my left were lots of sea-worn stones, about the size of a fist. There were also two big yellow poles – I don't know what they were for – in front of the stones. I looked in that direction. All of a sudden a beautiful energy came bouncing out of the stones, every colour, you name the colour, it was there. Millions of little glowing balls of coloured light bouncing up and down. The angels with me told me to call Megan over. I was excited. I knew that finally I was going to be allowed to show Megan something of what I see. She came running when I called, her hands covered in sand. I got up from the wall and knelt down beside her, looking in the direction of the bouncing lights. I put an arm around her, bringing her in very close to me. 'I'm going to show you something,' I said gently. 'I want you to look between the big yellow poles down there, and look out onto the stones.' She did as I said and the angels lifted a veil for her. She started to giggle. She couldn't believe what she was seeing. 'I can see balls bouncing up and down, hundreds of them, and they are all shiny and all the colours of the rainbow.' There was an angel beside me, whispering. I told Megan to watch the balls, as I knew from what the angel said that they were going to move out and bounce among the people. As the balls bounced out among the people she saw the mist as well, and she grew even more excited. She wanted to go and catch the balls and play with them, but I held on tight to her so she wouldn't follow her natural instinct.

All of a sudden the balls, the mist and the angels (which Megan hadn't been allowed to see) disappeared. She was very disappointed that they were gone, but so excited at having been shown them. She insisted on going and collecting a few stones to bring back to Johnstown with us, but I'm afraid grey stones is what they were and continued to be despite her ten-year-old hopes that they might be magic.

Chapter Fourteen

Meeting two spirits

I continued to see people who needed help. They would hear of me by word of mouth and be given my telephone number. One day, a husband and wife came. As I opened the door, I got a terrible shock. For a brief second in front of the husband stood a spirit – I knew this spirit was a great- or great-great-grandfather of the man in front of me. I wasn't shocked at seeing a spirit. No, I was shocked that I recognised this spirit, as one who had done terrible things to two spirits with whom I had shared my life for twenty years.

The story started to flood back to me, but I held it away while I saw the man and his wife. What they had to say relates to the story, so I'll tell you a little more about it later. After the man and his wife left, I sat lost in thought in the barn, reliving the story of two spirits who had been a part of my life from when I was seven and visited Granny in Mountshannon for the first time until I was married with children. It's quite a long story, but it is extraordinary, so let me tell it to you.

I was about seven the first time I visited Mountshannon House, the youth hostel in County Clare where my granny worked as a caretaker. A big old eighteenth-century grey stone house with big windows, it was at the edge of a village called Mountshannon on a small hill overlooking Lough Derg, a lake on the River Shannon. There would have been grounds surrounding the house originally but by this time they had all been sold. But there were still coach houses you reached through a big stone arch and a beautiful if wild and unkept garden out the front.

On that first day I went exploring the house with only angels for company. I felt strange. Something didn't seem quite right. As I walked up the main ground-floor corridor and glanced down a passage off it I felt uneasy. 'I don't like it down there,' I said. 'Why have you brought me here?' Sometimes the angels want me to do things I just don't understand. At that moment, my grandmother called me, so I got no answer.

It was on the following year's holiday that I saw her for the first time. I was out in the big old stone courtyard and looked at the small ground-floor windows at the far end of the house. I saw a beautiful, young, fair-haired woman looking out of the window at me, smiling. I'll always remember it. She seemed to shine. I called the angels and said, 'She looks beautiful – just like an angel. Can I go and play with her?'

'No,' they told me, 'not this time.' Why not, I wondered, what was different? I was really confused, I just didn't understand. Why couldn't I go and play with her?

Then Michael appeared. 'Come here to me and sit down beside me,' he said, 'and I'll tell you something.' We sat on a big piece of stone like a drinking trough in front of one of the old coach houses. As we sat there the swallows were flying in and out of the coach house behind us.

'What is it?' I asked. 'What do you need to explain to me?'

'Lorna, you have to listen,' he began. 'There is a long, long story and I can't tell it all to you now. I know you can see that young woman up there. She is not an angel like us, she is different. She is a spirit and there is another spirit in there as well. You are going to help them, but it is going to take time. Can you understand that, Lorna?'

I looked up at Michael. He made me feel so peaceful and safe, so I said, 'I think I do, in a sort of way.' He smiled down at me. 'Now don't be worried about anything, just go and play.'

That holiday went by slowly and each time I was in my grandmother's house I would avoid going down the passage off the main corridor on the ground floor. This passage was very different to the corridor. The corridor was wide with a polished dark wood floor and with paintings and potted plants down the side. The doors off it were enormous with elaborate wooden door frames. The passageway, on the other hand, was very narrow and dark with a flagstone floor and unpainted stone walls. It looked so long and dark, I could hardly see the pantries I had been told were at the end of it. I knew, even though the angels hadn't told me, that the beautiful young woman was down that passage. And I knew in my mind and heart that the other spirit Michael had talked about was a man, and that he was there too. I was afraid of them. I knew they wanted something from me, but I didn't know what. I learnt no more about them on that holiday, though.

The year I turned nine, my third summer holiday down in Mountshannon, the angels started to tell me stories about these two beautiful spirits. One of my favourite places in the old house was the place Granny called her conservatory. I'm not quite sure that we would, call it that today. A small space with a big window, at the end of a corridor, it was always very bright and full of my grandma's plants and flowers. Sometimes, when I was down there, Michael would come to me and the other angels would gather around me and they would show me something of the past. This day, Michael asked me to look out the window. I did and I saw the landscape change, it was as if Michael had pulled back a curtain. They showed me this beautiful young maiden. I know this seems a strange word for a nine-year-old but the word 'maiden' came to my mind when they were talking of her – I didn't even know what it meant then. I turned around and asked Michael, 'You said she was a beautiful young woman and yet I would say that she was a maiden. Does a maiden mean a young woman?' Michael nodded.

I looked again and was shown her walking through the fields. Michael told me her name was Marie. She was bringing a few cows in. She was carrying a stick, not just a small stick, but a good heavy stick. The angels told me to look closely and try to remember everything. So I memorised that scene. I can even remember the details of her dress. It was light in colour, white with little browny-orange flowers; there was a pocket on the left-hand side and it had a collar that looked kind of square. Her hair was long and straight; it didn't seem to have a curl in it, and it blew in the wind. She was very white, very pale in complexion. Her eyes were blue. She was very slight in build and her legs looked skinny. She wore flat shoes. They weren't boots, because I remember asking the angels why she wasn't wearing boots in the field on a damp day. They never answered that but just smiled.

I was afraid. Why were the angels telling me all this? I

knew that whenever the angels told me something like this it meant I would be asked to do something. I really didn't want anything to do with it.

Over that summer I learnt a lot about Marie from Michael and the angels. It was then that I saw the young man for the first time. I was walking up past the coach houses and I saw him peer out, but only for a moment. It was at the same little window where I had seen Marie, a window near the old pantries. I walked on, pretending I hadn't seen him, but then I caught another glimpse of him out of the corner of my eye at another of the little windows.

The angels had taught me how to take in appearances quickly, so with only those two brief glimpses I could tell he was dark-haired with sharp features. I couldn't be sure, though, how tall he was because I only saw his face and shoulders. I didn't know what to make of him. I felt afraid and walked past the windows as fast as I could and then broke into a run until I reached the gate and climbed over into the garden. I felt safe there with the big trees and lovely flowers. There were rabbits and birds and sometimes, if I sat under one of the big trees where the branches sloped down, I could look into a blackbirds' nest, and see the chicks or the eggs before they hatched. I sat in the garden giving out to the angels, reminding them that I was still only a little girl and could get frightened.

The day before we headed back home that summer, I slipped through the kitchen and into the house so I could look down the passage, even though I didn't dare to go down. I could see the pair of them in the distance standing side by side. It was cold down there, very, very cold, and it was as if their pain was travelling up the passage towards me – as if it might hit me. I said the prayer the angels had taught me, 'Jesus, Mary, I love you. Save souls.' I took two or three steps backwards. I looked briefly again but I was too scared to keep looking and rushed up to a big window at the top of the corridor. It was light there and I could look across the fields of cows over to Lough Derg. I felt safe there. The angels seemed to be all around me, like a blanket, or a mist around me. I couldn't see any individual angel; I could just feel the presence of many.

Back in Dublin, I wouldn't even think about those two spirits in Mountshannon, but then it would come to holiday time and I would start to think about them again. I still didn't really understand what was going on, but somewhere inside I knew that there was some heavy hurt involved with those two spirits, and that one day I would have to walk down that passage I kept avoiding. The thought of it terrified me.

Chapter Fifteen

Back in time

The next summer when we went to Mountshannon on holiday we didn't stay at my grandmother's. We stayed in a house in the village, which was empty. We visited Granny's house a lot though, and I wasn't allowed to forget the two spirits. I knew I was going to be asked to do something. This upset me and made me scared and sad.

Sometimes when I was sad like that Hosus would appear. One day, when I was in the little conservatory, he appeared and said to me, 'We know your heart is sometimes heavy and you are such a little thing, but you have to remember God made you different, and this will always be your life.' Hosus continued, 'You will always have to do this work, because you are needed.'

I looked at him crossly. 'But I really don't want to. Why couldn't God pick someone else? Why does he want me?'

Hosus just laughed at me and said, 'One day you will know why yourself. But you have to go down the passage, you know.'

I said, 'No! I'm never going down that passage for anybody. I'm afraid, it frightens me.'

Hosus said, 'But you have seen the spirits and you know that they are beautiful. You know they are good.'

'But I feel something bad happened. I can't put it into

words but I feel it in my heart, and it makes me want to cry.'

Hosus looked down at me sadly. 'You will have to cry because it is your tears that they need to set them free. They need you and one day they will go with you, but you have to go down the passage.'

But I didn't go down the passage that day. I said, 'No way!' to Hosus and I turned around and walked out of the conservatory, down the corridor and into my grandmother's dining room. I never even looked down the passage, let alone walked it! I can be stubborn sometimes. I sat down in the chair on the left of the dining room table. My grandmother walked in from the kitchen; she didn't say a word, but simply put a cup of tea and some fresh bread and jam down in front of me, and went back into the kitchen, leaving me alone.

One day, after I had been helping my grandmother to shine the floor, Angel Michael appeared. He took my hand and we walked down to the conservatory. When we were there gazing out the window he told me to look to the left. I looked to the left in the direction of the orchard and everything changed again – it was like looking at a big screen. I knew I was standing in the conservatory with Angel Michael holding my hand but the time and the place changed completely. I could see a group of women out picking blackberries in a rough, hilly area and there in the middle of them was Marie. She looked about sixteen. A young man came walking across the fields; he was tall, elegant and well dressed. I knew it was the man I had seen at the window. Marie straightened up and stood looking at him. It was as if she couldn't take her eyes off him. He gave her a big smile and she blushed crimson. I could see and hear the other girls teasing her. Another girl, who looked so like her I thought she must be her sister, said, 'You'd better get that smile off your face before you go into the house, someone will notice.' Then I was shown them finish picking the blackberries and Marie running home ahead of her sister. As she came in her mother said, 'Your cheeks are very red, Marie; you shouldn't be rushing around like that.' But her mother didn't seem to be too bothered, telling Marie, 'Get those nice blackberries all cleaned and we can get going on with the jam making.'

The scene changed again; I was shown Marie in a grocery shop. It was dark and dusty with a big wooden box and with crates and sacks on the ground. Marie was at the counter, buying groceries I think, when the young man walked in. He gave Marie such a big smile. It was obvious they couldn't keep their eyes off each other. The shopkeeper obviously noticed, as she said to Marie, 'You had better hurry home, young lady. Your mother is waiting on that sugar and butter.' Marie blushed and ran out of the shop looking very embarrassed. The young man followed her and caught up with her on a quiet road that seemed to go to her parents' home. They walked and talked, looking very comfortable together, and no one saw them.

For much of this holiday I was fighting with the angels, still saying, 'No, no, no, I'm not going to go down the passage. It will hurt and I'm too little. You should have asked someone bigger; you should have asked an adult.' I know I haven't explained that pain or hurt. I didn't understand it myself as of yet.

One day, Michael appeared when I was playing with a small injured hawk I had rescued. The bird was with me all the time that summer. Michael walked around the garden with me and my bird and then through my grandmother's kitchen. My grandmother and mother were there, baking bread, but no one seemed to notice me. We walked into the conservatory where all the plants were blossoming. I knew I was going to be asked to do something.

'Can't I just stay here with the bird, petting it and enjoying the sunshine?' I begged Michael.

'No!' was all he replied.

I looked at him. 'No, I'm not going down the passage,' I said stubbornly.

'I don't want you to go down the passage,' he replied. 'I just want to walk around the house with you.' I just looked at him. Michael's eyes were so bright, it was as if you could see for miles and miles inside of them, as if you went down a long, long road, as if you were passing through time itself. His face always shone so brightly and he took my hand, and then he let it go, and put his arm around my shoulder. Angels can make themselves so human that as a child I frequently forgot that they were angels. They were my best friends. Michael took me by the hand and we walked back down the main corridor and turned right into a room, which I had only been in once before and then only for a minute. Michael pushed the two big heavy doors open. Now when I think of it I realise how often Michael and the angels do things like open doors for me. Anyone watching would have thought that the doors opened by themselves.

It was a large room with a fireplace. There was very little furniture but there were big old-fashioned chairs down the opposite end by the fireplace. Through the big window I could see a grapevine hanging. The room was full of happiness and joy, but there was sadness there too. I couldn't quite figure it out and I looked up at Michael and he said, 'Do you feel it?'

I said, 'Yes.'

Michael continued, 'We have to give you little lessons every now and then, because there is so much that you need to learn and so little time for you to learn it in.' He motioned to me. 'Walk towards the fireplace and tell me what you see, and feel.'

As I walked towards the two chairs by the fireplace I suddenly saw an old man and a woman sitting in them. They were dressed in heavy, elegant-looking clothes. They seemed happy. I turned and looked at Michael, and said, 'Don't they see me?'

'No, they are actually in Heaven,' he replied, 'but you need to see them. Can you tell me anything else about them?'

I turned and looked at the old woman. She probably wasn't that old, it was just her style of dress. 'Yes, her hair is a greyish brown and straight,' I said. 'She has it up in a kind of a twist not like a bun, and she has a pin in it. It's not like the clips we use. It's like a long pin, and half of it looks as if it's covered in diamonds.'

'That's right, but what else do you see?' Michael asked.

I looked at her face more closely. 'I know,' I said. 'That's *his* mum, isn't it?'

Michael smiled and nodded. She turned in my direction, and for a moment I thought she could see me, but Michael said, 'She's not allowed to see you.'

She called out a name, 'Edward', and a little boy of no more than five ran over to her. He had a tanned face and looked quite podgy to me, not much like he had looked when I'd glimpsed him in the window. I turned and looked at the old man – he wasn't really old either, he just kind of looked old. I watched him looking at his little son playing with a wooden carriage on the floor in front of him. I couldn't understand it then, but I could feel loneliness. And suddenly I understood that somehow, someway, he knew that this precious son would be taken from him and that he would miss him terribly.

Edward's father sat there in the chair so upright and so stern, a man with authority, watching his young son play on the floor. In truth he was behaving as fathers were supposed to back then – not showing his love and affection. Regardless of this behaviour I think his little son knew how much he loved him because he turned and smiled up at him. I turned and looked at Michael in puzzlement. 'The chairs are very different to what is here,' I said, 'and the fireplace is different.'

'Don't worry about that,' Michael said. 'What matters is what you feel in your heart. You have to feel this mother's and father's love and hurt, and set their son free. God is using you as a soul catcher, Lorna,' Michael said. 'Edward and Marie have chosen to stay because of what others did, and you need to feel their hurt in order set them free.'

I looked back at the child Edward and his parents – they were gone.

'Before we leave,' Michael said, 'tell me what you feel now.'

'I hear music and laughter and lots of voices,' I said, 'but a lot of those voices are recent.'

Michael smiled and said, 'You're right. Your grandmother has brought a lot of light and happiness into this big old house with her work with the hostel. She is gifted too, but God has used her in a different way, because she was not strong enough to do what you are doing.'

I laughed and replied, 'Will you go away, my grandmother is the best!' and Michael smiled and agreed with me. We left the room, and headed towards the big old stairs.

Before I tell you about going upstairs, let me just explain one thing. I was there in that house in Mountshannon with Michael. But I don't believe it was the same house as Edward's parents lived in. Sometimes, when the angels draw back the curtain to show me something, I can be in one place but be shown a completely different place. When I was shown Marie or Edward the scenery used to change. For example, the conservatory had a view of the lake, but when I was shown Marie or Edward I never saw a lake. Perhaps the house in which the story of Edward and Marie unfolded doesn't exist any longer – so many old houses in Ireland have been destroyed over the years.

The hostel had a very big staircase – well, to me as a child it seemed enormous. It was very wide, and there was a return and the stairs turned to the left up to the big dark landing. We continued walking through the house and Michael brought me to a locked room I had never been in before. Locks were no deterrent to Michael, the doors simply opened in front of him. It was a very elegant room, although it had a mouldy kind of smell. I don't think the windows had been opened for years.

'Do you feel anything in this room related to the spirits downstairs?' Michael asked.

'I'm not sure, Michael,' I replied hesitantly, 'but there is something, something of long ago, I can feel it.' I looked around the room for a moment. 'I can see a hand reaching out from the bed there, somebody very, very old and very feeble. Michael, are you trying to tell me that the feelings in this room are related to the spirits downstairs? If they are, I really don't want to know!' I said.

Michael just smiled and said, 'But, Lorna, you know the answer, you always know the answers because we give them to you.'

I gave in. 'Yes, they are related then.' I started to understand, although you might doubt that a ten-year-old could comprehend this, that I was being called upon to help not just the two spirits, who were there in the house, but also those who had been around them – and their descendants.

I felt burdened and worried about what I was being asked to do as we walked back down the stairs. Michael put his arm around me and hugged me. I needed his hugs very much that day. We went back into the conservatory, where I felt safe, and I must have fallen asleep because I was woken by some hostellers walking up the corridor. I smiled at them as I headed through my grandmother's kitchen and out of the house, across the courtyard. I didn't look back but went straight up the hill and back to the house where we were staying.

As I sit here today, dictating this story, Michael is beside me reminding me of what happened all those years ago and he is saying, 'Lorna, you can explain further as you go on telling the story because as you tell this story, you will understand more and more of it yourself.' I am always learning – we are all always learning, the angels are always teaching me and they will teach you if you let them and that is very, very important for all of us.

Chapter Sixteen

Walking down the passage

Summer holidays came again. This time my family was staying in a little bungalow on a big old farm on the edge of Lough Derg, a beautiful big lake. I liked that place. There were cows and everything, but the walk to my grandmother's was much longer. The angels continued to show me visions of Marie and Edward – and it was always as if I were seeing it on a big cinema screen. One day in the conservatory Hosus told me, 'Look out towards the lake.' I did and the lake disappeared and in its place I saw hills. Then I saw Marie and Edward on horseback. They were having a great time and I could hear Marie's laughter echo across the hills. They followed the road over the hill and then disappeared out of my sight. Then everything came back to normal. Hosus said goodbye and disappeared.

Another day I was with Michael in the conservatory and Michael was holding my hand and suddenly the time and the place changed completely. I saw Edward and Marie walking alongside a river, where there were lots of rocks; they were holding hands. As they walked the noise of the river was getting louder and louder. I could hear them talking at times, Marie telling Edward about her little brother being sick, about the slugs eating the vegetables. I also heard them laughing a lot. Then the river got really loud and I could see they were at a waterfall. They sat on a rock by the waterfall and I saw Edward kissing Marie. I could see they were very happy. Over the image I could hear Michael speaking. 'They are in love, Lorna, and their love is made in Heaven.'

'I know, Michael,' I replied, giggling, 'but I don't often see girls and boys kissing and to me it looks funny.' I have to laugh recalling my reaction.

Then Marie and Edward started to walk back along the river, Edward kissing Marie over and over again, saying he loved her and that they would never be apart. I heard Marie, with tears in her eyes, say to Edward, 'I'm afraid that when your family finds out they will separate us. I know your family won't allow us to be together. They think I'm common, and not good enough for you.'

Edward wiped away her tears, telling her not to worry, telling her he loved her. They kept walking along the river-bank. When they reached the point where they had to separate I heard Edward tell Marie he loved her and would see her soon. And then the vision was gone. I turned to Michael. 'I can feel their love. It makes me feel really good. So why do I feel all this hurt and pain?'

'Lorna,' Michael replied, 'you'll understand as you get to know Edward and Marie better that their love for each other makes them inseparable. No matter what hurt and pain their love may cause them.'

The angels were around me all the time, twenty-four hours a day. They were everywhere – everywhere I walked, every-where I looked – but most of all they were around my grandmother's house. Even though I knew I had to walk down the passage eventually, I was very afraid. I was afraid of what

I was going to see, of what I was going to feel – all the pain and hurt. I said to God, 'I know you are there all the time, but I need some more reassurance. I'm still quite little.'

One afternoon I was sitting on a stone at the coach house, drawing a picture of a swallow's nest that was just inside the entrance of the coach house. Hosus appeared and greeted me. I was delighted to see him. He asked me to look at the little window where I saw Marie for the first time. I looked and there she was. Suddenly everything changed. I saw Marie, carrying a basket, coming out of a shop in town. Her way home seemed to be long and boring. The road was very rough. Then I saw Marie step off the road and go into the woods. I could see her standing there, surrounded by trees and bushes. She looked anxious.

'What is happening?' I asked Hosus.

'Marie is meeting Edward in secret,' he replied.

'Is this one of their hiding places?' I asked Hosus. He didn't answer, as at that moment Edward came through the trees and I saw them embrace each other with great passion, as if they had not seen each other for a long time. They sat on the ground beneath a tree, still kissing. With an arm around her, I heard Edward tell Marie that he was going to talk to his father about them. Then Edward took something small out of his breast pocket and took Marie's hand, asking her would she be his wife. Marie looked delighted as she slipped the ring on her finger and said yes. Then I saw Marie take the ring off her finger, saying she couldn't wear it publicly yet. She rooted in her pocket and found a piece of string and Edward tied it around her neck. They kissed and said goodbye. Then I was shown Marie in the yard of her home and as she reached the door she put her left hand to her chest feeling the ring under her clothes. Then everything came back to normal again.

'Hosus, they got engaged.' I said happily. 'That means they can marry now.'

Hosus looked at me sadly, saying, 'Lorna, they will never marry.'

He told me to look up at the window again. I did and for one split second time seemed to stand still. I was shown a beautiful sunny day and Marie and Edward together again in a quiet place. They were embracing, kissing and making love. I didn't fully understand what they were doing, but I saw nothing wrong with it. The vision disappeared and I stood there a little embarrassed and shy – I had never seen a couple joined in love before. I turned to Hosus. 'Is Marie going to have to baby now, even though they are not married?'

'Yes, Lorna, they will have a baby,' he replied and disappeared.

I did walk the passage that summer – on our very last afternoon there. I didn't realise at the time that it would be my last afternoon ever in that house. Shortly afterwards, my grandmother gave up her job there because of ill health and we never holidayed in Mountshannon again.

I stood at the end of the passage, scared and surrounded by angels. As I stood there I took in the hurt of those two spirits. I started to walk forward down the passage, where I had never dared go before. And it was as if the angels around me were forming a great temple, their bodies forming pillars and their arms a great arch. The two spirits, those beautiful two souls, were inside this. It was as if I was in another world. I don't remember a lot about what happened but I remember I felt the two spirits grab me and hold on to me.

I felt enormous emotional pain and hurt. I have no idea how long this lasted. Then I started to walk back up the passage towards the light and they came with me. All of a sudden everything was over. I was back on the corridor looking back down at Edward and Marie as they stood at the end of the passage arm in arm. I could see them, but this time it was different. I knew that they weren't really there, not in the same way. I didn't quite understand it but I knew they were now free to leave my grandmother's house.

As I left Mountshannon the following day, in the car with the rest of my family, it felt as if those spirits, those two beautiful souls, were following me. I knew that they had been set free, that they could go straight to Heaven. But they hadn't gone. I didn't quite understand what was going on. Why were they following me rather than going straight to God? As you read on, you'll understand why. Let me just say now they didn't want to go straight to Heaven. With my help, they wanted to break the bondage of pain and hurt that was holding many families back, to break the chains, to let them be free, so that what happened long ago would not continue to bring pain and ill fortune to future generations.

Chapter Seventeen

I was their gatekeeper

Shortly after arriving home from Mountshannon we moved into a newly built house in Leixlip on the outskirts of Dublin. My parents had never owned their own home, but finally, due to a series of events, they were able to buy one. We were all so excited. I could still feel the presence in a strange kind of way of the two spirits from Mountshannon. It was as if they were travelling, going somewhere, yet they did not come to me. Somehow I knew they were going to the new house, and would be waiting for me there.

The day of the move to Leixlip, I was the last one to leave the old house. Da had gone off with a car full of people and things, and I was waiting for him to come back to bring me, my rabbit and my cat Tiger to the new house. I was there alone in the house making a cup of tea when Hosus appeared and I looked at him with tears in my eyes and said, 'I know that they are waiting for me in the new house. Why? Why do I have to continue for so long to feel their hurt? I don't like it and sometimes it scares me. I'm scared, scared of the unknown.'

Hosus consoled me. 'Don't be thinking about it; you know they are beautiful spirits. Things have to happen to set everyone free. You are the only one who can set them all free. You have been made their gatekeeper.' Hosus told me to close my eyes. I woke up when I heard my da knock on the door.

I was very nervous during the journey, because I knew they were going to be there in the new house. I understood that they were good and there was no need to be afraid, but I still was unhappy about it. My father drove the car to Leixlip and up into the housing estate. As we came closer, I could picture the house in my mind, even though I hadn't ever seen it or been shown a photograph. I knew exactly where he was going to turn and which house he was going to stop at. I remember opening the car door and feeling so strange. The knowledge that these two spirits were going to live with me twenty-four hours a day upset me. I rescued my cat from the boot and assured her that everything was OK. Then the hall door opened and my mother was standing there saying, 'Hurry up, come on in.' I walked into the hall very carefully, not because I was carrying my cat in the box but because I felt that I had to be alert, so the spirits would not give me too much of a fright. I didn't know where they would be.

Where were they? I put the box down and opened it and took out poor Tiger who was very upset. I walked her around the brand-new dining room and the kitchen, showing her everything, telling her again it was all all right. They weren't on the ground floor – I had looked all around. The cat settled down quickly enough and went all around the house, sniffing and smelling everything. She had more courage than I had because I had still only been downstairs. I didn't want to go upstairs. But eventually I couldn't avoid it any longer and went into the hall. Edward was standing there on the stairs. 'Why are you standing there?' I asked him and his reply was, 'This is where I always will be for as long as I have to be here.' I told him he made me nervous and he said, 'I'm sorry, but I need to talk to you each time you go up the stairs. That is part of what we need to do – and it's part of your life too! You have set Marie and me free but we are not going until all the others are free as well.'

'I don't like this – I'll run up the stairs every time then,' I replied. 'I feel your pain and when you mention the others it's as if they're here too, even if I can't see their faces.' With that I took a deep breath and ran up the stairs two steps at a time, as quickly as I could. He reached out to touch me. When I reached the top of the stairs I cried out, 'Made it!'

The bathroom at the top of the stairs became very important to me – like a sanctuary! It was small but it was the light switch, a pull string, that was the really important thing for me. That first evening I realised that just as I reached the top of the stairs, I could put my hand into the bathroom and pull the string and have some light. Already I was planning all kinds of strategies in my head.

I had to go back down the stairs that evening. As I did, I took a deep breath and said my usual prayer, 'Jesus, Mary, I love you. Save souls.' I could feel Edward touch me. It was as if life was being taken from me – flowing from my soul, as if he was receiving my grace and passing it on to others. Deep down I knew the others were there waiting, waiting to be set free. Knowing this didn't stop me from going as fast as I could, though, and when I got down I immediately turned on the hall light, and went into the warmth of the kitchen.

Much to my distress my parents decided that I shouldn't go back to school after we moved to Leixlip. I had loved school and learning, and now I had nowhere to go to escape the spirits. Edward was always on the stairs and I would often say, 'I see you there! Just leave me alone!' He would just smile at me. He was always so well dressed, elegant and neat.

There was a phone in the hall in the house and one of those old telephone stools. One day the phone rang and as there was no one else in the house, I answered it. It was my aunt. As I was talking with her, Edward started joking with me through the banisters, whispering bird sounds in my ear, trying to distract me while I was on the phone. 'Look at the little mouse running across the floor,' he cried out. I jumped with fright – even though I had once kept mice as pets. I always remember that day because Edward was very carefree, gentle and playful.

A few months after we moved into the house in Leixlip, Da came up with the idea of my going and working with him in the garage in Rathmines. I was thrilled. I loved the idea of going to work. I also felt so relieved that I would have an excuse to get away from the spirits for some of the time. The night Da suggested this I went up the stairs – running as usual – and for the first time ever on that stairs I wasn't disturbed, not one little bit. Nor was I the next morning coming down. I smiled, because I knew that Edward realised I was being allowed to leave the house. I loved work in the garage and got on well there and each night, when I had to go up the stairs to bed, I would rush up the stairs and on reaching the landing would immediately reach my hand around through the bathroom door and pull that light string. It's silly now when I think of it. I knew I had nothing to be afraid of, but when it was dark at night I didn't like going up the stairs. Sometimes the bulb would be gone in the hall or the landing or both and my parents weren't very quick in replacing them. It was as if that's the way it was meant to be – that the darkness was to be there as well. And it didn't matter how fast I ran up the stairs, I would be stopped, as if everything was in slow motion or time itself had stopped. I would feel all the hurt and sadness of that young man. Edward in a sense was pouring out the sins, pouring out the anger, the hate, of those who had hurt them. He was trying to clear the sins of others. It was as if I had to feel all the hurt myself humanly to make up for the sins of those who had caused the tragedy and of those who hadn't stopped it. These sins had been passed on to future generations. In a sense I was being asked to pay for the sins of their fathers' fathers. That's the only way I can explain it. God works in such strange ways. Sometimes it would puzzle me and one day I went off on my own to pray. The angels moved away and I asked God, 'Why all of this?' and the answer He gave me was, 'Why not, if that's what they want?'

This went on for the seven years I lived with my parents in that house – every time I went up the stairs I saw and felt Edward and all the pain. At different times Edward showed me different parts of the story.

One night as I was going up the stairs to bed he showed me himself arriving at his parents' home. He allowed me to know what was on his mind. He was going to tell his father about Marie. I was shown him calling out to his father and then going into a room that looked like a library with a big fire burning. His father was standing there with two other men – his uncles, Martin and James. He was surprised to see them there. He knew immediately that something was wrong. He walked over and greeted them, shaking their hands. They seemed very cold. Another man Edward didn't know now walked in and his father asked this man to tell Edward what he had told them. The man spoke nervously. He had a cap in his hand and was twisting it tightly. He said he had seen Edward with a young girl called Marie in the woods. His father ordered the man out of the room in an angry voice. I could hear his father and two uncles raise their voices in anger. His father roared at him about disgracing the family. He called Edward all kinds of hurtful names. He laughed at the idea of Edward considering marrying a common girl, at him even thinking it might ever be allowed.

And then Edward let me go, and everything went back to normal and I ran up the stairs and reached my hand around the bathroom and pulled the string for the bathroom light to go on. I felt devastated. I just sat on the loo crying for a few minutes, knowing that my tears were prayers too. Then I prayed out loud, knowing I was their gatekeeper. I gave out to God and the angels, saying it wasn't fair. 'I saw so much love and joy in Edward and Marie – and then to see their love torn apart.' As I sat on the loo the angels eased my pain, so when eventually I did go to my bedroom I was able to sleep.

Lots of times what Edward showed me was the love that Marie and he had for each other, but anytime Edward took my hand going up the stairs I knew what he was going to share with me was going to cause a lot of pain. On one occasion as he took my hand he showed me his two uncles and his father discussing what was to be done with Edward. As far as they were concerned Edward was a disgrace. His duty was to marry a girl with land so that the families would grow richer. By taking up with a poor girl he was jeopardising the wealth of all the family.

Edward was called to talk with his father again – this time with his mother present. She tried to keep the peace but her efforts were to no avail. Edward's father said that anyone who supported this girl or her family would be thrown out of their homes and he'd do his damnedest to make sure they starved. He then told Edward that he was no longer a son of his, that he would never speak to him again, and that he was being sent away. Edward pleaded with his father but to no avail. Within hours he was gone, escorted off the land by the two uncles. Before he left, though, Edward did have the chance to give a sympathetic servant a letter for his trusted friend Daniel. In it he asked Daniel to take care of Marie and tell her why he had to go away and that he would write to her.

The two uncles took Edward to work on a run-down estate owned by one of them. Edward worked very hard, thinking that if he proved himself to his father, his father would eventually accept Marie. He wrote letters to Marie every day telling her he loved her with all his heart – that he hoped that sometimes when she was alone she would put the ring, the token of his love, on her finger and that one day they would be together again. Edward didn't know that none of these letters were getting to Marie. They were all intercepted by one of his uncles, who read them aloud, laughing, and then burned them.

Sometimes, Marie would be standing beside Edward on the stairs. One evening, returning from the cinema, I ran up the stairs as quickly as I could. I only got about halfway up when I saw Marie standing on the stairs with Edward. Then everything moved slowly and time seemed to stand still. I saw a pregnant Marie in her home. She was probably six months or more. She was in the bedroom she shared with her three sisters, and they were surrounding her, trying to comfort her and protect her from what was going on downstairs. I heard a lot of raised women's voices from downstairs, accusing Marie's mother of hiding her pregnancy. Voices saying Marie should be sent away and never allowed to return, that it would be a blessing if the baby died at birth.

I was then shown downstairs. The house was full of women from the town, but Marie's mother was a strong character and well able to deal with them. Then the door slammed opened and Marie's father came in, followed by a small crowd of local men. Marie's father didn't seem to know how to handle the situation. A bit of him was very angry with Marie for putting the whole family in this situation. The men were very angry too. As far as they were concerned, Marie had no right to be involved with Edward. They felt that her actions – offending their landlord, Edward's father – were putting their own livelihoods at risk. Distressed as I was at what I was seeing, I was delighted that Marie's mother defended her daughter with such vehemence, telling the townspeople to get out of her house and never to cross the threshold again, that they would raise the child as their own. Marie's father now stood by her mother, shouting at them to get out. But he didn't quite know what to do. There was so much bitterness and hate against Marie, her unborn child and her family.

One day, after more than a year of his working on that run-down estate, Edward's uncle brought him a letter saying his mother was unwell and he was to return home. Before he left his uncle threatened him, warning that if he had anything to do with that girl, his life would be over and that his father and family would be better off without him. Edward rushed home and was relieved to find his mother a little better and able to sit in a chair by the fire. He kissed her forehead, saying he was glad to see she was much improved. His mother was very happy to see him, but his father still wouldn't talk to him and acted as if he did not exist. This caused Edward great pain, as he loved his father very much. That was as much as I was shown that day but some time afterwards Edward grabbed my hand on the stairs, and I was allowed to see more of the story. I was shown Edward visiting his friend Daniel in the town. It seemed to be just after he had come back to visit his sick mother. Daniel told him that Marie had had a baby. Edward was shocked. He hadn't known she was pregnant. He felt foolish at not having realised that this could happen. But on another level he was pleased to be a father. Now he just had to find a way for them to be together as a family. Daniel told him that he must not under any circumstances attempt to see Marie – that to do so would put her life, and the life of the baby, in danger. He told Edward that his father was acting on the threat to evict anyone helping her family, and that a few families had already suffered because of this. He told Edward of the great anger in the community towards himself, Marie and the child. He told Edward, 'Your father is a hard man. He shows no mercy.' Edward left his friend and walked through the town. He saw Marie and she saw him. They didn't speak but seemed to read each other's minds. She headed for the woods to the place where I had been shown her meeting Edward secretly. She hoped that Edward would be able to come – even if just for a brief moment. I was never shown the meeting, but I know from what happened later that they did meet. And someone saw them.

I had many encounters with Marie at this time too. Most of the time she was gentler than Edward, though, as she had already let me feel her hurt when I looked down that passage all those years ago in Mountshannon. Sometimes I would see Marie in our new dining room. She always seemed to be cleaning or dusting. The house in Leixlip was a newly built semi-detached, but I always felt that to her it was somewhere else. Sometimes I would see her move through the dining-room window, as if it didn't exist, into the garden and act as if she was hanging washing on the line or beating a rug.

Marie was always so bright and light. The sun always shone around her. Sometimes it was as if she was wearing an apron and the wind would catch it. She used to smile at me a lot. At times, when she smiled at me, I would feel tremendous comfort, like forgiveness, as if she was no longer hurt by all that had happened to her. Occasionally she talked to me without words. One day I was in the dining room and Marie told me about the first time she had ever seen Edward. 'He was so gorgeous, so handsome; I had never seen a boy that looked like that before. I didn't know who he was or his name, but from that day on I watched for him, hoping I would see him again. I didn't have to worry because I learnt later that he was watching out for me too. That's how the story started, Lorna, we fell in love. We knew we were meant for each other.'

Sometimes as I was walking from the bus stop coming home from work from my new job in a department store, I'd see Marie standing at my bedroom window. When I think of it now, I realise I never saw her at any other window than that window. As I came around the corner I would see her turn her head and look directly at me. Sometimes I would raise my hand and give her a little wave and then look down at the footpath and keep walking. When I glanced up again she would always be gone. Other times I wouldn't wave. I'd pretend I hadn't seen her, and would look down. On these occasions when I would look up she'd be still at the window – as if waiting for my wave, my acknowledgement, and then she would disappear. I smile now thinking of it.

Chapter Eighteen

The tragedy unfolds

I always remember the first time I brought Joe to meet my mother in the house in Leixlip. When we came in the hall door, I glanced up and saw the spirits on the stairs – both of them together, with their arms around each other – and they gave me a big smile, as if blessing us and wishing us well.

All this time I was going out with Joe, the two spirits were on my mind. In fact, they were always on my mind. It may be difficult to understand, but I was praying for them all the time, praying with every breath I took, knowing that I could never stop praying no matter what I was doing. When I was eating my dinner I was still praying.

The angels showed me more of the story one day when I was sitting in the garden feeding my rabbit. The angels pulled back the curtain and gave me a vision of something that saddened me deeply. I saw Marie's mother heading towards the river with Marie's baby held very proudly in her arms. I got the impression this was the first time Marie's baby had been brought out publicly into the community. There seemed to be some kind of festival and everyone was heading for the river. Some of Marie's younger brothers and sisters were carrying blankets and baskets with bread and fruit. After some time I saw Marie talking to her mother and then slipping away quietly. An angel whispered to me that it was the day after she had met Edward in the woods and she was going to meet him again. There were lots of children down by the river, playing and having fun or sitting down eating but yet, as I looked, there seemed to be something not quite right. I saw some women call out to Marie's mother for help. Marie's mother hurried over to help, carrying the baby in her arms. Seeing a child covered in blood on the ground she automatically, and without any hesitation, handed Marie's baby to a young woman beside her. There seemed to be lots of hustle and bustle as people tried to help. A few minutes later Marie's mother heard a scream from the riverbank. Everything had happened so quickly. Somehow Marie's baby had fallen into the river. Marie's mother was shocked. Frantically she got up from the child she had been tending and raced towards the river. The baby had been swept along with the current and Marie's mother ran along the riverbank. Some men ran towards her and stopped her, saying it was too late, that the baby couldn't still be alive – that they would get the baby's body. Marie's mother collapsed on to her knees, devastated and wailing. Some women came running up to her. Marie's mother looked up at them and to her horror saw they had smug expressions on their faces. She looked at the crowd silently watching her. 'How could you kill an innocent baby?' she roared at them. Marie's mother stood there and gathered her family in silence. They waited and waited for the men to return. When it got dark they walked home, shocked and in tears, clinging to one another. Marie's mother was saying over and over again, 'How am I going to tell Marie?'

The vision faded. I was numb with grief. I couldn't imagine

how any mother or grandmother would feel if they lost a child in such a way. I got up from the garden, leaving my rabbit loose, and ran to the loo and locked myself in, crying. The angels surrounded me, doing their best to comfort me.

As often as I saw Marie and Edward I never saw their child. I never saw that little spirit. I knew it had been sent straight to Heaven and was there, waiting for its parents to come. I often think of that little spirit in Heaven waiting on its dad and mum, who had chosen to stay as spirits on this earth in order to help those who had hurt them.

Eventually a time came when the spirits decided that others needed to know that they were in the house, that this was necessary for things to move on and unfold. Then Marie did something she had never done before.

One morning I was sleeping late. It was my day off from the department store and I had been out late with Joe the night before. In my sleep I could hear Marie calling, 'Lorna, Lorna . . .' repeating my name over and over again. Then I could hear her footsteps. It was as if I could hear her walking down the passage – her passage in Mountshannon. Suddenly, I knew she was on the landing. 'Lorna, Lorna . . .' She kept calling my name, gently but insistently. Suddenly I heard knocking on the door of my bedroom. I was terrified that she would wake someone else. I called out to Marie, 'Go away!' I heard my mother call out; Marie had obviously woken her. 'I'm awake, Mum,' I called. I sat bolt upright in the bed, afraid of what might happen next. Suddenly Marie pressed down the handle and opened the door wide, still calling, 'Lorna, Lorna...' That frightened me. Spirits aren't supposed to be able to open doors. In fact, it made me really angry. She walked the few steps over to the top bunk bed where I had been sleeping, calling my name all the time. I sat looking at her. I was shocked more than anything. She just kept saying, 'Lorna.' Now she was right beside me, facing me, and we looked into each other's eyes.

'Lorna, do you remember when you were a little girl, what you felt when I was allowing you to feel my life?' she asked. 'I know you blocked a lot of it out. I'm going to talk and I'm going to allow you to feel what you felt then, when you were a little girl. I'll make it as gentle as I can.' I felt scared as Marie said those words, and I guess she saw it because she put her hand on mine and all of a sudden I just felt peaceful. She started to give me a vision of what had happened.

Marie was walking near the river through an area where there were trees. The trees stood on each side and it was dark, with only a little sunlight coming through. The ground was wet and muddy. When she saw the men there, she didn't think much of it. There were four of them, four neighbours, whom she knew. But one of them grabbed her and started to threaten her, to tell her that she had to go away, that they wanted her out of the area and that if she wouldn't go they would beat her up. With that they started to push and kick her. She felt enormous fear rush up inside of her. She fought with every breath, and she struggled, trying to defend herself. I could feel all the fear rush up inside of her. It was as if I was inside of her, helping her in a spiritual way. I was inside of her even though I wasn't even born at that time! Somehow I was there – somehow the time difference was bridged. I could feel her fighting with every breath. I could feel her struggle to defend herself. I could feel every kick she received. She was matted in mud and soaked by the water beneath her. They kept on kicking her and she curled herself up into a ball. Then one of the men grabbed her by the hair and dragged her along, as two others hit her with sticks they had cut from the branches. I can still see it, the men running with her like that, with her arms up over her head.

The man who grabbed her hair was the spirit whom I had seen at my front door in Johnstown. This spirit was the great-great – I have no idea how many greats – grandfather of the man who had come with his wife seeking my help.

Marie did do her best to fight them off. She struggled. She may have been frail but her will to live was very strong. She thought of Edward and she called his name, and she thought of their baby.

I can still see this man. He must have been about fifty, holding her by the hair, as he let her battered body go and it slipped to the ground. I was able, back through the years – I know this is hard to understand – to tell her that her child, her baby, was gone. She heard me clearly. She knew this and stopped fighting to stay alive. So she didn't suffer longer than she had to. She let go. I know that Marie died there where she fell. I can still see Marie's body now. I can see her as I dictate this into the voice-activated computer. It was dirty, covered with mud and blood. I can see her guardian angel wrapped around her on the ground. I can see wings, not full wings, just parts of them. The feathers are muddy. Angels were there when this was happening, but they had been powerless to stop it. I saw the shock on the faces of the men when they stopped and realised what they had done. Marie told me it was an accident, that they didn't mean to kill her, they only meant to frighten her but they had got carried away. Yet one of the men came and gave her couple of kicks, as if to make sure, and they just ran off.

As I sat there in my bed in Leixlip, Marie's hand slipped out of mine, and I flopped back down in the bed and closed my eyes for a moment. Marie walked towards the window and disappeared.

Chapter Nineteen

Telling Joe and my da about the spirits

Joe and I bought the little cottage in Maynooth before we married and we moved in on our wedding day. I wondered what would happen to the two spirits. Would they move with me into the little cottage? And if they did, what would I tell Joe, who knew nothing about them at this stage? I needn't have worried. They didn't follow me. They stayed where they were in my parents' house in Leixlip. They weren't meant to come to my new family home in Maynooth. It wasn't meant to be – they weren't being allowed to interfere with my life as a wife and mother. It didn't mean they disappeared from my life though. At times, in the kitchen in Maynooth, I would hear the spirits of Marie and Edward calling to me from my parents' house in Leixlip, some six miles away. It was as if they were afraid I would forget them. But how could I? I was still praying every day and night for them to achieve what they wanted and so be able to leave. But the years went by and they were still there. Of course, I also often went down to my parents' house in Leixlip, and I would see them then.

One day, when Christopher was a toddler and Owen a baby, I went to visit my parents. We had no car so I had to get the bus – hard going with two children under three. As we turned the corner to the house I could see Marie at my old bedroom window and I raised my hand to wave. I always felt that she needed that acknowledgement, a sign she hadn't been forgotten.

Another day I went into my parents' house, as always, by the back door. There were two men there, and I smiled and said hello to them. I wasn't really introduced, but the angels whispered to me that one of them was called Paul and he would be involved in changing things for the two spirits. I played away with the children while listening quietly to the conversation. I realised that Paul and the other man came from one of the prayer groups that my da attended. I am sure they were good people in their own way but I just didn't feel quite right about them. I felt uneasy about them, and I think my da may have noticed that. I felt that, as far as the two spirits that were in the house were concerned, they were an intrusion. I felt like I had to protect Marie and Edward from these two men, but I didn't really know why. I left the children for a few minutes and went up the stairs. Edward was there, as always. 'What's going on?' I asked. 'I really don't like those men. I'm afraid you and Marie will be hurt in some way.' He replied that I shouldn't be afraid, that this was part of the change. He told me not to worry.

The conversation that day was all about God and Jesus. It gave me great pleasure to see my father becoming more interested in religion, getting to know God better. I felt very thankful, and I felt the two spirits were partly responsible, that my father was becoming more open. I could see changes happening in my parents' home – more talk of God, more people coming into the house. But that day I felt very protective of the two spirits that were there. I tried not to worry, but I couldn't help it.

One day when I was in Maynooth, minding my children, I heard the spirits calling me, just calling my name, as if from down a big long tunnel. I didn't know what was happening but later I learnt that on that day, my da saw something on the stairs. He didn't see what I saw but he was allowed to see, faintly, the lower legs and boots of a man. He felt there was someone there. I don't believe he was allowed to feel the hurt and pain, as I don't believe he would have been able to take it. Da didn't tell me anything about this, at this time, but he talked to Paul, who claimed that the house was possessed. He said that he had been feeling bad things in it. He had, in fact, been in my parents' house on and off for several years and had never said he felt anything, so I'm not sure whether he really did or not. When my da said he had felt it on the stairs, Paul said that yes, 'the evil presence', as he described it, felt strongest there. Da didn't seem to take the whole issue too seriously, but he occasionally prayed and sprinkled holy water on the stairs.

Time passed and I was still feeling very uneasy. I guess part of it was that I knew that it was getting close to the time when I would lose my friends, those two spirits, Marie and Edward. The two beautiful spirits had become my best friends, even though at times I was nervous about all that I felt. I didn't want to lose them. In one sense it was going to be like a death. I was sad at the idea that I would never see or hear of them again, but happy at the idea that they could leave this world of ours. I thought it was going to happen very quickly, but it didn't.

Mum and Da invited Joe and me and the children to go on holiday with them down to Mullingar, about fifty miles outside Dublin. We rarely had holidays so we were all very pleased about this. A few weeks before we went away, I was hanging washing on the line – I always seemed to have loads of washing to do – when this strong breeze came up and I knew immediately it was Hosus. He told me he had come to bring me a message. He told me that Da was going to bring up the subject of the spirits with me when we were on holiday.

I took a deep breath. 'What am I to say? Am I to say anything?'

Hosus replied, 'Yes, Lorna, you have to this time. Tell him that you know all about them, that they have been there a long time, and that a Mass needs to be said in the house.' I must have looked worried as he continued, 'Don't worry, we will prompt you. You'll know what to say but your da will find it very hard to believe. He'll listen to you only once, and he won't ever bring it up again. It's very sad, but you must tell him what we tell you on that day.'

I agreed I would, although I was very worried about the conversation, and sad my father would be so reluctant to talk about it with me. By this time I had told Joe a little about the spirits – really only that they were there, and had been for years, and that I was praying for them. I told him nothing about the pain and fear I had felt or about my role in the whole story. I told Joe that I knew Da was going to ask me about the spirits, and I told him I was really, really worried about it. Joe tried to calm me down.

Eventually, on our way back from the holiday, Da did bring up the subject. The car was packed with my parents, Joe, myself and Owen and Christopher. My da started to talk as he drove. He asked me and Joe whether we knew that there was a spirit in the house in Leixlip, somebody on the stairs. He asked whether we had ever noticed anything or heard anything strange. To my surprise my mum answered, saying that she often saw a young woman out in the garden. I don't know whether she really did or not – I've never been quite sure about it. Da looked at her in surprise. Apparently she had never told him that before, although she knew all about Da's experience on the stairs. I told my da that I knew they were there. I described Edward for him. I didn't tell them everything, but I explained there was another spirit there too. I described Marie for them and told them her name. I told him that the two spirits had been in the house since they moved in and had been in Mountshannon House when we had all holidayed there when I was a child. I also explained that they weren't bad, that they were good. I told him that I knew a Mass needed to be said, not only for those two spirits themselves, but for other souls that they wanted released. I said it would be wonderful if he and Mum could organise such a Mass. I didn't say an awful lot. Da just listened. He didn't ask any questions or make any comment. I was very disappointed about this. I felt that maybe he was apprehensive and wanted to protect me. I would have liked to talk more, to share with him some of what had been going on in my life, but he didn't ask me and I didn't feel able to go on explaining in the absence of questions from him.

Joe had been sitting quietly in the car and he told my father that I had told him all about this before and that I had described many things to him. My da talked to Joe for several minutes about God and about spiritual things, but he never spoke to me directly. That was the last time my da said anything about the spirits in Leixlip to me or to Joe.

That night, lying in bed in the cottage, I told Joe that I was disappointed that Da hadn't asked me more, that he wasn't more interested in the two spirits. Joe suggested that perhaps he was afraid. Da may have been afraid, but I still wanted that Mass said.

Chapter Twenty

A Mass is said in the house

I really wanted my da to organise that Mass; I knew it was very important. Months passed and I heard nothing. Then suddenly, when I was in my parents' house, I started to hear things in passing about a special Mass which was to be held there. I wasn't asked anything about the Mass or told anything, let alone invited to it. It was just that sometimes I would overhear things. I found this really hard. I was happy that there were plans for a Mass, but I was very upset and hurt that my family was leaving me out of it.

Over those months I talked to Angel Michael a lot, seeking comfort. I used to go to the church and light candles more often than usual. I asked Michael why I was being ignored and not invited to the Mass. He told me that he and the angels and my parents' guardian angels were working on getting them to invite me to the Mass. 'Your mother and father,' he continued, 'seem to be listening to others more than they are listening to us. But we will keep trying to get them to invite you. It would make things easier, Lorna, if you were at the Mass to pray for the release of those souls, but it won't make a big difference in the end. If you are not invited to the Mass, there is something you'll be able to do afterwards – so don't worry about it.'

I left it in Michael's hands and I prayed hard to God that

I would be invited to the Mass. Over the following weeks I was invited down less and less to my parents' house, and when I was there, being honest, I felt that I wasn't really welcome, that my parents didn't even want me there, and that other people didn't want me there either. The angels consoled me, saying, 'Don't mind that, Lorna. Remember that the spirits there are pure, they are only doing good, and nothing evil can harm them, but some of your mum and da's friends don't understand that.' They told me to keep on living my own life as wife and mother, and to go to my parents' when I was invited. Despite their comfort I was still fearful of what might happen. I was fearful for those beautiful spirits who had become my friends — fearful that something would go wrong for them.

A week or two later Mum told me that she wanted to do some extra cleaning of the house and would I help? She never told me what it was for, but I was happy to go. She also told me that they were repainting part of the house and asked if Joe could help. Da was getting old and wasn't able to do as much himself any more. I asked Joe and he agreed to help too.

That cleaning day, Mum never once mentioned the Mass, let alone invited me to it. But I had to smile because one of her neighbours, a lovely tall woman with a little boy full of life, called in to talk to Mum about the sandwiches she was making for Sunday. Mum carefully took her into the dining room and closed the door behind her. Again, Mum said nothing. Another neighbour came calling. This time to talk about cakes she was making for Sunday. Again, no mention of the Mass or an invitation from my mother. I saw Edward on the stairs that day and he took my hand. I was shown the last piece of the story. It was evening and Edward was walking fast through a village. There were houses on either side, some with lights on. I know he was on his way to meet Marie. He was just on the edge of the village when I saw several men with big sticks come out of doorways, yelling at him that he had been warned never to see Marie again. To my horror, I recognised one of them, a big, heavy, blocky man. He was one of the men who had beaten Marie to death. An angel told me that this was the same day that the baby had died, that somebody had seen Marie and Edward meet again and that they had decided to teach them both a lesson. The men used language that was so foul I can't even repeat it. They called Edward and Marie every name under the sun. They called their child a bastard.

Edward was scared, but he was also very angry and was fighting back. They kept hitting and kicking him. I saw blood coming from his mouth and nose. When he tried to stand up, they knocked him down again. They were yelling, 'You should have stayed away from her. We can't have our children going hungry because of the two of you.' I know that people in the cottages nearby must have heard what was going on but no one came out, no one tried to stop what was happening.

Edward was beaten and kicked in the chest and stomach continuously. Then I saw him fall to the ground, senseless. The men turned and walked away at a leisurely pace. A few minutes later I heard Edward's name being called frantically and I saw Daniel hobbling along using a walking stick as support. Someone must have told him what had happened. Daniel fell to his knees beside Edward, dropping his walking stick. He cradled his arms, saying, 'What have they done to you?' Edward opened his eyes a little, muttering something his friend could not make out. Daniel knew it had to be something about Marie so he said, 'Yes, I will take care of Marie.' My heart nearly broke hearing this. I knew that Marie and their baby were already dead. I saw Edward's beautiful soul rise up out of his body as Daniel, in tears, cradled his body. I heard Marie's voice calling Edward and saw the two souls embracing each other. I could see lights coming from doorways as people watched what was going on – not saying a word or shedding a tear.

Edward let go of my hand as I stood there on the stairs. It was like slow motion for a second and then I raced upstairs, grabbing the string of the bathroom light, pulling it, out of breath, almost falling into the bathroom, closing the bathroom door behind me, turning on the cold tap, throwing water into my face. Sitting on the loo I cried, giving out to the angels and to God. I was also remembering the scene of Marie's death, her lifeless body wet and covered in mud.

Michael appeared. He bent down in front of me, taking my hands in his, relieving some of the pain that was aching in my heart. 'Pray, Lorna,' he said, as his right hand reached up to my face, wiping away some of my tears. As I sobbed I could see some of my tears dripping onto Michael's hands. Michael said, 'Lorna, even your tears are prayers exploding into millions of prayers of light, hope and love.' As I looked into his eyes my tears started to dry up and I became calm. Michael was calming me with the peace of Heaven.

'Now, Lorna,' Michael said, 'go and finish cleaning for your mum.' I did as I was told and went with a heavy heart to help Mum clean the house for a Mass I wasn't invited to, one that I wasn't even supposed to know was happening.

Joe came after work, and helped Da paint the sitting room.

As we bundled the children into Da's car that evening, I looked back at Mum standing on the doorstep and could see her guardian angel – a bright light behind her. I knew the angels were looking after her. As we turned the corner I could see angels all around the house. They were all around it like a ball. They were there because this special Mass was going to be said the following Sunday evening.

That evening in bed, I talked to Joe about how I had felt, and how bitterly disappointed I was that my parents didn't want to invite me to the Mass. Joe hugged me, saying, 'You know what they are like. You know that all your life they haven't included you in most things.'

'Joe, that doesn't worry me – but this does, this is an extremely important thing. I know how important this Mass is and yet I don't understand exactly what is going to happen at it if I'm not there. I'm not sure if they are going to do it right.' Joe comforted me, and eventually I went to sleep.

The days that followed passed quite slowly and I was constantly in prayer. Those two spirits were on my mind so much. Sunday came and still no invitation. I remember going to Mass in the local church in the morning and receiving Communion. I knew the Mass in my parents' house was that evening. The day seemed to go so slowly. I was going around in a daze. Joe just seemed to take care of everything that day. He cooked lunch and then took the children for a walk so that I had some peace. I dearly hoped my da would call up that day. It would have meant so much to me if he had, but he didn't. Despite the strength of the connection between those two beautiful spirits and me, I wasn't allowed to travel spiritually to be with them for the Mass. I was being kept away.

I stayed in that strange daze all evening, but around eleven I turned to Joe in bed and said in a shocked voice, 'The spirits are still in the house in Leixlip! I don't understand it. They were supposed to leave with the Mass. Something has gone wrong.' Joe put an arm around me. The angels must have put me to sleep immediately, because it was morning when I woke.

Chapter Twenty-one

The last journey

The next few weeks were very confused. I knew the spirits were still in my parents' house in Leixlip. They were on my mind more than they had ever been. It was as if they were clinging to me. I prayed and I prayed and begged, 'Lord, please help them to go free. Surely they have done all they have to? They are pure. Surely the past families that were involved in any way and their children, and children's children, have been forgiven?' As I prayed, it was as if bolts of lightning were striking me. I felt the angels' wings go up around me and my hair being fuzzed up. I knew that the most important angel of them all was there. He didn't say a word, he was just reassuring me that everything would be all right.

Life went on as normal. Christopher started school and then, a few weeks later, early one September morning, I sat bolt upright in the bed. I suddenly knew that we were at the beginning of the end – the last part of the journey of the two beautiful spirits. As I sat up in bed it was as if the walls of the cottage disappeared and an awful lot of angels rushed in. They smiled at me and told me they were here to help, to give me extra strength as what followed would be hard. And I could feel within me that it would be.

I did all the normal things that day: made breakfast, took

Christopher to school, played with Owen, but I wasn't really present. I could feel the house in Leixlip. It was as if life was trying to burst out through the stones of its walls. I knew the two spirits were leaving the house. Then it felt as if the house was alive, and it was being blown up like a balloon. It was a permeable balloon, though, as if it had tiny holes in it and the life within it was oozing out. It would fill up and empty again. Then suddenly it stopped. It was as if the two spirits were finally free of the house. I could feel their power. They were free to go straight to Heaven – their work was done – and yet they didn't! They had one last journey to make.

It felt to me as if they were walking . . . very, very slowly. God had given them the gift of feeling as if they were alive again and their bodies were being allowed physically to feel the excitement of human life once more. I could see and feel what they were experiencing. I could feel the effort required each time they lifted their feet, each time they bent their knees. It was as if their bodies were a great weight and they were pulling them along. It was hard for them to make their human bodies become alive and to make that journey because, in a sense, their bodies weren't meant to be still here on earth. It was as if they had really to pull themselves along physically. It was very hard for them and yet they enjoyed enormously the sensation of feeling humanly alive again.

As they journeyed, I felt all their aches and pains as my own. My legs felt so heavy. My body felt so tired and so heavy it felt as if I was making the journey. But I could also feel great joy, great excitement, great longing as they moved. I cried for happiness as – and this I still find overwhelming – I realised where they were going on this final journey. They were coming to Maynooth to me. They were coming to thank me. I felt so privileged and honoured, as if I had been given a wonderful gift. I felt like a child who has been told they are being given a very special gift. I was full of anticipation and joy. I felt them step by step as they came from the house in Leixlip, through the estate, past the shops, through the other housing estate, past the railway track, on to where the canal was, and up along the canal. The walk from Leixlip to Maynooth is five or six miles. I could go on for hours describing every blade of grass they saw, every bit of life, every particle of air that touched their human bodies. They were in their bare feet, I remember, feeling the earth and the grass beneath their feet, between their toes as they came along the canal. Sometimes I would even feel something – a leaf perhaps – sticking into their feet, or a scratch on the leg from a branch.

Sometimes, when they stopped for a moment, they just stood still to enjoy where they were. They were enjoying feeling human, and I was enjoying it with them, despite the physical toll it was taking on me. I felt joy as I experienced any little drops of rain that fell on them, the heat of the sun that shone on their bodies, the wind against them. I heard any birds that came close to them. I felt their appreciation and excitement at feeling all these things we living people take so for granted. I was so excited that they were coming to me.

Day followed day. They were going so slowly over that five or six miles. Sometimes, if Joe was at home, I would tell him, 'They are on their way, Joe. They are coming to

Maynooth to say thank you. Would you believe that? I am so excited, I wish they would get here!' On one hand I was looking forward to them coming to Maynooth, to say hello and to say goodbye, and yet my eyes would fill with tears when I thought of them leaving.

Physically, it was really tough for me. One day, after about a week of this, I called out, 'Oh God, I feel so heavy! How close are they now? I feel I can't cope any more. I can't take the weight of them coming, and yet I feel so happy. Where are they?'

One of the angels surrounding me replied. 'Lorna, we know you can do this. We know you can feel every step and that it's wearing you down, but you have to hold them up, and you can do it. They have to come. It's so important to them to come to say thank you. We're sorry it has to take so long, but they are along the canal now, you know – where the tall trees are growing.'

'Yes, I know,' I replied. 'I can hear the cars on the road near that stretch of the canal sometimes. I just wish they would get here soon. How much longer will it be?' I could walk from Leixlip to Maynooth in two hours, taking my time, and yet their journey so far had taken over a week.

'Another few days,' the angel replied, 'maybe a little more, but we want you to stand up straight. We want you to think of them now, all of the time. Remember this is all part of their journey and part of your journey.'

'Well, you must never leave my side,' I replied. 'You'd better all stay around me. I know I can do it, even if sometimes I feel that my body can't take it and I get cross and give out to you. I know this has to be finished, and I know the spirits will come soon and I'm looking forward to it.'

A few more days passed; I felt their journey all the way up along the canal. When they reached the bridge in Maynooth, I knew they were there, oh how I knew they were there! 'Do you know how close they are?' I asked Joe. 'They are at the bridge in Maynooth. I can see everything.' They looked so beautiful. As they got closer and closer to Maynooth they got more and more radiant. Even after they had reached the bridge in Maynooth – a short walk from my home – it still took a few more days for them to arrive. I always remember the tarmac under their bare feet. On another part of the lane there are little pebbles and I could feel them beneath their feet. 'Ouch, that hurts!' I muttered to myself. 'Can you just walk a little lighter?' They were getting so, so close now, it was wonderful. I was looking forward to them arriving – and yet I didn't feel worthy of it. I didn't feel I had done enough to help, but still I was so excited.

Sometimes over those days I saw Joe look at me in a very worried way. Once he said, 'Lorna, you don't seem to be with us?' I turned and replied, 'How could I be, given that these spirits are on their way here?' I had told him about their journey, but it was of course very difficult for him to understand. I always remember him saying to me one day around then, 'Lorna, sometimes I don't really understand what you are talking about, but I love you and I do try.' I smiled back at him. 'I know, it's hard for me to understand too. I'm trying to figure it out myself.'

He worried about me, saying I didn't look well; I would reassure him, saying it wouldn't be much longer and that the angels were looking after me. I think that made him feel OK, but I was saying to myself, 'Dear God, you haven't any idea, Joe, how hard I am trying, how hard it is to stay alive!'

I felt my energy was really, really drained down. I will always remember the day they finally arrived, although I can't actually remember anything else of the day – what day it was, what time of day it was, whether Joe or the children were in the house. All I can remember, and will remember until the day I die, is my encounter with those two spirits. I remember just feeling such, such excitement. I wanted to run out to meet them, but I couldn't, I wasn't allowed to. I had a vision of them as they came past the hedging in front of the few cottages near us, then on to our gate. I was lost in time; I was just waiting and waiting. I could feel everything – every breath I took seemed to get lighter. It was as if the closer they got to me, the more life was poured back into my body. I was starting to feel alive again.

'Lorna, Lorna, Lorna. We're here, Lorna!' I heard, and I jumped for joy. Tears rolled down my face. There they were, standing at the gate. They looked so human and yet so bright, and they were calling my name and waving. I rushed out the hall door, down the path towards the little gate and opened it. They threw their arms around me and I cried and laughed, and they – would you believe it – cried and laughed too. There was so much joy and so much excitement. I felt like dancing. My feet felt light. I felt like I was sixteen again. I was so, so happy. A light enveloped the three of us hugging each other on the little path outside the cottage. There was so much love in the embrace we gave each other. They were flesh and blood again for this moment and I could feel them physically. I was overwhelmed. It was just so wonderful.

Standing there outside the cottage, embracing the two spirits, I was suddenly given an understanding of why it had to happen this way, an understanding of all the things that I had been told by the angels previously about my being their gatekeeper. The Mass had not been enough to release these souls. I was their gatekeeper and I hadn't been there. I know it's hard to understand, but from the first time I saw them in Mountshannon the connection had been made. I was their protector.

This story is all about love – God's love and the love within my soul which made me their gatekeeper. And their love. The scale of the love involved is beyond all human comprehension. It's beyond unconditional love. Marie and Edward made the decision not to go to Heaven, where they belonged and where they longed to be. Instead they chose to stay in this world because of their love for the people who had murdered them, and for the people who had ignored what was going on and all their descendants – generations and generations who were affected by this evil. They stayed out of pure love. You have to remember that the child died before Marie did and yet Marie decided to stay. And she didn't just stay for the man she loved. She stayed out of love, to clear the stain of sin for future generations. For me this is unbelievable. I have never met any other souls that have done this. All I can say is that Marie and Edward must have been such good people when they lived.

Suddenly, as we stood there by the gate of the cottage, we were surrounded by other souls – the souls of those who had committed the murder. These souls seemed to get brighter and brighter and then just disappear. It was as if they were giving thanks for the stain that had been removed from the souls of their descendants. I know that these souls had come back to say sorry and thank you. They were sorry for the part they had played in the murder of these two good people and their innocent child. The angels tell me they had been sorry for it even while they still lived. But sorry as they might have been, they had been unable to clear the guilt that stained the souls of their direct descendants. They required God's mercy and the love of others to do this. The sins of our ancestors – of our fathers' fathers – means that some families carry guilt for hundreds of years. Even if they know nothing about what happened, they carry that deep hurt, that stain on their soul. This is why we should all remember to pray often for the souls of our ancestors, and should talk openly about things that happened in our families' past.

Marie and Edward and I clung to each other there outside the cottage. They were thanking me, telling me of their joy at going home to Heaven, at being reunited after all this time with their child. I was full of joy, but crying at the same time – I didn't want them to go. They had been such a big part of my life for almost twenty years. They were reassuring me, talking back to me, telling me of their joy at going to Heaven, going home to God where they had always wanted to be. The light enveloping the three of us faded and they disappeared. They were gone to Heaven where they belonged.

Now, as I remember this, I am sitting in the old barn in Johnstown. It has been twenty years since I last saw the two spirits. I was completely jolted back by seeing the spirit of one of the men who had participated in the murder. I also recognised him among the spirits who surrounded the spirits of Marie and Edward and me as we said our joyful and tearful farewell. I had never seen Marie and Edward since that day. I think of them often though. I miss them in the same way as I miss close family members who have died. I talk to Joe all the time, but I don't feel any need to communicate with Marie and Edward.

I felt very grateful to the angels for sending the great-great-grandson of one of Marie's murderers to see me. What he told me about his life that day in the barn was a tremendous comfort. He told me a lot about his family and his life. He told me he had grown up in a tough family and that his father kept getting fired from jobs because of stealing and had eventually ended up in jail. He told me how a lot of the family drank – men and women – and got into fights, and how they would go out of their way to cause trouble. There was so much misery surrounding the family that one of his uncles used to say that there was a curse on it.

This man had been in lots of trouble himself as a young man, leaving school early and having big difficulties getting and holding jobs. He was good-looking and attracted lots of women but when annoyed, he would hit them. The relationships never lasted long. Now, though, his life had turned around. He described how, some twenty years before, an employer had given him a chance and trusted him, and from that point on his life had blossomed. He had lived up to the trust that was placed in him and his career had flourished. He was now happily married to the woman with him and they had two healthy children. His life had changed dramatically. He told me that he had never been happy as a child or young man, that he had never looked on the bright side of life, but that now he did. He told me that his siblings were getting along better too.

I realised, listening to him, that his life had changed dramatically for the better at the same time that the two spirits and I were completing the healing work on the sins of the fathers' fathers. I was overwhelmed, knowing that this man's life had changed from the moment the spirits had left and knowing that this was a direct consequence of the work of those two spirits and me.

I was so grateful to the angels for allowing this man to come to visit me, and for giving me this demonstration of the difference that had been made. And I know the difference was not just for this man but for hundreds, perhaps thousands, of people who were direct descendants of those involved directly or indirectly in the deaths of Marie, Edward and their baby.

The past is fixed. It has already happened and you can't change that. But you can pray for something that happened in the past, you can pray to help to alleviate the suffering that was caused. I am constantly reminded by the angels that we need to pray for the sins of our fathers' fathers. We need to pray for the suffering they underwent, to help them – but also to make things easier for ourselves as the wrongs carried out by our ancestors can have an influence on us here today.

Chapter Twenty-two

Someone to help you

Since I was a young child the angels had always told me that I would write a book. One day, when Ruth was a baby and I had been pushing her in her pram along the lane near the cottage, Michael had talked more to me about this. He told me that the angels needed me to write about certain things. I stopped pushing the pram, looked at Michael and replied, 'Deep down in my heart, I know that I have to write about my experiences with you angels and all the knowledge that God and you have taught me, and all the experience you have given me.'

Yes, deep down I knew I had to do it, but the thought of it terrified me! I continued; 'Michael, I am afraid of being ridiculed and laughed at.' As I thought of it more and more obstacles came into my mind. 'Anyway, Michael, I can't even read or spell properly! How on earth could I manage to write a book?' Michael laughed at me, saying I was not to worry. 'Help will come. God is sending someone to help you, and the Angels will guide this person to your door. God already has Angels working with this person, guiding and preparing them, helping them to learn the skills that are needed.' I looked at Michael. 'They'll sure need lots of skills because I know nothing at all about writing or publishing books.'

Then, as we reached the gate of the cottage, Michael

smiled at me and said, 'When the time comes and this person arrives at your hall door, we'll tell you.'

'Is it a man or a woman?' I asked curiously.

'No more questions, Lorna. God has angels working hard to make sure you get plenty of help.' Then Michael disappeared.

The angels never let me forget about the book. They reminded me again two or three weeks after Joe died. I was out having dinner with the children and the angels were whispering in my ear to try and cheer me up. One of the things they whispered to me was a strange-sounding company name. They told me it was the name of the company that would publish the book I would write. It wasn't a name I had ever heard of. I couldn't even pronounce it. To be honest I had forgotten the publisher's name by the time I left the table. However, I did remember that they had told me one, so I knew that even if I wasn't in any state then to think about writing a book, the angels hadn't forgotten.

Before we left Maynooth I finally got to meet the person the angels were sending to help me, although I would be well established in Johnstown before any work would start.

One Sunday morning both Megan and I had slept in. We had intended to go to early Mass that morning, but it wasn't to be and we went to a later service instead. As I opened Megan's bedroom door two of my angels were sitting on her bed as she slept. It was such a lovely sight to see. I smiled and asked them what they were doing there. Angel Michael said, 'Good morning,' without words. Megan sleepily turned on to her back, muttering, 'Mummy.' Angel Hosus, who was sitting closest to Megan, reached out and stroked her head and she stirred a little and turned again. Hosus put his finger to his lips and Megan went fast asleep again. The room was full of the light of the angels. I said a silent prayer that every person would someday be allowed to see the incredible light of the angels in their own home.

Now Michael stood up and took my hands, saying, 'Lorna, we can't stay too long. I have come to tell you that a man your dad knew, called Finbar, will call you, asking could you see a friend of his. This friend will ask you to see others and you must see them all. One of them will have a lot of the skills that you will need for the future,' Michael gave a big smile, 'for when you start writing about God and the angels.' But I really didn't want to even think about the challenges of writing a book.

'Lorna, don't be afraid,' said Michael. 'God will give you all the strength you need and, remember, you will have all of us angels with you.' He looked at me again and continued, 'Stop holding your breath. Breathe!'

I took a deep breath. 'OK. Is it a man or a woman?'

'You'll have to wait and see,' said Michael. 'Now hurry up and get Megan ready for the late Mass.' Michael let go of my hands, Hosus moved gently away from Megan, and they disappeared.

At Mass that morning, I prayed to God for the strength and courage and confidence to do what God was asking of me – to write a book. As I prayed, I asked God why he had chosen me, an ordinary person, and not someone else. I did not get an answer. I only heard the voice of an angel whispering in my ear, saying, 'God heard your prayer, Lorna.'

A few days later Finbar did call, asking me to see a friend of his. I agreed. He said that this friend would also bring someone else with them. A time was agreed. After I hung up I realised I hadn't asked the name of the people, or whether they were male or female. It had completely slipped my mind. I called out to the angels, 'I don't understand why you won't allow me to know beforehand!' But they didn't answer.

When people were coming to see me, I normally tried to arrange for someone to mind Megan. But this day Megan had a day off school and there was no one to look after her so I told her to stay quietly, watching television, and asked the angels to try and keep her there.

A little before eleven, the Angel Elijah walked into the kitchen, saying, 'Lorna, they are almost here,' and then he disappeared. I did not even get the chance to ask a question. I was a little anxious and yet excited. When I heard a car pulling up to the gates, I went to the hall door and opened it. I saw two women emerge from the car and the light of both their guardian angels opened up. The two women approached with the two guardian angels fully visible behind them. As they approached the door one of the guardian angels dimmed its light. The other woman's guardian angel remained open until she had stepped into the hall and said hello, then it dimmed its light too. I spoke to the angels without words, asking, 'Which is the woman who will help with the book?' The angels didn't answer me as the women introduced themselves as Karen and Jean. Jean sat in the hall while Karen came into the kitchen with me to talk in peace.

I discovered afterwards that Megan did something she very rarely did. She came out and sat beside Jean, telling her all about her dad's death and her brothers and sisters. Apparently, Jean played happily with Megan for the twenty minutes or so that I was talking with Karen. When Jean walked into the room to talk with me the light of her guardian angel opened up again immediately. I have spoken before about how guardian angels are neither male nor female but can give the appearance of either depending on the circumstances. Jean's guardian angel was very beautiful and stood like a giant; it changed human appearance from male to female every few minutes. When the angel assumed its male appearance it showed great strength, dressed in clothes of pastel-coloured silk which changed colour. Then the angel touched Jean's head, smiling down at her with such love and care. When assuming a female appearance, her angel was even more beautiful. A scarf was draped over her head and face and every part of the guardian angel seemed to glow like sparkling gold. The light of this guardian angel filled the room and every time the angel moved, it was as if a breeze rippled through this light. As Jean was talking to me, her guardian angel spoke to me without words, saying, 'Jean is the one who is going to help you and who has some of the skills that are needed. Before Jean leaves she will ask if she can be of any help to you or your family. Don't hesitate to tell her, Lorna, that you plan to write a book, and maybe she could help.'

That is exactly what happened. As Jean got up from the table, she said just what the angels had said she would say and handed me her business card. I told her I planned to write a book and maybe she could help. Jean's response wasn't quite what I hoped for. She laughed and said, 'You have the wrong person – I know nothing about writing or publishing books.' The angels told me I hadn't got the wrong person – that Jean would be the person who would help, whatever she might think now.

* * *

Jean and I had met occasionally over the time since I had asked her to help with the book. Every so often we would have a cup of coffee together. I hadn't forgotten her – the angels made sure of that – but for a couple of years after we first met Jean continued working full time as a business-woman. Then, gradually, as the angels had told me it would happen, she changed her career. After a while she started working on her own as a consultant.

It was in January 2004 that the angels told me I was to ring Jean. I asked her was she free for lunch? She told me that a meeting had just been cancelled so she was. The angels were already at work. As I drove to meet her I was very nervous: nervous of asking her for help, nervous she would say no.

We talked about the book over lunch. I told her that I had a whole load of material recorded on tape, but that I needed help. Jean offered to work one day a week with me helping me with the book. Neither she nor I had any idea of how many years it was going to be to publication. If she had, perhaps she might not have said yes!

The following Thursday, and every Thursday after that, she travelled from Dublin down to Johnstown with her laptop. That was the beginning of a long relationship with lots of hard work. Most of my recording was done in the barn downstairs. I would work in the morning when Megan was at school, but when she came home I devoted all my time to her, except on Thursdays when Jean was there. Many nights the angels woke me from my sleep in the early hours of the morning and got me to go down to the barn to write for an hour or two before letting me go back to bed.

* * *

One sunny winter's day early in 2005 I was working out in the overgrown garden, pulling long grass and weeds from among the gorgeous pink and red wild roses. The sun was shining. I heard a voice saying, 'Lorna, you should put some gloves on.' When I turned around Angel Michael was walking towards me through the long grass, dressed like a gardener with a pair of gloves in his hand. He handed the gloves to me. I was delighted. 'Where did you find them?' I asked. I put them on. Michael told me he had found them in the cupboard with the toolbox.

The sun caught Michael's eyes and made them even more stunning than usual. 'Have you come to help me with the roses?' I asked him with a smile. He told me he had come to talk with me, so we walked back into the old farmhouse. I made two cups of tea and put one in front of Michael as we sat down at the table in the barn, smiling, knowing he couldn't drink it.

'I'm worried about finding a publisher for the book,' I said. At this point Jean and I had been working on the book for almost a year. We now had lots of material – but we had no idea how we were going to get it published.

'Don't concern yourself about that. You have already been told that the books you write about God and angels will be bestsellers around the world,' Michael continued. 'Can't you remember the name of the publisher?'

I was very embarrassed, I had forgotten. I did remember an angel telling me a name several years earlier, but even then I found it hard to pronounce, let alone remember. I shook my head. 'You know how hard it is for me to remember names, never mind say them. I am only starting to pronounce Angel Elijah properly now.'

Michael laughed at me, saying, 'Not to worry, Lorna. Jean will buy a book with publishers' names and you will recognise the name of the publisher when she reads a list of them out to you.'

'Why can't you tell me now?' I pestered Michael.

'Because it's not necessary,' Michael replied with a smile. 'The one thing I will tell you is that the editor of your first book will be called Mark and he's the best. You just keep writing, Lorna. Jean will meet someone one evening when she's out. And that person will be a friend of Mark's. Lorna, you must always pray that all the people that God is asking to play a part in making your books bestsellers will listen.' Michael stood up from the table, saying he must be going. We walked back out into the garden and Michael disappeared.

Chapter Twenty-three

Finding Mark

After Jean had been working with me on the book for more than a year she arrived one day with a big directory of publishers – *The Writers' and Artists' Yearbook*. She showed me a list of UK and Irish publishers she thought might be of interest. She asked had I any ideas about who was supposed to publish the book? We sat at the table, and she went through the pages, reading out the names of publishers. When she read 'Random House', I remembered what I'd been told by the angels and said, 'That's the publisher!' Jean was less than unimpressed. She read out, '"No unsolicited manuscripts,"' saying, 'Great, Lorna, only one of the biggest publishers in the world – how are we going to do that?' I told her she would meet someone who would know someone at Random House. Jean looked at me rather doubtfully. 'Where on earth am I going to meet someone with links in the publishing community?' I told her to trust and not to worry about it and to be alert and keep listening. Don't let it pass by.

A month or so later, I got an excited call from Jean late one evening. 'It's happened,' she said. Jean had gone to meet a friend, Peter, from Italy. They'd met for dinner in a restaurant in Dublin and various people had joined the table. The chat had been around books and publishers, and there was some discussion about a literary agent in London whom

Peter knew. Jean remembered what I had said about being alert, about not letting opportunities pass. She asked Peter whether this literary agent had any interest in a book about angels. His reply had been, 'No, but my friend Mark, who is an editor at Random House, is fascinated by them.'

Jean was so excited on the phone to me. She couldn't believe this was happening. She said that Peter had promised to send an email to Mark the next day. After I hung up I was jumping with joy. I thanked God and the angels and asked Peter's guardian angel to make sure he wouldn't forget to send the email and that Mark's guardian angel would keep him open and receptive to the contact.

Peter kept his word and made contact with Mark the next day. So he was definitely listening to his guardian angel.

That was the beginning. But there was still a long way to go. In fact, from the first contact Jean had with Mark in April 2005 it was more than three years until publication. The angels never told me how long it would take. I think if Jean or I had realised how long it would be, and how much further work was involved, we might have despaired. But now Jean made contact with Mark and sent him some of the material we had prepared. He was interested and open and it was agreed that the first step should be a meeting. It took three months for the meeting to happen, but eventually it did.

The day arrived for the meeting in London. I stayed overnight in Dublin with Jean and we took a taxi to the airport. As Jean and I walked through the door at Dublin Airport there was a group of angels, wishing me well. The angels were making me smile and taking my anxiety away about meeting Mark.

Airports are very confusing and strange places, so I was very glad to have Jean with me. After we checked in and went through security we went to have a cup of tea. The light of Jean's guardian angel opened up and other angels appeared around her. I could see they were keeping her calm. She was as nervous and excited as I was, even if she was trying to appear cool. I asked the angels that were around her to help Jean in every way.

Eventually we arrived at the offices of Random House in central London. We waited in the reception area. At times I could feel my knees shaking. I sat there turning the pages of a magazine, pretending to be reading it. All the time I could feel an angel's hand on my shoulder. The angel whispered in my ear that I would be fine. A man walked into the lobby and I knew straight away it was Mark. The light of his guardian angel was slightly bent gracefully over him, and I could see three other angels around him. He seemed quite shy and very polite.

Mark ushered us into an area of the canteen where we could sit and talk in peace. A colleague of his joined us and he introduced her as Hannah. We sat at low tables. One of Mark's angels whispered in his ear and he said, 'Lorna, have some tea,' and offered me a biscuit. I said to his angel, 'How am I going to manage to lift the cup of tea without my hand shaking too much?' His angel said, 'We will help you, no one will notice.' Fortunately, Jean started talking so I didn't have to say very much to begin with. Beside each person sat an angel writing down every word that was spoken by the particular individual. The angels were keeping a record. I spoke to Mark's angels without words, asking, 'Why are they doing this?' They told me I was to focus only on him, that he was the most important person at this meeting. They assured me of his character and his brilliance as an editor. They reminded me to smile, which did make me do so.

Then Mark's guardian angel opened up. He was very tall and stooped over him. His face was shiny and smooth. I was allowed to see his guardian angel's eyes – which isn't always the case. It was fascinating – when Mark was talking about my book, I could see an enormous depth in his guardian angel's eyes. But when he talked about other books he had edited – and Mark has edited an enormous variety of best-sellers – the depth faded. It was as if Mark's guardian angel knew that my book was a very important task. Mark's guardian angel wore robes of different styles and colours, and they changed each time he talked about a different book he had worked on. It was as if there was a different robe for each book. When he talked about what was to become *Angels in my Hair*, though, it was as if he was wearing all the robes – one on top of another.

We talked about my life, and about the orders I had been given to spread the wisdom that God and the angels had given me. I told him that God and the angels had told me that I would write a global bestseller. If Mark was doubtful, he hid his doubt well, and I know that all the time his guardian angel was there stooped over him, reassuring him.

The book Jean and I had sent in outline was a book of this angelic wisdom – with chapters on connecting with your guardian angel, guardian angels and death, and lots of other subjects. Mark said this was interesting but not extraordinary. What he was interested in, and what he would consider publishing, was my life story.

The meeting lasted about an hour and we promised to come back with a revised outline. As we left the doors of Random House the angels told me that Mark and Hannah were standing watching us – wondering if I was for real!

I was exhausted, but happy. I felt we were on track, and knew, even if Mark didn't know, that we would give him a book that he really wanted to publish and that would become a bestseller. The angels had originally told me that the book would be the story of my life. I had suggested this at an early stage to Jean but she had been sceptical, so instead we had gone down the route that Jean suggested. I reminded Jean of this as we had lunch in a cafe nearby, chatting about the meeting. 'It's impossible to work with someone who is always right!' was Jean's irritated reply. I know she briefly felt like kicking me, but that irritation passed almost immediately as we planned how we would get Mark the material he wanted.

Megan became good friends with two children from one Johnstown family in particular – the Murphys. They had a girl just younger than Megan and one a little older. Megan loved being with them and they were very good to her, taking her regularly on outings. Mrs Murphy was great at baking and Megan frequently came home all excited with a present of a cake for me.

I didn't often take Megan and the Murphy girls off on outings but one day I decided to take them all to the adventure centre in Carlow. This is a play area with bouncing castles, climbing bars and bowling and lots of children have birthday parties there. When we were there we met some other school friends of Megan's with their parents. I left those parents keeping an eye on the children and went into the centre of Carlow to do some shopping.

I had parked and was on my way to the shops when the angels brought my attention to a very well-dressed lady on the other side of the road. She was middle-aged and looked strong and full of character. Walking beside her was an ancestral angel. I have told you about various different types of angels, including guardian angels and healing angels, but I haven't told you about ancestral angels – angels that are linked to particular families.

Ancestral angels are appointed by God to a particular family for eternity and will never abandon that family. Not every family has an ancestral angel. In fact, fewer than one in a hundred families do. Ancestral angels are extremely powerful and they will step in if a family is threatened. They have much more power and a different kind of power than a guardian angel. Sometimes a family has one because that family, or someone in it, is destined to play an important role in humanity's development.

The woman's ancestral angel was very tall and strong, dressed in steely grey armour, as if for battle. He looked so powerful – a real force to be reckoned with. I didn't see wings. He turned and glanced at me sternly, and then, as if he recognised me, he smiled. From his glance I could feel his power and I knew he was accompanying the woman on a mission that was important to her family. From what the angels around me said, I believe there was a threat to the family business and she was going into battle to save it. For the ancestral angel it wasn't about the business per se. It was about the impact that losing the business would have on the family. This was not supposed to happen and the ancestral angel was there to do its best to protect the family.

I didn't see the woman for very long. She turned the corner, and I've never seen her since. I have no idea if she saved her family business or not. I continued on and did my shopping and went back to the fun centre where the girls were.

I sat watching the children playing ten-pin bowling. There were no adults playing and as it was very busy, much as I love bowling, I didn't feel able to play. I thought about ancestral angels. I have been seeing them since I was a very young child and over the years Michael has told me more and more about their role. Ancestral angels work in different ways; they may be working in a family now to influence something that will happen far in the future of that family; they may work with spirits within the family that lived in the past, perhaps hundreds or even thousands of years before. Ancestral angels are also very active when there is a feud within the family. As I say, ancestral angels don't necessarily work equally with all members of a family. They may only work with a few members of a family or even an individual in a particular generation – and then it may only be for a day or two in that person's lifetime. In fact, they may not work with anyone in a particular generation. But whatever happens, they stay with the family – watching.

I remember as a child walking in the countryside and seeing an ancestral angel with a father and son. The father held the hand of his son, who was five or six years old. The ancestral angel looked as if he was dressed in armour, but in this case it seemed to have a red sheen. Again, I didn't see wings. He was powerful, but looked gentler than the ancestral angel

I saw later in Carlow. I understood that this ancestral angel was there for the son not the father. I understood that for some family reason it had been decided that the boy would go and live with an unmarried aunt. I wasn't told why – perhaps there were too many children in the family and it was difficult for the parents to cope? The ancestral angel was working hard to ensure the son didn't go to the aunt but stayed where he belonged with the main family. It was as if he needed to be shaped within that family for some future task and he wouldn't get that living with his aunt.

An ancestral angel is concerned with the extended family. As families grow over generations the chain of connection can be fairly thin, but it remains nevertheless. An ancestral angel often connects people who are blood relations but have no idea that they are. An ancestral angel will, of course, use this connection to bring about change for the good. Angel Michael told me that the extended family is important and families should strive to stay connected. They should never look down upon any part of their family, thinking they are uneducated, poor or inferior in any way. Extended families have lots of ups and downs, particularly over generations, and the ancestral angel will work with them. Michael also told me that the names of ancestral angels are always kept secret by the angels. The families themselves are never told them, and unlike your guardian angel's name, which you do know deep down (even if you don't know you do!), you will never guess the name of your ancestral angel if you have one. Should anyone ever tell you the name of their own or your ancestral angel – no matter how well connected they may say they are – you will know they are not telling the truth.

Michael once showed me a group of ancestral angels standing closely together in a circle on a small hill in County Meath, fifty miles outside Dublin. They were talking. They glowed brightly. They all had wings that were partially open. Each one had a suit of armour, but they were all slightly different in shape and I believe that the armour represented something of each family. I know they all had weapons, different ones for each ancestral angel, but I wasn't allowed close enough to see what they were. They stopped talking and turned towards me, giving me a stern appraising look. Then a smile grew on each and every one of their faces until they were beaming at me. I wasn't allowed talk to them and they disappeared. Michael wouldn't tell me what they were doing, or why I had been shown them.

You may be a member of a family that has an ancestral angel but, remember, fewer than one in a hundred or so families do. Your guardian angel will know. So don't hesitate to ask him and, if you believe you have an ancestral angel, you can call on his help for family-related issues.

Shortly after I met Mark for the first time, a friend gave me a very generous present of a laptop, which was voice activated so I could just speak into it. I had to do a lot of training and practice so that the computer would recognise my voice. It wasn't easy because one's voice changes at times, but it was certainly easier and quicker for Jean than recording everything on tape and typing from scratch. Sometimes this laptop mishears me and this is something I always give out to the angels about. I ask the angels for the technology to improve so that the computer recognises my voice at all times, but I guess that might be asking for a miracle. The truth is

I find it hard to pronounce a lot of words correctly, so the technology can't really be blamed. The angels sometimes laugh at me and tell me not to complain.

Every so often when I was working, the barn would become full of angels trying to pull me away from my work. They would tell me I needed a break – I'd tell them to go away and say that I needed to get more done. They wouldn't go away, though. They would start trying to distract me by appearing on the computer screen, making faces, pulling at my hair or moving my chair. They would stick at this until I'd laugh and take a break, perhaps getting up and going for a walk. Some days they didn't allow me to write at all. God and the angels would have me doing other things.

Jean came and stayed in Johnstown for a week that summer in order to get the second outline ready for Mark. Megan always enjoyed it when Jean came to stay. Jean would get up early in the morning but I would stay asleep until about nine and when I came down and opened the door to the barn, Jean would be hard at work, typing and editing. There were always lots of angels there keeping her company. The first thing I would see when I opened the door and looked into the barn was rows of white angels sitting at old-fashioned school desks at the far end of the long room. They were busy writing, dipping their quill pens into the inkwells. Each morning a different one of them would look up at me and wave. All the angels would then start turning white pages in slow motion, in time together, and then they would start writing with their pens again.

Jean was always sitting with her laptop at a big wooden table to my left near the kitchen door, working away. Her guardian angel allows in all these beautiful angels to give her all the help she needs. There would be other angels all around the table, helping her not to feel tired or get frustrated in any way. Beside her, to her left, there would be another angel with a laptop, typing away. I have never told Jean this. That angel was there beside her whenever she was at her laptop working on stuff to do with me. I have to smile at all the angels that are there with her in the light of her guardian angel, doing their best to help to keep things going as smoothly as possible.

Eventually, in March 2006, nine months after I had met Mark for the first time, he took the proposal to the meeting that makes publication decisions. I was praying so hard. I knew that the book was supposed to be published by Random House, but I knew that for it to be approved, other people had to listen to their guardian angels and say yes. The meeting went well. Mark told Jean that others had asked to see the outline of the book. One evening, about a week later, Jean rang me. She had an email from Mark. We had a formal offer for the book. I was so thrilled. Finally it was going to happen. The book the angels had asked me to write more than twenty years earlier was finally going to be published.

Chapter Twenty-four

A *narrow stairway to Heaven*

At times, Jean and I would sit and talk about all the things that had to be done to get the book written and published, and to get word of it known. We had problems at times – Jean tells me I should call them challenges! But I know that without the help of the angels the problems would have been much bigger, so I thank them constantly.

Every day I ask the Angels to help us to get my books into as many people's hands as possible all around the world, to help me in my job of spreading the message of God and his angels. I ask the angels to speak to people's guardian angels, to give us a helping hand. And I am still amazed, even today, at all the different people who have come forward – people of all ages, nationalities and professions, offering to help and expecting nothing in return, just wanting to be part of it, just wanting to help. Everyone who has helped to spread the word of God and the angels has been chosen. I'm sad to say there are some who were chosen and asked by their angels to help but didn't listen.

One bright summer's day I took a break from writing and went for a walk along the river in Mount Juliet. It's a beautiful river and I had walked some way when an angel touched my arm and told me to walk through the trees, that there was someone there to meet me. I made my way through the trees and brambles by the riverbank. There I sat on a branch of a tree that looped down to the ground, watching the river currents and two swans.

I heard my name and looked to the right. I jumped up with excitement. It was Angel Elisha. As always, she gave me the appearance of being made of feathers of light. The last time I had met her was six years earlier when she had told me that God wanted me and Megan to move down to Johnstown. Now I called out her name.

'Sit back down, Lorna, and I will sit beside you,' Angel Elisha said. I looked at the branch. There wasn't any room. Angel Elisha knew what I was thinking and smiled as she sat down. All of a sudden there seemed to be plenty of room.

'It seems such a long time since I've seen you, Lorna,' Elisha began. Then she continued, 'I have been hearing a lot about you and your writing about us angels. You have a long way to go yet and lots of hard work. I know at times you feel disappointed when we tell you a certain person is going to help you, and then they don't. We are encouraging them all the time to make the right decision and to give you help, for them to be part of this journey. But you know we can't force them. They have free will to say yes or no and sometimes they just don't listen at all. You are never to be disappointed when this happens, Lorna. We will find another person to say yes. Now keep on walking and don't forget to smile.'

I got up off the branch and said goodbye. As I walked through the trees I stopped briefly, turned around and looked back. Angel Elisha was still sitting by the river. She waved and I waved back and then continued walking until I reached the path.

*   *   *

One evening, Megan came home all excited from playing with a friend. The friend's dog had had puppies six weeks previously and now they were looking for good homes for them. Megan begged me to let her have a puppy. I was hesitant about it and told her about all the work involved in minding a puppy, and all the love she would have to give it. Megan was adamant she wanted one. I wanted Megan to learn something about responsibility and caring for a dog, but secretly I was also thrilled at the idea of having a dog. I have always loved dogs. As a child I had always had pets, but never a dog. When Joe and I married one of the first things we did was get an Alsatian puppy – Heidi. Heidi lived to be thirteen. After that we had a collie mongrel called Trixie, but she died after a cow kicked her. Much as we both loved dogs, we didn't get another one. Joe was so ill and we had enough on our plate without a dog as well.

Megan agreed we would wait a few days before making a final decision about getting a puppy but she went about planning for it as if it was happening anyway. She found an old blanket and a box for the puppy to sleep in, and in the supermarket she announced that Ruth had given her the money to buy a ball for the puppy. Clearly it was all decided and there was little point in fighting against it. So the next day around lunchtime we drove over to her friend's house. Megan disappeared into the house and her friend's mother came out and invited me in for tea. Megan came into the kitchen with this small black and white puppy in her arms. Her friend's mother told me it was a cross between a sheepdog and a springer spaniel. We went into the back kitchen to see the other puppies, but Megan held on tight to this particular one. This was the one she wanted. Half an hour later we headed home with the puppy; by now Megan had named her Sapphire.

Sapphire was so playful and friendly. Megan and I both loved her from the start and Megan was true to her word and looked after her really well. I have always loved walking and Sapphire gave me an excuse for going on really long walks around Johnstown.

Occasionally, Jean's German partner, Mano, came to stay in Johnstown with her. When he did he loved walking with Sapphire and Megan, and he used to try and teach Sapphire to obey orders. They had little success, though. Sapphire was full of energy and had a mind of her own. All the little joys of normal everyday life, making friends, getting a puppy, having a homely home, helped Megan get over her grief. I too was enjoying life more.

Early in 2008, a month before the book was published, I was invited across to Random House in London to meet the sales team and some of the other managers involved in the launch of the book. Jean and I sat in Dublin Airport drinking coffee, waiting to go to our gate. I told Jean I was very nervous – that I had very little experience of meetings. As I said this, Jean's phone bleeped, indicating she had a text. Jean laughed as she read out a text from Mark saying that some of the sales managers were too nervous to meet me on their own, and wanted to do so in a group. All I could do was laugh. We were *all* nervous.

This time I met Charlotte as well as Mark. Charlotte is a wonderful editor who works with Mark. They met us in the reception and we went up in the lift to Mark's office. I hate lifts. My tummy seems to turn inside out, and they make my head light. But the lift was packed with angels. I don't know how we all fitted in. I kept talking to the angels without words. I told them I couldn't feel my feet on the floor, and they said not to worry, that they were carrying me. When we got out of the lift and walked along the short corridor and into Mark's office the place was filled with the light of angels. It nearly blinded me and I had to look down at the floor for a second. The energy field around Mark was glowing every time I looked at him and this made me smile.

The meetings went well and afterwards Mark invited Jean and me to lunch. After lunch Mark and I spent time talking on our own and it was then, sitting with Mark in his office, that I got to know the three beautiful angels that work with Mark. These are in addition to his guardian angel. They are angels that his guardian angel has let in to help him to live his life to the full. One angel was on the left and took notes. Occasionally, this one sat on Mark's desk. The second angel was on his right. There was a third angel who was there all the time and moved around. When Mark stood up to walk, this third angel seemed to walk through him, in front of him, guiding him on the right path. This angel spoke to me all the time I was there talking with Mark, telling me about Mark and his life. I told him not to tell me too many secrets.

The first angel, the one that sat on his desk some of the time, gave a female appearance, extremely beautiful, tall and slender. Its role is to teach Mark to live life and not to be too serious. The second angel looked like quite a mature man, and was dressed like an old-fashioned clergyman. His role is giving Mark knowledge to help him to do his work as an editor and an author in his own right. The third angel gave a male appearance of great strength, tall and military

– despite his long curly hair. He seemed to be dressed in gold and had a sword strapped across his back. At times his arms were full of books. Not reading books as we know them, but books full of pathways. All three angels have been with Mark every time I have met him. Before we left, Mark gave me some books for Megan and Ruth. I knew they would be thrilled with them.

We flew home that same night, exhausted but happy. Everyone was playing their part and things were moving in the right direction.

One day, I was working about the house, doing the normal housework that still had to be done – book or no book. I took a break and went out walking. The angels were going to work the miracles to make my book the international bestseller that they kept telling me it would be.

I saw Angel Amen standing at the gate of a field. I was so pleased to see her. She told me to go into the field and she walked into it herself. I followed and we stopped by a big old tree. She reached out and took my hand and at that moment a stairway appeared. It reached down to the grass beside where we stood and it seemed to go up forever. We were suddenly on the stairway. I have no memory of stepping on to it. It was narrow – much narrower than any other stairway to Heaven I have seen – but then some of them have been massive. It was extremely bright. Both the steps and the sides of the stairway were radiating light, in some ways a bit like the sun. Every so often I would catch a glimpse of the reflection of Angel Amen and me, side by side holding hands on the stairs. The stairs curved at various points and at each curve there were several very tall angels standing like sentries. The stairs seemed to go on forever, but I wasn't getting tired or feeling any effort at all. Suddenly, Angel Amen said, 'Stop. We are here.' And it was as if the rest of the stairs upwards disappeared. There were no doors or floors, or anything like that that we could identify in the normal world. We walked into an enormous open area filled with angels and I walked through them. It was as if there was a never-ending host of angels there.

Suddenly, I was back in my body, back under the tree in Johnstown. On my own. I never got a chance to ask Angel Amen why she had taken me up the stairs that day. I can only think it was to give me encouragement and support.

Chapter Twenty-five

The American gathering angels

I will never forget the first time I saw the final published copy of the book. It was on a Sunday morning and Jean and I were on the plane from Dublin to New York. Mark had previously been over to New York to talk the book up and set up appointments with American publishers. In the end, we were able to choose between competing offers from two of the largest publishing companies in the US! Now we were on our second trip to America in one month, finalising the US contract. For someone who had hardly been out of Ireland before starting to write *Angels in my Hair*, I was travelling an awful lot. Having had an international business career Jean is a very well-seasoned traveller, which makes things much easier for me.

We had just taken off when Jean gave me a big smile and told me she had a present for me. Out of her bag she took a copy of *Angels in my Hair*. I was totally and utterly shocked. I couldn't believe it! I knew publication was close, but I hadn't really imagined holding the book in my hands – and I certainly wasn't expecting it there on that plane. I rubbed the cover and flicked through the pages. I nearly burst out laughing with excitement. All around us on this plane there were angels chanting, 'Angels in my hair . . . Angels in my hair.' With Jean, I read every word on the cover and I laughed. I read all the endorsements, and gave thanks for those who had the courage to endorse me when I was still unknown; I read the acknowledgements and my dedication 'for my children'. I gave out to Jean, asking when she had received the book. How could she have kept the book hidden in her bag? Why hadn't she shown it to me the minute we met at the airport? She laughed and said she had got it on the Friday and we hadn't seen each other on the Saturday. She said the moment after take-off seemed like an appropriate time to give it to me – and it gave me lots of time to savour the success. I did savour the success and thought about little else on that seven-hour flight to New York.

We were only in New York for three days and we worked very hard most of the time. We did, however, have one half day free and Jean took me to visit the Metropolitan Museum. It was an enormous building and when I walked in the main hall there were lots of people and lots of angels. The angels smiled at me and seemed to be very pleased to see me there. We wandered around, looking at things, and then I followed Jean into a vast bright courtyard. It was as if we were in the open air but there was a roof. As soon as I walked in I knew something was seriously wrong. I was really uneasy but I didn't know why. The feeling was so strong that the angels around me had to hold me up. If they hadn't I think I might have collapsed.

In the middle of the room was a big old building. Jean told me it was called the Temple of Dendur, that it was very ancient and that it had been brought to America from Egypt. Jean didn't notice that something was wrong with me and wandered off to have a look on her own. I still had no idea what was wrong, I looked around, but I couldn't understand it. I went up a few steps to where the temple was and walked through an arch. I stood in front of two big pillars. As I stood there it was as if everything became very quiet and there was no movement. Although there were lots of people in that part of the museum, it was as if they all disappeared temporarily. The big pillars seemed to grow as if reaching up to the sky and between them a door appeared. It opened inwards. I took a deep breath. Inside, on guard, stood an enormous angel. He was extremely tall, and very thin and – strange as this may seem – he was pointy. His head was actually pointy. This didn't take away from his beauty, though. His clothes were dark and draped over him, covering his body and legs. I didn't see any wings. Most often when I see an angel I see their clothes move. In this case there was no movement at all.

He called my name. His voice was very thin, as if coming from a long distance, and yet he spoke forcefully. I felt a pressure against my chest as if he had hit me energetically. He told me that the Temple of Dendur did not belong there. That it was being defiled. When he said that, I stepped back and looked around. I was amazed at what I saw. I was shown Egyptian spirits from the past walking around the room and the temple. They were surrounded by angels, one of whom told me that many of these spirits had worshipped at this temple when they were alive. Even more amazing to me, I was shown American spirits and it was as if they were there trying to make amends – trying to protect this sacred place from tourists, to stop tourists from touching things that they shouldn't. These American spirits – who looked as if they came from different centuries – were surrounding the tourists and visitors. Their presence seemed to make the tourists step back or stop touching. In some way or other it seemed to make them treat the Temple with more respect.

I looked back at the tall angel again. He told me that he had come to give me a message, and that he had been sent by the Angel of the Nation of Egypt. The message was simple: 'This Temple does not belong in America. It needs to be taken back to Egypt.' I felt very sick and weak; I wanted to sit down but I was told by the angels that I couldn't. I saw people sitting by water that ran like a moat around the Temple and asked my angels if I could go and sit with them, but they said no. Finally, I asked them to find Jean and tell her it was time to leave this horrible room. They must have done so, as she appeared shortly afterwards, suggesting a cup of tea in a cafe. It was with enormous relief that I left.

On our way to the cafe I went to the ladies room. When I was there I asked Angel Michael about what I had seen and the message that the very tall angel had given to me. He explained to me that when the roots of any country are torn up and brought to another country, it imbalances the country and, as a result, creates imbalance in the world. The Angel of the Nation of Egypt wanted the Temple back in order to help bring the countries surrounding Egypt together. (I'll say some more about angels of the nation when the time comes. All you need to know now is that these are very special and powerful angels, appointed by God to guard the needs of a particular country.) I didn't understand what Angel Michael meant. He explained a bit more. He said that this temple and other treasures in other countries are meant to be back in Egypt. Egypt and the surrounding countries need their past inheritance to be brought back so that they will develop a deeper understanding and appreciation of each other's cultures. This understanding will help to reduce divisions between countries and lead to more peace in the Middle East. Michael told me that the Egyptians need their past back in order to open up their future. The angels have also told me that this temple that I saw in the Museum – the Temple of Dendur – will be sent back to Egypt at some stage. They haven't told me when, though.

Americans don't need the past of others to bolster themselves. They are a different race, in many ways more advanced. They may be made up of a mixture of people from different nationalities, but these people have blended together to form a new race. America needs to show leadership by giving back this Egyptian temple, showing the independence and strength of this new race. Americans are a chosen people, even though many people in the world may not be happy to hear this. They have been chosen and gathered from all around the globe by a special powerful force of angels. This powerful force of angels has driven the development of America. People who went to America were to some extent chosen, including – strange as this may sound – those brought there as slaves. The angels have been gathering people of all nationalities to this one continent to help fulfil mankind's destiny. This is why I have been told to call these special angels the American gathering angels.

American gathering angels are quite distinctive in appearance. The first time I saw them was here in Ireland when I was a child. In America I saw a lot of them. They all show me a male soldier-like form. They wear an armour that covers their legs. It's a silver colour with a darker colour, like that of pewter. On their chest they wear a large crest, like a shield.

This is deep blue in colour and there is some other design element on it that I can't quite describe. They wear a band across their forehead that disappears into their hair. All of them seem to have dark hair but the hair length seems to vary, although I have never seen any hair below shoulder length. Some of them have wings. As I say, these special angels were created by God to gather souls for America. I don't know exactly when God created them but they were already at work long before Christopher Columbus discovered America. The American gathering angels were all created at the same time and unlike most angels they stay on earth all the time. Guardian angels, for example, bring the soul they are minding back to Heaven and rarely return to earth. Healing, teacher and prayer angels come from Heaven when they are needed and go back to Heaven when they are not.

The Native Americans are a part of this new race. The people who were chosen to come to America by ship didn't understand that Native Americans were an integral part of the new world. The angels have told me that they worked hard to try and stop massacres, but we humans can behave disastrously at times. We are prone to think that we are superior to other races and Native Americans suffered greatly in the past. They are still kept on the outside today. This needs to be changed. Native Americans need to be drawn into the mainstream. They have a spirituality that is different and is needed for the evolution of mankind, for the body and soul to become one.

Angels Michael and Hosus have also explained to me about slavery. Outrageous though this might seem, it had a part in making sure that the right mix of people were brought to the new world. The slave traders never realised that they were being used to bring to America people who had been chosen – people who could never have come to America by other means. This was a part of America's path. This does not excuse turning another person into a slave, taking their freedom or dignity, whipping them or working them to the bone. Yet, hard as this might sound, it was a part of these individuals' paths. And these individuals and their descendants are a vital part of what makes America what it is and what it will become. America is where humanity's future will unfold. Decisions made in America will have a determining effect on human evolution and this is why America, alone of all countries, has these special angels – the American gathering angels.

Chapter Twenty-six

The angels celebrate with me

Jean told me she thought it was really important that I celebrated the publication of *Angels in my Hair*. I don't think she realised how shy I was at the thought of it. From that day on, however, the angels pestered me constantly, whispering in my ear every day that I had to have a launch party. I would tell them to go away and not to be bothering me.

One day, there was a knock on the window of the old farmhouse. It was the Angel Kaphas.

'What are you doing here?' I asked and I went to open the door. He stood on the doorstep with a big smile.

'Lorna, you don't need to open the door for me, I can come in anyway.'

I smiled back, saying, 'I actually forgot.' With every movement of Angel Kaphas I could hear the beautiful music that always comes from him. It soothed me and calmed me down as he encouraged me to have a launch party, and assured me that, whatever fears I had, I would in fact enjoy it.

'I am very shy and the thought of it makes me very nervous,' I told him. 'I wouldn't know what to do or what to say to people.'

'Lorna,' Angel Kaphas said, 'you have worked so hard, it's time for you to have a celebration and we angels deserve a chance to celebrate too, as it's our book as well.'

How could I refuse the angels this? 'All right then, seeing as you angels will be celebrating too.' Angel Kaphas disappeared, leaving the sound of music fading in his wake as always.

So Jean organised a party in Carton House – an eighteenth-century house outside Maynooth, which is now a hotel. It was held in a beautiful old room overlooking a rose garden and, beyond that, a golf course. On the ceiling were lovely, elegant paintings of angels. Very appropriate. I invited all the people who had helped to make the book a reality. So many had helped in so many ways without looking for any reward. It was incredible for me to realise how many people, who had been complete strangers, had stepped in to help. I thank God and the angels for all of them, because without their help I couldn't have done it. Even to this day, there are people in different parts of the world whom I have never met, who have reached out to play their part in spreading the message of *Angels in my Hair*.

When the day of the launch arrived I was terrified. The angels kept touching me to stop me from shaking. Ruth came and did my hair and make-up and helped me to dress. She told me I looked great, but I was still very nervous. I arrived at the party with Megan and already there were lots of guests there enjoying themselves. I rather shyly went around saying hello to people. Shortly after I arrived my mum came in. I wasn't sure she would come. But she looked fantastic and was so proud of me.

In no time the place was absolutely packed – I don't mean with people, but with angels. I smile at that now when I think of it. The angels were mimicking everyone – the guests drinking, and the waiters and waitresses going around with trays of drinks and finger food. They even danced to the violinist in the corner of the room. I could see the angels helping to relax people. I wasn't the only one there who was nervous. I would see an angel starting to laugh, and then almost immediately afterwards the people who were standing beside started to laugh. The angels did a brilliant job of keeping the atmosphere light and joyful. Christopher, Owen, Ruth and Megan helped too, mingling and making sure everyone was enjoying themselves and no one felt left out.

Suddenly there was a tap on a microphone and I was called over. Jean and Mark were standing together by the big old fireplace. I went and stood to their left. I remember Jean with the microphone in her hand. She looked so delighted that all our hard work had paid off, that after all those years the book was finally published. She was glowing with excitement and achievement. I had never seen her looking quite like that before. I felt so proud of Jean that day. As she spoke the light of her guardian angel opened up behind her. Other angels that were around her were mouthing the words of her speech as she spoke.

Then Mark spoke and as he did the light of his guardian angel opened up as well, and the angels around him were mimicking him too. Every now and then one of the angels would look at me and say, 'Yes, Lorna, he's talking about you.' I didn't recognise myself in the wonderful compliments Mark and Jean were paying me.

When Mark finished Megan handed me a huge bouquet of flowers. I didn't know what to say; I was overcome, both by the occasion and the tributes that had been paid to me. So I just thanked everyone – God, the angels and all those who had been so supportive.

Photographs were taken afterwards and one of the angels surrounding us, who had a pen and paper in hand, like a newspaper reporter, blew me a kiss. I giggled, rather embarrassed. Never in my life had I had a celebration like this for me – a party where I was the focus of attention. It felt very strange and a bit unreal but it was fantastic and an evening I will never forget.

Chapter Twenty-seven

Pilgrimage to Mecca

About a month after the launch, I did my first live television interview in a studio in Dublin. I was terrified at the prospect and asked my angels to keep me calm. They kept telling me I had nothing to worry about but I was still very worried. It was morning TV and we needed to be there early so I stayed in Dublin overnight with Jean and we got up very early to make sure that we got there in good time. We had loads of time, so Jean found a cafe that was open and insisted I eat something. To be honest I was sick with nerves, but I did manage to eat something.

I remember nothing of the interview except for asking the angels, during it, to stop me shaking so much. They must have, as Jean said that I had done fine and my terror hadn't been obvious.

After the interview we went back to Jean's house to do some more work and then decided we deserved lunch out. Over a lovely lunch in a nice restaurant with a view of the River Liffey in the centre of Dublin, Jean asked had I ever been to the Chester Beatty Library? When I told her I didn't know it, she explained that it wasn't really a library. It was more of a museum and it had a wonderful exhibition of religious items and books from different religions from all around the world. Some of the exhibits were very old. I was very happy to go and visit, so after lunch we set off.

As we walked towards the building I saw a very bright light in the distance. I realised there was a massive angel standing at the doorway. We walked across a lawn to get there. It was busy as it was lunchtime on a beautiful day. I was walking a little ahead of Jean, focused on the angel in the doorway ahead of me. Suddenly I felt someone take my hand. I got such a shock that I bumped into a man walking towards me. It was Angel Michael taking my hand. As we went in the door I said hello to the angel, who was dressed in armour. He was like the doorkeeper to this library. I know if he stands in front of anyone, they change their mind and do not go in.

We went upstairs – Michael still holding my hand – and in through some big swinging doors. The light inside was dim. I was astonished, completely taken aback, because this was a holy place. I hadn't expected that at all.

As I walked further into the big, dim room, it was as if I was stepping back through time, as if I was being torn from one place to another. I felt this enormous stillness, knowing my soul was being brought forward, my body becoming lighter with every step. My soul was wrapped in God's angels as I was put into a state of prayer. I realised why Michael was holding my hand. He was there to keep my body func-tioning, and to keep me conscious on one level. Because of him I could walk around looking at the different exhibits and even smile and talk if I had to. Jean didn't seem to notice anything strange about me. I told her I would wander around on my own and she left me in peace to do so. So I might have looked normal, but the state I was in was far from normal. Michael didn't say a word, even when I asked him questions or complained that I couldn't do this. As I walked, my soul moved ahead of me in front of my body. I found myself standing a short distance from a big screen. I began watching a film of a Muslim pilgrimage. There were thousands of people, all dressed in white and praying. Angels lit up the screen and it expanded, becoming bigger and bigger, filling all the space ahead of me.

In a flash of light my soul was transported spiritually to that place and time. I was surrounded by people praying and the power of their prayer electrified my soul. I was a part of the prayers that were being listened to by God. I knew my body was standing in the library, even though I couldn't feel any connection to my body, but I was also watching my soul there among the other pilgrims praying.

An angel told me the place was called Mecca. I watched the prayers of tens of thousands of Muslims on their pilgrimage to this sacred holy place. I could see the light of the guardian angels of each and every one of them beaming brightly. I could see millions of other angels too. No one prays alone – your guardian angel always joins with you when you pray. Other angels always join in your prayers too – and that is why I saw these millions of angels. We can also ask the angels to join us in our prayers – thereby increasing the power of the prayer to God. Occasionally I am asked whether we should pray to angels? I only *pray* to God. I *talk* to angels. I ask them for their help and I ask them to pray to God with me.

As each pilgrim prayed, I could see the words of his prayer being taken by his guardian angel and given to one of the millions of angels there to carry prayers to the throne of

Heaven. The angels that carry our prayers up to Heaven are prayer angels. They never show me a human appearance and their light is somewhat different to other angels. They move upwards and then disappear, leaving a trail behind them. They move so fast it's as if they are part of a never-ending stream. An angel carries each and every prayer – or prayerful thought – upwards.

The stream of angels carrying prayers heavenwards was never-ending. It didn't cease for one second. The power and glory of what I was seeing was indescribable. The power of prayer can move this world of ours towards peace, towards unity, towards a better world. Those Muslims were praising God, praying for what they believed was right. And their prayers were being listened to.

I continued to see my soul in amongst all these Muslims praising God. Then I saw my soul reach out and touch the Sacred Stone. From the depth of my soul came a cry, a prayer of unity, a call for all religions to join together. Imagine seeing all religions of the world joining together, all religions under the one umbrella, the way my soul knows they should be? Imagine people from other religions joining the pilgrims at Mecca in prayer? This is one of the possible futures that I have been shown for mankind. There are others, which would lead to chaos, but this is a future I profoundly wish and pray for – all mankind living in peace and unity, all striving together for a better future for the world.

As I stood there watching, my human body started to feel God's love. The feeling of love became overwhelming. Then, with a flash of light, I was jolted back to the present. The film screen went back to normal size. I was surrounded by the dim light of the library again. I wanted to cry out, to say no! I didn't want it to end. My soul was enjoying being in the midst of such fervent prayer. As my soul stepped back into my body I started to feel alive in my body again. I became conscious of Michael's hand in mine. Michael turned me around, and I walked slowly away from the screen. With each step I felt a bit stronger. I could feel my feet on the ground again. I also became conscious again that there were other people around. It had felt like I had had the place to myself. Shortly afterwards Jean came over and suggested we leave. I smiled and nodded. She walked ahead of me and I followed. As I stepped out onto the streets with the Angel Michael still holding my hand, the beautiful angel standing guard acknowledged me. Jean was unaware of what had happened and left me to go to the bus on my own. I really needed to sit down for a little while and went into a cafe. As I entered, Angel Michael said he had to leave. The touch of his hand faded slowly as I thanked him and he disappeared.

I sat in the cafe thinking. The angels had always told me that it didn't matter what religion anyone belonged to. The truth is that it's the forces of evil that create divisions between one religion and another, making one religion feel that their beliefs are superior to another's. God and the angels have told me that there are many stairways to Heaven. No one religion controls access to Heaven.

Chapter Twenty-eight

Glowing babies

I had made the house in Johnstown reasonably habitable. Being honest, though, the outhouse and garden still left much to be desired. I'd go out every so often to try and tidy the outhouses that were full of stuff – half-finished tins of paint, bags of hard cement, an old fireplace – you name it, it was there.

Shortly after the book was published I was out in one of the sheds tidying when the Angel Michael appeared, saying, 'Do you want a helping hand?'

I was delighted to see him and greeted him, saying, 'I sure could do with some help.'

Michael smiled at me, saying, 'Lorna, I want to talk to you about the Angel Gabriel.'

I looked at him in surprise. Michael had never mentioned Angel Gabriel to me before and I had only met Angel Gabriel on a few rare occasions. The first time was when I was about five and living in Old Kilmainham in Dublin. I had been playing with my friend Josie in her father's old garage. Well, it was called a garage, but in fact it was a big old yard with wrecked cars piled high towards the back of it. At the front there was a little room with no roof, only walls. We were allowed to play there. On the day in question, I was sitting on an old wooden box, playing on my own with my doll. I was surrounded by angels, one of whom told me I was going to have a visitor.

Suddenly I saw a very bright light in the opening in the wall that served as an entrance. Within that light I could vaguely see what looked like a doorway. It was enormous. A light was approaching the doorway. At first I couldn't see it clearly, but as it got closer I could see better. It looked like the moon in the night sky. It was extremely bright but not so much that it hurt my eyes. Then the light gradually dimmed and got smaller and an angel walked through the doorway towards me. For a split second I thought the moon was coming towards me . . . This angel's eyes were enormous – big, bright and shining. Saucers full of love and understanding. I was fascinated by his eyes and face. I stood up and stretched out my arm to touch his face. But I was unable to reach him as he was like a giant. His glowing smile grew more glowing.

I stood there looking up at him. I was a little confused about this angel. He was bigger than any angel I had ever seen and I couldn't see him clearly as his human aspect was very faint. He spoke in a soft and gentle voice. 'I am the Angel Gabriel, Lorna. Sit back down on your wooden box and I'll sit beside you.' I did as he suggested. He sat beside me on the other wooden box and took on a slightly more human appearance and size. He looked like a working man with heavy jacket and trousers. Nowadays, I suppose I would say he looks like a biker. So he looked more human than he had done, but his face and eyes still glowed in a way that no humans eyes ever have.

'Is that better, Lorna?' he asked.

'Yes,' I replied, 'but I can hardly see you in that light.' He didn't answer. Instead he did something angels don't do very often he reached out and took my doll. Angels rarely interact in a physical way.

I loved this doll. She was called Lena and was made of

rubber and had black painted hair and a plastic ponytail. After a few minutes of admiring her he handed Lena back to me saying, 'Lorna, don't be afraid.'

'I'm not,' I said, and Gabriel's face and eyes became even more radiant.

'Lorna,' he said, 'you are always going to see me within a doorway of light. That's how you'll know it's me.' He continued, 'I want to tell about glowing babies so when in the future you see them, you will recognise what they are. Glowing babies are very special. They are babies whose souls the world will never be able to contaminate.'

'What does contaminate mean?' I asked Angel Gabriel. I was, after all, only five.

Gabriel burst out laughing. I've never seen an angel laugh as he did and he made me laugh too. As he laughed he appeared to change rapidly back and forth between his human appearance and his angelic appearance. And he had such a hearty laugh. It was as if everything around us was vibrating with his laughter. It made me feel happy.

Then Gabriel stopped laughing, and for a split second it was as if time stood still. Then he reached out to take my doll Lena up again.

'Lorna, if your doll fell into some oil it would become contaminated, because the oil would soak into the rubber she is made out of,' Gabriel began.

'I understand,' I said, showing my doll's stained foot to Gabriel. 'Lena fell into a puddle of oil here in the garage and no matter how hard I try it never rubs off.' I looked up at Gabriel again, adding, 'I know my doll doesn't have a soul, though.'

Gabriel said, 'It's the baby's soul that cannot be contaminated. When you get a little older, Lorna, I'll tell you more.' With that, Gabriel disappeared.

Since then I had met Gabriel several times and each time it was linked to glowing babies. So I was intrigued at what Michael was going to tell me now in the outhouses here in Johnstown. He looked at me with a smile. 'Lorna, I'm going to show you something special.' With that, the outhouses disappeared and we were surrounded by a mist. Michael changed his appearance from quite human to an extremely powerful archangel. Archangel Michael showed himself to me as extremely tall with a golden crown upon his head, shining like the sun. He wore robes of white and gold that draped loosely with a gold belt with a black buckle around his waist. On his feet he wore thonged sandals which criss-crossed up his legs and on top of each foot was a golden crucifix. In his left hand he held a magnificent shield with a crest upon it. The shield looked three-dimensional, as if it wasn't just one shield, but many hundreds of shields. In his right hand he held an enormous sword with a gold handle shaped like a crucifix with red and green emeralds at the top of the hilt. The blade of the sword glowed, reflecting gold and silver. Archangel Michael's dark hair was shoulder length and flowed as if there were a gentle breeze. His sapphire blue eyes radiated love and peace and on his face was a smile that I can only describe as a smile of Heaven.

Michael looked magnificently powerful. His appearance was very similar to the one he had shown me in the old cottage in Maynooth when he gave me the Prayer of Thy Healing Angels,[2] which has helped so many people. The only significant difference was that on that occasion he had a scroll

---

[2] The Prayer of Thy Healing Angels can be found as an appendix at the back of the book.

with the prayer in his hand, whereas this time he had a sword and shield. I felt very safe seeing him with his sword and shield. I knew that whatever happened I would be completely protected.

Within the mist that surrounded us an extremely bright light like an open doorway appeared, but I couldn't see Gabriel.

'Michael, why can't I see Gabriel?' I asked.

'You will in a moment, Lorna, but first I must tell you he is not just Angel Gabriel but Archangel Gabriel.'

It took my breath away. I knew that Michael was an Archangel and for some reason I had been able to accept that, but I had never expected to be allowed to meet another Archangel here on earth.

I looked towards the bright light like an open doorway and, coming towards me, getting bigger and brighter all the time, was another light. It was like looking out into the universe and seeing the moon travelling thousands of miles, coming closer within the light of the doorway. Then Archangel Gabriel stood in the light of the doorway surrounded by crimson lights, like the moon but a billion times more imposing. He looked completely different to what I had been shown before. I don't know, even now, why it was that he decided to show himself to me in such a powerful and brilliant way. His face was astonishingly beautiful. It reminded me of a very bright full moon. Within the face were two enormous bright eyes, round like saucers, reflecting the essence of love and compassion. And deep within his eyes it was as if I could see the pages of a beautiful book being turned. It was as if his face was split in half, the way two pages of an open book are split by the spine.

To me, Archangel Gabriel represents the book of life – and this was reflected in his appearance. It was as if he was an open book with the pages constantly changing. His fair hair looked extremely fine, falling gently around his face at times. He was draped in a fabric. This looked to me like silk. It criss-crossed down the centre of his body like the binding of a book. The colours were not of this world. The best description I can give is that they were like colours reflected in water, constantly changing with the light. Then I got a glimpse of his wings. They were enormous, with a constant rippling movement of light. It was like an abundance of angels' wings all moving in rhythm. He had a book in his right hand.

Archangel Gabriel came forward slowly, from beyond the doorway, and yet within its light. Then he stepped through the bright light of the doorway and, as he did, his appearance changed, giving me again that familiar faint appearance of the biker. His face or eyes didn't change though. We greeted each other.

'Why didn't you tell me you were an archangel?' I asked.

'Lorna, because it was not the time for you to know or for me to tell you,' Archangel Gabriel replied. 'Only the Archangel Michael could do that.'

'Gabriel, do you mean Michael is the boss?' I asked mischievously.

'Yes, Lorna,' the Archangel Michael said and laughed. We all laughed. The laughter from the two archangels was like thunder. I had never heard them laugh like that before. And with that laughter Michael disappeared.

'What's that book you are carrying?' I asked Gabriel.

He looked at me and replied, 'Lorna, no questions.'

'I should have guessed that there was something different about you,' I said reflectively. 'You have always shown me such a faint and faded appearance.'

Gabriel smiled. 'Lorna, it won't be too long now before you see another glowing baby. But this baby will have been allowed to grow up a little.' With that Gabriel disappeared.

I was intrigued as I went back into the old farmhouse. All plans of cleaning up the outhouses were gone – yet again. I was thinking about the first time I had seen a glowing baby. I had been about ten, and Gabriel had visited me a few weeks beforehand to tell me it would happen. I had been walking home from school in Ballymun. The angels told me to walk across the fields. There was a little river in one of the fields and a little lake or pond with an island in the middle of it. Beside the pond were a few trees and part of an old tree trunk that had fallen years before. The angels told me to sit there, so I climbed up onto the tree trunk and sat watching a rabbit nibbling on grass nearby.

An extremely bright light appeared like a doorway to my left. I knew immediately it was Angel Gabriel and I was delighted. As Gabriel walked towards me the light dimmed, and with each step his human appearance became a little clearer. He was wearing the same clothes as he had the previous time I had seen him and his human appearance was still very faint. As he greeted me I reached out to touch him. Even though he was right beside me I didn't seem to be able to reach him. Gabriel smiled at me.

'No, Lorna, you cannot touch me.' I asked why not, but Gabriel didn't answer.

'I have come to talk to you about glowing babies. Do you remember, Lorna, what I told you when you were little?'

'Yes, about my doll being spoiled by oil,' I answered proudly. 'You used another word, Gabriel, but I can't remember it.'

'Contaminated,' said Gabriel.

'Are there any glowing babies in the world now?'

'There have been some over the years, and a few more have been born recently, including one here in Ireland. I'm here to tell you that shortly you will see your first glowing baby. These babies will be very special, but they will have something wrong with them.'

'Do you mean that big word I've heard them use about me?'

'Yes, Lorna. Some people may think the babies are retarded, but they will be wrong. While these children will be physically disabled or have a disease, they will in fact be mentally perfect. These babies will glow brightly, which is why I call them glowing babies. People will not be able to see this glow, but everyone around them will be attracted to them because of it. They will all want to hold the baby or be in its presence. Every time you see one, I will be there with you.' Then Gabriel said, 'I want you to look into my eyes.'

'I am looking at you. Your face is very bright,' I replied.

'Lorna, look only into my eyes.' I did as I was told and Gabriel continued talking.

'Most of these babies will die as babies or as young children and they will never grow up because God will not allow their souls to become contaminated by the world. With time, God may choose to allow some of the glowing babies to grow into adults.'

Still looking into Gabriel's eyes, I replied, 'Even though I know these babies are going to die, looking into your eyes only fills me with love. I don't feel at all sad.' Gabriel smiled and disappeared.

I climbed down off the log and one of the angels who had been with me all the time said, 'You know, don't you, Lorna, why you didn't feel sad?'

'Yes,' I said, 'because I was looking into Gabriel's eyes.'

A few weeks later, on a Sunday morning, I was coming home from Mass on my own when the angels told me to walk through a housing estate that wasn't on my normal route. Suddenly I saw a glowing light like a doorway beside a garden gate. The light dimmed a little and I saw Angel Gabriel. We spoke without words. 'Lorna, look!' I did as Gabriel said and saw a baby's pram in the garden. Because of the angle I could see a glowing light coming from the pram but couldn't actually see a baby in it. Surrounding the pram was the mother and some other children.

'Ask the mother if you can see the baby,' Gabriel said.

I walked towards the gate and the mother walked towards me. I smiled and asked the mother if I could see the baby. I was surprised and delighted when she walked back towards the pram, reached in and picked the baby up to show me. I noticed its head was abnormally large and seemed to be bigger on one side than the other, but the baby was definitely glowing. It was very beautiful. The mother walked over to me, carrying the baby, and saying in a whispered voice, 'Everyone seems to want to hold my baby.' She had tears in her eyes, but I could see she was trying to keep them in.

'I know your baby is very special,' I said to her, as I touched his little hand. For a moment the mother and I were alone with the baby. Then the children surrounded us. I knew Gabriel had kept them away for those few precious moments.

Two women came along the footpath, one of them calling out to the mother, 'We'll take care of that baby now. You go and have a rest!' The mother didn't even have the opportunity to respond before one of the other women reached out and took the baby from her arms. They were very bossy and I felt sad for the mother. It was as the Angel Gabriel had said: everyone wanted to be in the presence of that glowing baby.

I was just outside the gate when Gabriel disappeared. I turned and looked at the baby again and asked all the angels to help the mother and to watch over her and her little baby.

I sat drinking tea at the old table in the barn in Johnstown, thinking about that glowing baby I had seen all those years ago. Knowing that there was no way it could still be alive I said a prayer for the mother, who was undoubtedly still grieving, and for the rest of the family too. But now I was excited about seeing a new glowing baby, and at the hint that this one might have lived a little longer.

It happened a few weeks later – in Glasgow. Jean and I had gone over to do some interviews. We stayed in a hotel in the port area and I did a photo shoot there. In the afternoon we went into the city centre and I had an interview with a journalist who asked fascinating questions – very different from the usual standard ones. It was an interview I really enjoyed.

After the interview I went strolling on my own in a large and crowded shopping centre near the hotel. Suddenly I saw that bright light like an open doorway appear in the distance ahead of me. The angels around me told me to stay where I was. I did as they said. Gabriel spoke to me without words,

'Don't come any closer. You're going to meet a glowing child.' I was thrilled and wondered immediately what age this child would be. I was sad, though, when Gabriel continued, 'This child won't be here in this world for much longer. God will be taking her very soon.' I wanted to walk towards Gabriel as I expected to see this child near him.

'No, Lorna, stay where you are and turn around and look the other way,' Gabriel told me. I did and I saw girl of about sixteen, full of energy and beaming with life, walking with her parents towards me. She looked perfect and beautiful. Her guardian angel opened up and there were loads of other angels around them. The place was crowded with them and yet of course there was loads of space for the angels and her.

The young girl glowed so brightly that I found it hard to understand that no one else could see the light that was coming from her. I could see all the knowledge and wisdom that the soul within her held. This young girl was too advanced for this world. She was truly a young person of the future, but God wasn't allowing her to speak of what she knew. Her guardian angel told me that she had a congenital disease, which had stopped her living a normal life.

She saw me and walked in my direction and gave me a big smile and a hug. It was as if we were lost siblings meeting for the first time. On one level, we were both complete strangers, but on another we were not. The parents caught up with the young girl and smiled at me as if a little uncertain as to what they should say to me. The angels told me that the parents knew spiritually that their daughter was special, but on a human level they couldn't understand.

I was standing close to this young person and it was as if

the angels were protecting the four of us – the girl, her parents and me – wrapping us in a healing embrace. I prayed, unknown to them, as angels poured down the grace of God upon this young girl. I was again told that she would be leaving this world soon. We all said goodbye, and I watched them walking through the crowd and past Gabriel. As they walked past him, Gabriel disappeared.

I headed back to meet Jean, thinking about glowing babies. I asked the angels silently how many more I would see as I travelled the world, and wondered if I would ever see a glowing adult. I got no answer. In the year since then, I have been shown one other glowing baby and a glowing child of about five. I am so thrilled when I see them.

Chapter Twenty-nine

A throwback from the future

I went to see my doctor because I hadn't been feeling great. He said he would arrange for me to have some tests done in a hospital in Tallaght, near Dublin. I thanked him, left the surgery and walked out to my car.

Angel Hosus was already sitting in the passenger seat. I smiled. 'I'm glad you are here, Hosus. I have to go to hospital and I dread the thought of driving there since I don't know my way from Johnstown.'

Hosus said, 'Lorna, don't worry.'

'I'm not worried about the tests,' I replied. 'It's only getting to the hospital that concerns me, especially when I have to drive on my own.' Suddenly, the car was full of angels. They spoke simultaneously, as if in a chorus, 'Lorna, don't you know, we will be with you.'

I'm always nervous driving somewhere for the first time. The angels know this and try to mind me.

'Don't concern yourself, Lorna,' Hosus said. Hosus and I chatted about other things as we drove home. He made me laugh quite a bit. He always can think of something funny to say. When I pulled up outside the house, Hosus disappeared.

A few days later, Ruth came to visit and I told her about my tests in Tallaght Hospital and without hesitation, Ruth suggested that her boyfriend, Brendan, should draw a map. Apparently he had worked near Tallaght for some months.

One day, shortly before my hospital appointment, I was doing little bits and pieces around the old farmhouse alone. I thought of going out for a walk but when I walked into the barn, there was Angel Michael. We sat and talked for a little while, and then Michael said he had something to tell me. I looked at him with interest.

'When you're at the hospital, we are going to show you something important. Something that could become part of the future of mankind, depending on the choices humans make. At the hospital, take in as much detail as possible of what you see and hear.'

'Michael, will I be shocked by what I see?' I asked.

'Yes, Lorna, you will.'

'Can you tell me more, Michael?' He told me no, and disappeared. I was disappointed. I would have loved to have known a little more.

A few days later I drove to the hospital using the map Brendan had given me. I got no more information from Michael or any of the other angels about what I would see and experience at the hospital. I prayed to God that I would not find it too upsetting. In my prayers I talked to God and asked, 'If this is something of the future, what can I do?'

'Remember, Lorna, I am watching over you,' God said. He didn't answer my question though.

I smiled and said, 'Thank you.'

The drive to the hospital went smoothly. As I drove into the car park, a car was pulling out and a tall angel was standing in the parking space. As the angel guided me into the parking spot, I said, 'Thank you.' It seemed the angels had arranged everything. As I got out of the car I could feel the spiritual protection of God's angels surrounding me.

As I walked towards the main entrance of the hospital, a few people of different ages were coming and going. I was told to follow the yellow line to reception. Everything seemed to be squeaky clean and extremely bright. As I walked along the corridor the nurses and doctors and even a few patients who passed by seemed to be glowing brightly with a light that radiated about two inches outside their body. I couldn't help but smile as I watched the angels accompanying them. When, eventually, the yellow line brought me to the reception area, I found it was silent. I stopped and looked around. Everything looked as if it was completely new. Everything was abnormally bright. There were rows and rows of empty seats. No one around. I couldn't even see an angel, even though I knew they were with me. I walked over to reception. There was no one there either. Then I noticed a little bell on the counter and I rang it. After a few minutes I called my angels. They appeared. 'Where is everybody?' I asked. One angel raised his hand to his lips. At that moment, the receptionist came out to the counter. She glowed brightly too. She asked could she help? I handed her my doctor's letter. She did something on a computer, handed me a ticket and told me to sit down. Someone would see me shortly, she said. Then she disappeared to the back office.

So I had the whole waiting room to myself. It wasn't actually a room. It was part of a corridor, like a hallway, with about twenty rows of seats. Loads of the angels now went ahead of me towards the seats and started to sit down in different positions, as if waiting for appointments. They nearly made me laugh out loud, but that didn't matter as there was no one around.

Then I saw the Angel Michael sitting in a chair at the furthest point away from the reception area. 'Do you want me to come and sit beside you?' I asked. He said, 'No. Sit about five rows in front of me.' I did as Michael asked, and sat down. There were some magazines on the chairs. I picked up one and was flicking through it when Michael came and stood behind me. He put his hand on my shoulder. 'Relax, Lorna. Everything will be fine.'

'Michael, I can't relax,' I said. 'It's too quiet. No one has passed this way. Anyone would think the hospital was deserted.'

Michael laughed, saying, 'No it's not!'

Just then, three nurses and a young doctor, talking quietly, came around the corner. I don't think they even noticed me.

'Michael, I've been sitting here now a good fifteen to twenty minutes,' I said. 'It's making me a little apprehensive about what God is going to show me.'

Just then, an elderly lady and her granddaughter came walking towards the reception. They rang the bell and the receptionist came out. As they were talking, I could see two angels were supporting the elderly lady. Her whole body was trembling, so much that I thought her walking stick would break. I could see one angel was trying to help her not to tremble, while the other seemed to be trying to comfort her by talking to her. As they walked slowly past me, the angels allowed me to hear what the old lady was saying to her granddaughter. 'I'm afraid. Won't you stay with me?' the elderly woman asked. My heart went out to the two of them, particularly the elderly lady.

As they walked around the corner and out of my sight, I asked the angels to take her fear away.

Angel Michael sat beside me.

'Maybe everyone is on their tea break?' I suggested.

'Be patient, Lorna, it will happen soon.' No sooner had Michael said this than everything in the atmosphere seemed to stand still. I could see all the particles of the atmosphere in the air around me and a young man, apparently in his prime, strolled around the corner into the waiting area. He stood for a moment and then walked over to reception. Every move he made seemed to be in slow motion. I knew that wasn't for him, but for me, so that I could see him clearly and take in everything about him. He was in his early thirties.

'He looks fine,' I said to Michael. 'He doesn't look sick to me or anything like that.'

'Pay attention, Lorna,' Michael replied. 'You will soon see.'

The young man was given a ticket, as I had been, and told to sit down and wait. He looked at all the empty seats and then walked towards me. He sat about two rows in front of me, but facing me.

I had been sitting there for some time, but hadn't realised that my seat was facing the opposite way to the other seats. So now we were facing each other. I was astonished by what started to unfold. This young man suddenly changed. As he raised his head, everything was again in slow motion. He no longer looked human. There seemed to be implants in his head, like clamps separating parts of his brain. I could also see that parts of his brain were missing. His skull was not wholly made of bone and he was no longer all flesh and blood. I was so distressed by what I was seeing that I felt like crying out.

'He is a throwback from the future,' Angel Michael said to me.

'What does that mean?' I asked in an upset voice.

The young man stood up again and walked back to the reception desk. I saw that the rest of his body was not all flesh and blood either. But it was not wholly mechanical. It's hard to describe, but it was as if there was something invisible inside his arms and legs which made them unbreakable – something made of steel or some reinforcing material we have never heard of yet.

Michael stayed silent as I watched, then continued. 'We're showing you what some people might look like in the future. As you can see, this man is real, but he is different to any human alive today. We have superimposed on him what his great-great-grandson might look like.' Michael turned from the young man to me and asked, 'Remember when the young man walked in – what did you see, Lorna?'

I looked at Michael and thought about it. 'I saw a tall young man who was well built and strong. I didn't see any sickness in him and he seemed bright and intelligent as well.'

'It's because of those family strengths and characteristics that his family could be chosen in the future,' Michael said. I looked at Michael, puzzled.

'Lorna, remember,' Michael said, 'in his exploration of science and technology man can make life better, but he can also use science in the wrong way. Mankind must learn to do things for the right reason, and not for the sake of power and control over others.'

As the young man turned his head to the right I saw more.

'We are letting you see into the young man's mind now. It's empty and dark, all except a little bit of light. Can you see it, Lorna?' The shock of what I was seeing and feeling nearly took my breath away. It was as if that tiny speck of light was his conscious mind, but the shocking thing was that it was surrounded by a total void – darkness. As if a part of him had been locked away in a room where he could never access it. And he was aware that he was missing something. He seemed to be screaming in his mind as he searched the emptiness that filled it.

'Oh my God!' I exclaimed to Michael. 'Why would anyone do this? Why would one man want to take away another's ability to think for himself, to dream or to love?'

'Lorna, remember, no one has the right to take away another human being's right to live a fully human life. No one has the right to turn another human being into a machine. If in the future human leaders choose to go down that path, they will probably select certain families to become less free, more like slaves. These will be families which for some reason are thought to be inferior in some ways, though fit and strong. That young man's family was chosen in one of the world's possible futures. But remember, that future is not fixed. It can be changed.'

I sat looking at the young man, thinking of his family losing their freedom to be fully human – to love, laugh, cry and have the freedom to make their own choices.

'I wouldn't like to live in a world like that,' I said to Michael. I suddenly had another thought. 'Michael, if man makes that choice will he still have a soul?'

'Yes,' Michael replied, 'a human being's soul is the one thing no scientist or technological progress can ever take away. The human soul belongs to God. God will not allow anyone to take away a human's soul, no matter what poor choices humankind may make.'

I wondered about the flicker of light I had been shown in the man's brain. Was that the soul holding on to what was left of his consciousness?

'Lorna, you must pray that man listens to God and his angels,' Michael said. 'Man's scientific and technological progress is brilliant – but it must never be used to take away any human being's freedom.'

I sat there, looking at the young man. Michael put his hand on mine. He squeezed it, then disappeared. There were so many thoughts going through my mind, as I looked at the young man. I only glanced every now and then in case he caught me looking.

The fact that I was shown this throwback means it is a real possibility. It was horrible to see this and to know that it was not done to give him a better quality of life, but to take that quality away. It was done by man, wanting to take control of other humans – to turn them into slaves.

Science and technology have done wonderful things – medicine and treatments to cure diseases and destroy cancerous cells, technology for replacing hips and knees, creating artificial limbs. I pray for continued success for all those wonderfully gifted people who search for cures and discoveries that make life easier, and give people back dignity. This work is fantastic and very important. But we mustn't overstep the boundaries. We are responsible for the future of our children, and future generations.

I was startled by a nurse calling my name. I turned and looked at the man. Now he looked normal again. I got up and walked towards reception. I must have looked pale as she asked me if I was OK.

The tests were fairly straightforward and lasted only about half an hour. It took me about two hours to drive home and I was relieved when I got there. I was – and continue to be – upset by what I was shown that day.

Chapter Thirty

Answering people's questions

Book signings are fascinating for me. They are exhausting – as I try and talk with everyone individually for a moment or two – but fascinating. I am often amazed by what people tell me, and by what the angels show me. What people ask also often intrigues me.

I did a signing on a Sunday in the Dundrum shopping centre in Dublin. When I arrived I was shocked to see such a big crowd queuing and waiting. I was even more astonished by all the angels that were there. For every person that was there, there were about twenty angels. There was a magnificent light around everybody. It's very hard to describe. All I can say is that it was the light of love and care the angels had for each person there – man, woman and child. As I sat down at the table to sign books I silently asked the angels to allow miracles to happen for all the people who were there that day – and for their families and friends.

One of the people who was queuing was a boy of about twelve. He was in a wheelchair. Seeing all the angels around him and his mother I knew he was being well looked after. The angels kept changing the colour of his wheelchair. The boy was passing the time while he waited to talk to me by playing a Nintendo. What he didn't know was that there was an angel beside him playing with it too. I could see the angel's hands intertwine with the boy's hands. Another angel was touching his leg. The angel with his hands on the boy's legs turned and spoke to me, telling me that when his mother wheeled him up beside me, I must put my hands on his legs.

When they reached the top of the queue the boy and his mother came and sat with me. I spoke to them and I touched the young boy's legs. As I did, the beam of light behind him opened up and his guardian angel appeared. Standing with his guardian angel I could see several teacher angels. The guardian angel handed something to one of the teacher angels and he placed the object into the boy's chest. I silently asked the angels what was going on and what they were doing. I got no answer. I was only told to put my hands on the boy's legs and to bless him. That I did, and I asked for blessings for him and for his whole family. He was a happy young man.

Later, a young boy called Michael gave me a notebook with pictures he had drawn. He told me he had made them especially for me. As he said this his guardian angel showed himself to me, glowing so brightly that for a moment I had to look away.

Some people asked me questions about angels. One woman asked me about the difference between our relationship with God and the angels' relationship with God. It was a brilliant question, but I could only give her a very brief answer then. Let me answer it more fully here and hopefully the woman will read this book.

God made humans and God made angels, but we are very different. When God created man and woman he made them in His image. This phrase does not refer to our body – but to our soul. Our soul is a piece of God, a spark of His divinity, of His light that dwells within each and every one of us, regardless of faith or belief. Because of this spark of divinity we are all God's children and like any father He wishes all His children to return home safely to Him, to Heaven.

God created angels for their beauty and grace, to be His helpers, His messengers. He has tasked them in particular with helping to bring His human children back safely to Him in Heaven. The angels and I have talked about the difference between humans and angels many times. I still feel embarrassed saying that angels are creatures but that they are not created in His image. They are not God's children. We humans are superior to angels because we have a soul. The angels insist I must say this and not be embarrassed about it.

I have been shown the connection that exists between God and the angels. It's like a thread of light. It's as if God's light runs along a thread from God to each angel. Angels would not have this light without this connection to God. Angels have a deep desire to receive this light constantly and this is why they serve God unconditionally. Angels are answerable to God at all times. They do not have free will like we do, but they do help to create the conditions in which we can enjoy this unique gift.

When God sends a little soul to be conceived humanly, an angel accompanies the soul. This is, of course, their guardian angel, their helper, protector and most importantly the gatekeeper of their soul. God asks this angel to bring this soul safely back to Him in Heaven. So your guardian angel is an enormous gift from God. That's why I feel so sad if people ignore this gift, or deny it.

I understand some people wish to have a direct relationship with God. But why throw away a gift God has given you? Your guardian angel is there to help you in your connection with God. When you have a direct relationship with God, your angels are helping you, whether or not you are aware of them.

In the Bible Jesus had angels around him, helping. I know he had a guardian angel, as everyone born human does. Jesus called on his guardian angel and other angels for help. So why wouldn't we follow his example?

In other religious traditions spiritual leaders right through time have also called on the help of angels. Many of us don't understand how important the relationship between mankind and angels is. We have free will, but we have angels to prompt us to do the right things, to prompt us to do what God would want us to do in each and every circumstance. This is the task God has given angels and, because it is God's task, angels will never ever give up. Every time you pray you are talking directly to God. Regardless of your belief in angels, angels are praying with you at the same time, adding power and strength to your prayer. This is one of the tasks God has given the angels. We never pray alone.

Another question I was asked by a man at that same signing was why I refer to God all the time in my writings and don't talk more about Jesus. I gave him the short answer: 'Because that is what God told me to do!' I'm not sure if that answer satisfied him, so let me explain a little more.

When I started to write *Angels in my Hair* I was worried because I did not know what to call God in the book. I didn't know whether to call him God or Jesus or the Holy Spirit and I know He is called different names in different religions that I don't know. I know that for some people their primary devotion is towards Jesus. To me, Jesus is God. I knew that the book I was writing was for all religions, and I was afraid of offending someone by the name I gave God. I asked God for help and He asked me, 'When you are praying, Lorna, what do you call me?' I replied, 'God, of course.'

'And that is what you should call me in this book and in every book after that,' God replied. 'When you speak of me, you call me God because it is universal. I am the Father and the Son, and the Holy Spirit. I am God. Write and speak in simple words, Lorna, so that people can understand.'

There were so many questions that day – some deeply personal, some more general. An adoptive mother came to talk to me. She said she knew that I had written that babies chose their mothers and that they loved their mothers even if they never were born, or died very young. Even if they know that their mother will not keep them and will give them up for adoption. She wanted to know about adoptive parents. Were they chosen too?

The adoptive mother is chosen by that child as well. This is why it is so important that prospective parents listen to their feelings and their guardian angel during the process of selection – their connection with the baby is already there. This is why occasionally someone who has said they always wanted a girl will suddenly find themselves adopting a boy, or they will find themselves adopting a child of a different age to what they had anticipated, or a child that has disabilities. Adoptive parents are chosen, a baby has chosen them, and loves them already, and they need to listen; the angels are prompting them to make the right choice. The angels told me that this woman had made the right choice and that her daughter had chosen her and loved her dearly, both before adoption and now, when she was ten years old.

The highlight of that signing for me was a young man, perhaps in his late twenties, whose soul came forward as he walked towards me to get his book signed. The angels with him told me that reading *Angels in my Hair* was the first time he had been made spiritually aware. I was so excited at seeing his soul and the excitement within him about his new discovery of himself. I met him quite early in the signing – probably in the first hour – but he stayed there for the whole signing. I could see him out of the corner of my eye for hours; I would get a glimpse of him, but the angels wouldn't let me look. Hours later, when I finished the signing, he was still standing around – now with his wife, whom I hadn't met. He was glowing as if the light of his soul was beaming out through him. I wanted to stand and stare at him, but the angels told me to keep moving.

I was exhausted at the end of that signing, but I felt good. I knew that things were happening, even if in some cases they were miracles in disguise. I had met so many people. So many people shared with me their worries and concerns and I implored God and the angels to answer their prayers. That day, I saw so many angels working with people, becoming employed alongside their guardian angels to help them.

Chapter Thirty-one

The boy in whose soul an angel dwells

I got a call from my mother one day, to say that Molly – a cousin of my father's – was in hospital in Cork. Mum was very anxious that she would have at least the odd visitor and asked me would I go and visit her. I was reluctant to – it was a two-and-a-half-hour drive each way – but an angel whispered in my ear that I should go.

I set off a few days later. The traffic wasn't too bad and I got there in good time. But the hospital car park was quite full, so I had to drive down to the far end to find a space. The car park was full of potholes and it had been raining, so I walked towards the hospital avoiding the puddles. Michael appeared beside me and asked, 'Do you remember how, years ago, God asked you to pray for a person who has an angel dwelling in their soul?'

I looked at him. How could I forget? Years earlier, when Megan was only a tiny baby, Angel Michael had told me that I would be shown someone very special and that I would have to pray for this person's protection for the rest of my life. That day I had asked Michael what was so special about this person. 'All I can tell you', Michael had replied, 'is that an angel dwells in this person's soul.' I had been shocked, overwhelmed by the thought that there was someone here in this country in Ireland, where I live, with an angel dwelling in their soul! Michael reached out and took my hand. As he held my hand he told me that it wouldn't happen for a little while, but that God wanted me to be aware that one day I would see this person. I wanted to know more but Michael wouldn't tell me anything else. He just reminded me that God wanted me to pray for this person and then he had disappeared.

As I walked up the ramp from the car park my attention was directed towards a woman dressed in a navy coat, hurrying along ahead of me. She was taller than me and slim, with black hair. I only saw the back of her. Just as I reached the hospital entrance, I felt a few drops of rain. Going up the stairs inside the hospital a woman in a dark coat passed me by. Again, I only saw the back of her. I asked the angels whether it was the same woman, and they told me it was. I asked the angels why they were not allowing me to see her face. This concerned me a bit. The angels gave no answer. I was tempted to walk around to see whether I could see her face, but at that moment a nurse turned to me and asked could she help?

When I got to Molly's ward, she was delighted to see me. While we chatted I held her hand and said a silent prayer for her to get well. One of the catering staff came into the ward serving tea, and offered me one too. We sat there drinking tea and talking, which was really nice, but then Molly started to get anxious. She fretted about the traffic, saying it was very heavy and that I should go before it got too busy. An angel appeared, sitting at the far side of Molly's bed. I watched the angel taking Molly's hand, and at the same time the light of Molly's guardian angel opened up for a second and she became a little less anxious. I took a last sip of my tea. As I did, I saw another angel appear at the door of Molly's ward, telling me it was time to go. I kissed Molly's cheek and left. When I reached the door, the angel there told me to look back. I did and saw that Molly was already asleep with an angel holding her hand. It was a lovely sight to see.

The sun was shining as I walked out of the hospital and down to the car park. I noticed a lot of angels gathering around me. I asked them what they were doing there but they ignored me. On my way down the ramp to the car park Angel Michael appeared beside me. 'Molly may not want you to get stuck in the traffic,' he said, 'but I'm afraid God has other plans.'

I looked at him. 'The traffic doesn't seem so bad to me,' I said. I looked at Michael again and saw him smiling. 'Do you mean I'm going to see it now?' I asked. I was so over-whelmed, I could hardly breathe.

'Lorna, it's OK, take a deep breath,' said Michael, nodding his head.

'Am I going to see it here in Cork?' I asked in a shaky voice.

Again Michael nodded. 'No more questions, Lorna. Get into the car.'

As I turned on the ignition I looked around. Only then did I realise that I was unable to reverse out of my spot because there was a line of traffic blocking me. The place was full of cars, all of which seemed to want to exit at the same moment. There was very little movement. I could do nothing, so I sat there and prayed.

About ten minutes later an angel told me to put my car into reverse. I did so and shortly afterwards a car honked its horn, allowing me to reverse my way out. Now I was in the line of traffic trying to reach the exit onto a busy street. About half an hour after I had walked out of the hospital, I reached the top of the ramp out of the car park and on to the main road. I was there with the handbrake on, waiting for a gap in the traffic so I could cross the road, when suddenly everywhere was thronged with angels. As I waited, I watched them moving in and out between the cars, but there were no gaps in the traffic. Angel Michael appeared beside me. 'Lorna, you see the white van on your right. He will indicate to you to cross the traffic in front of him. Don't worry about blocking traffic!' Michael disappeared again. There were about six cars in front of the white van but eventually it reached the entrance of the car park and what Michael had said would happen, happened. I drove out onto the road, blocking the near-side lane for a few moments, and then another car allowed me into the opposite line of traffic. I sat there in the traffic again, hardly moving.

I could feel the presence of all my Angels – Michael, Hosus, Elijah, Kaphas, Elisha and many more. I was told to keep on looking straight ahead of me. Angel Michael spoke to me without words. 'Watch the bus!' he said. As he said this, I saw the double-decker bus coming towards me sway a little in slow motion and then crash into an empty parked car. I watched the driver get out of the bus. I could see he was confused, wondering how he could have hit it. All the traffic coming towards me had stopped now, leaving the road to my right clear of all cars.

Things started to become incredibly still. I felt the presence of my angels become extremely strong. There was nothing moving – no cars, people or birds. Everything was completely still. Not even a leaf on a tree moved. The only thing I noticed was the light of an energy coming up from the ground like a mist. I was told to look to the right and there I saw the woman with the navy coat I had noticed earlier. She was walking along the footpath about twenty feet away. She was walking as if in extreme slow motion and everything around her was especially still. She started to walk out on to the empty road beside me. I watched her very closely, afraid I might miss something that God wanted me to see. My whole body felt extremely light. I could not even feel the seat I was sitting on.

'What am I to see?' I asked Michael. After what felt like an eternity to me, Michael told me to look to the right again. I could see a young boy. He seemed to be moving normally, taking his time as young boys do. This boy was tall and skinny, with black straight hair and he was dressed in a school uniform. He was probably around ten. The woman was still moving in extreme slow motion. She was halfway across the road when she turned and called out to him. I knew instantly that she was his mother. Her voice was muffled, so I don't know what language she spoke. It may not even have been English. As the boy stepped off the pavement to follow his mother it was as if he slowed down too and was hardly moving. Each movement he made appeared to me like a multitude of waves of movements. It was incredible to watch. He was moving within a crimson light tinged with deep blue, which extended about three feet around him. His feet didn't seem to be touching the ground. It was as if he were walking in another time or place. As he walked his appearance changed from a young boy to a tall and handsome adult and then back to the boy again. His appearance switched like this several times. Suddenly the young boy stopped in the middle of the road about five feet away and turned and faced me, giving me a big smile. His face lit up and the blue crimson light surrounding him seemed to explode and lift him off the ground. The boy's soul came forward with an incredible burst of light and with it came the angel that dwelt within his soul.

For a fraction of a second I saw the angel on its own. It was enormous, with huge wings and was draped in creamy-coloured fabric with a tint of gold in the creases of the fabric. The most incredible aspect of its appearance were its very deep and bright eyes. Then – within the explosion of blue crimson light – the boy, his soul and the angel within his soul merged and became one. This merged entity was enormous. It dwarfed the buildings on the street. It seemed to move upwards and then suddenly descended back to the ground. The boy's eyes flashed dramatically and I could see into an enormous depth of blue crimson. I can never forget those eyes. Writing about it now, I realise for the first time that what I saw were the eyes of the angel looking out through the boy's human eyes. I was exuberant. Of all the things I had seen that day, this surprised and delighted me the most.

The young boy came back to normal and stood on the road in front of me, acknowledging me with a smile. Then time started moving at its regular rate. The woman walked quickly on and the young boy ran after her. The traffic started moving again. I was overwhelmed by what I had seen. I don't know how I continued driving. At the first possible moment I pulled in and called out to Michael, asking what all this meant.

'An angel dwells in this young boy's soul, Lorna.'

I asked Michael how many times it had happened before.

'Very few; it happens very rarely,' Michael replied. He continued, 'Remember Angel Elijah, who first came to you as a child, who walked across the water and told you about Joe?' I nodded. How could I ever forget!

Michael continued, 'Elijah was one of those very rare people who had an angel dwelling in his soul. Many people knew him as the prophet Elijah. God can send Elijah as an angel with a message when he chooses. That's what he did with you.'

I looked at Michael uncomprehendingly and he continued. 'Normal souls aren't sent back as angels, and angels don't have souls, Lorna. The prophet Elijah and this boy are very rare and special.' As Michael said those words he took my hands and gave me such a wonderful smile, and I smiled back.

I said, 'Michael, I can't imagine you and the angels being any more special than you are already.' Michael smiled.

'Let me finish. On very rare occasions like these God has allowed an angel to dwell in the soul of a man and become a part of his soul. God has allowed this to happen again. You must pray for this young boy as he grows and goes out into the world. Pray that he is allowed to live and to do what God wants him to do. There is a possibility that he will be destroyed. This is why he needs your prayers so much. You need to pray that he will be allowed to live.'

I had so many questions for Michael, but he disappeared. I know that some things are beyond our human comprehension. I know we will never understand everything. As I drove back home, thinking of what I had just seen, I prayed with all my heart that that young boy would have the chance to grow up and fulfil what God wanted him to do.

I still pray for him every day because this young boy is part of the future of mankind. He has a role to play in bringing peace to this world, in bringing an end to war, hunger and famine, and in bringing justice to all people, allowing every person to have a fulfilled life.

Chapter Thirty-two

Jimazen

The year after the book was launched was hectic. I was doing lots of interviews and seemed to be travelling back and forth to London frequently. I was also, of course, still a mother. Megan was still only twelve and very demanding, like all teenagers. Fortunately, Ruth and the other children gave me tremendous help and support, otherwise life would have been impossible.

The angels had warned me that writing a book would be hard work, but they had never explained just how hard and demanding the work would be, and they certainly hadn't warned me just how much work there would be after publication. I had rather naively thought that all I had to do was write the book and that was it.

One Saturday, the spring after the book was published, I decided to take some time for myself. I had to visit some married relatives who live in a house in a valley in the middle of nowhere in the Wicklow hills. The scenery in the area is spectacular, so I set out early with the plan of keeping my visit short and having some time in the Wicklow hills by myself.

It was spring but it wasn't very warm. The day was a little overcast, but at times was bright. There didn't seem to be any threat of rain. The roads up there are very narrow and

I took turns at random. I found myself on the top of one of the mountains. Irish mountains are very small by international standards, so we sometimes call them hills and sometimes mountains. The highest in Wicklow is less than a thousand metres high. I was at the top of this mountain and pulled in and parked the car. There was nothing much growing there – a little gorse and heather, and lots of rocks and stones. It was very wide and open and in the distance I could see other hills, some of which were higher. I could also see down into a valley where there was a river.

Suddenly, everything got very bright. Initially I thought it was the sun, but then I realised it wasn't. Everything went silent and it was as if everything stood still. I knew Angel Jimazen was about to appear and I was filled with fear.

From the first moment I saw the Angel Jimazen I was scared of him and of what seeing him meant – and I still am. Jimazen is very powerful and very important to our earth. He is the gatekeeper of our planet. In many ways you could call him the guardian angel of the earth.

We have to realise that our planet is alive and very beautiful. It's a gift from God but a gift that we share with others. Controversial as this may sound, our planet has its own life force or spirit. Some traditions refer to this as Mother Earth. Jimazen is the angel who does everything to quell and soothe Mother Earth, to keep her still.

My introduction to Jimazen was different to my introduction to any other angel. I was very young at the time, about five years old, and still living in Old Kilmainham. I was standing in our garden looking over the wall at our neighbour's apple trees, and playing with a few little pebbles.

Suddenly, loads of angels came around me. They said, 'Lorna, look. See the angel over there.' I stood on my toes, gazing in among the apple trees, but I couldn't see anything.

'The angel must be hiding,' I said to the angels surrounding me. 'All I can see is all the light falling from the apple trees on to the grass and wildflowers.'

'Lorna,' said the angels, 'look above the apple trees.' I did, and I saw this enormous angel, like a big male giant, standing about fifteen feet away from me above the trees. I have no idea how far up into the sky he stretched. He was dressed in gold and red protective armour with a tinge of black. His face looked stern but yet in some way gentle. I stepped back from the wall and the angels around me whispered in my ear, 'It's OK, Lorna, don't be afraid.'

This angel looked down at me and smiled. 'Lorna, I am Angel Jimazen.' He reached out his left hand and touched me. For a split second it was as if I was beside him, standing beside his enormous foot, and the next moment I was back at the garden wall. It was really scary.

Jimazen said, 'Breathe, Lorna!' In his right hand he held an enormous wooden stake that was almost as tall as he was. It was very big in every way, but then so was he. The stick started to grow in length, going downwards and touching the ground. He tapped the earth with it and the earth trembled. I felt this faint tremor under my feet and then he disappeared. I was terrified; I had never felt the earth move like this before and I turned and ran as fast as I could into the house.

The angels around me whispered in my ear that it was OK, but I was still terrified. Luckily, Mum was in Da's bicycle shop at the front of the house when I ran through it. She offered me some bread and jam, which comforted me a bit and helped me to forget my fright.

I don't have to be out in nature for Jimazen to appear. I could be, but equally I could be somewhere like my kitchen. I dread his appearance as, over the years, I have learnt that it means that he is having difficulties controlling the spirit of the earth because of something we humans have done. In other words, his appearance means we are in trouble! And most often, some time afterwards I will hear of a natural disaster somewhere in the world – be it earthquake, floods, landslides, volcanic eruptions or whatever.

Jimazen has taught me that we who live on this earth must stop destroying our planet. We must stop destroying the rivers and the air we breathe with pollutants, cutting down her forests, drilling into the earth, tearing holes in her surface to take out too much oil, gas and other minerals.

Mother Earth is desperately trying to shield herself and not to destroy the precious life that lives on her and within her. But the level and speed of the damage being done to her by us is too great and she's not being given the time to heal herself. Under these circumstances she cannot avoid reacting to protect herself, twisting and turning in an effort to heal herself. But when she does this she destroys the life that lives on her and grows from her.

I have noticed as I have got older that Jimazen finds it harder to control the spirit of the earth. Angel Jimazen is angry with us for not listening. He tells me he is finding it harder and harder to control her because we humans are tearing her apart more and more. We are killing her.

Back there, standing on the Wicklow hills on this spring

day, I knew that Jimazen was going to appear to me again and so I was filled with apprehension.

The earth shook. Jimazen appeared above me, standing some thirty feet away from me. He was a giant as always and as usual I saw no wings but in his hand he held his staff and his face looked angry and frustrated. He communicated to me without words that he was desperately trying to control the spirit of the earth – but that this time he was not sure he could succeed. He had come to warn mankind.

For some reason that I don't understand, he asked me to pray to God. I don't know why a powerful angel like this needs my prayers. He asked me to pray so that the twists that the spirit of the earth would make would not be too destructive, that too many lives would not be lost.

Then he was gone. I stood there shaking and very distressed. I was trembling so much I have no idea how I made it back to the car, but suddenly I found myself sitting there in the warmth. I must have sat there for an hour or two praying. I began thinking about what I had been shown in the past about the spirit of the earth.

The first time I had been shown the spirit of Mother Earth I was fourteen. I was out walking Shane, the neighbour's Alsatian dog. Suddenly, Shane stopped and lay down on the path beside me. I didn't know why. I suddenly felt Jimazen's presence and I realised that he had appeared up above me. He tapped the ground with his staff, as he had done the first time I met him and, as he did, I heard my name being called in a gentle and loving voice. I knew instantly that it was the voice of Mother Earth.

The earth opened up and I could see into its core. In the centre, curled in on herself a little like an unborn baby, was

Mother Earth. She was absolutely beautiful, long and sleek and very smooth with emerald colours of blue and green running into each other in veins of gold. Just looking at her I had no doubt that she was female. She looked back up at me. She was absolutely beautiful, gorgeous. She had a vaguely human appearance. She didn't have a head as we do. Rather her face was within her body. She didn't say anything more to me but just smiled and I was allowed to watch as she turned very gently. I couldn't see arms like our arms. Rather, she seemed to have lots and lots of arms – but not in the way an octopus has tentacles. Instead, it was as if there were lots and lots of sails made of silk billowing out from her. As I watched, she seemed to get longer. Moving ever so gently, she stretched out her sail-like arms to parts of the planet that needed healing.

The spirit of the earth is like a mother feeding her young that live above her. We live on the earth's crust – which is her skin. Other life dwells within her. All life is very precious to her – including people, animals, trees and flowers, the oceans and rivers, the mountains and deserts. We are asking too much of her. We can't just keep pulling at the earth, taking and giving nothing back. We know that if we keep overloading a human organ like the kidney, we get sickness and perhaps ultimately death. The same is true with the earth. When we put too much pressure on her she responds and she needs to fight back for her own survival. Global warming is exactly this. It's nature's response to how we are mistreating the environment.

Angel Jimazen tells me we must stop. He has told me, 'If Mother Earth is not given time to recover, time to heal, the likelihood is that one day she will have to give an enormous twist and turn in order to survive. That, more than likely, will destroy an enormous amount of life.' Jimazen is an extremely powerful angel with an enormous job to do that requires great power. He is beautiful, but he scares me. I find it extremely hard to explain what I feel around him. He is a very passionate and emotional angel and he shows his emotions to me in a way that no other angel does. He also lets me feel his power in a way that no other angel does. He roars and gives out about what we are doing and he feels enormous frustration because he is unable to stop us. I'm scared of his power, and yet I know how important he is to the survival of the earth and the human race.

The Angel Jimazen feels the pain of the spirit of the earth. He has great compassion for Mother Earth and for us but in many ways he is in battle with the earth, trying to control it, and calling on God to help him. I see him in battle sometimes, something that I have never seen with any other of God's angels. But when he is fighting with Mother Earth, trying to pin her down and stop her convulsing, he is doing it out of love.

Jimazen is like roaring thunder above the earth. When I see him he only stops and stands still for a few seconds. But, one day, Jimazen stopped for a moment and showed me what I can only describe as a shield of light around the world. It was made up of a series of straight lines of light that went from one point to another. The width of these lines looked to me to be not much bigger than a pencil line. I have no idea of the distance between each point. There were loads of them and they seemed to criss-cross each other constantly. One line is never on top of the other. I have asked what this shield is for and the angels have told me it is to keep particles away from planet earth.

Jimazen told me that the points where the lines intersect are called 'corners of the earth'. There are loads of them. How can there be so many corners in this pattern, I do not know, and I don't understand – but that it is what I was told. At each corner, there is an angel. These angels have the task of helping Angel Jimazen and they never leave their corners. Jimazen moves along these lines of light. He is the only angel I know who moves in this way. He is working all the time to keep the shield intact. He takes enormous pride in his job and he never leaves earth. Most angels come and go but I don't know if Jimazen has ever been anywhere else, other than on the earth. All I know is he has been there since earth began and will be there forever, or for as long as the planet earth exists.

Some people are doing tremendous work in relation to the environment, but we all need to do our bit. We all need to sit up and realise that this is the responsibility of all of us and if we don't take it seriously, future generations will pay a terrible price. Imagine a situation where your grandchildren or great-grandchildren have to live in a bubble or in a closed and confined area where everything – including the air they breathe – is controlled. It is possible for us to change how we treat our environment. I have been shown a possible future where the planet earth is so green, the air so pure, and so very different to today, with such an abundance of so many wonderful natural things. But to reach this future we have to start acting and act fast.

It was dark when eventually I headed home from Wicklow with a heavy heart.

Chapter Thirty-three

Reincarnation

I went to Amsterdam to do media interviews and a public talk, and to meet the Dutch-language publishers. Jean was with me and we stayed in a fantastic hotel by a canal. Apparently the hotel was famous with authors and it even had a library full of books signed by authors who had stayed there. I was thrilled when they asked me to sign my book and add it to the library.

On our first day we headed out to find somewhere for lunch. As I left the hotel Angel Michael took my hand, whispering in my ear, 'You are going to see something very special over the next few days. Something you don't see very often.'

I smiled and said back, 'I like surprises.' I had thought that the something special probably meant the sights of Amsterdam. But no, the angels had much more surprising things in store for me.

I loved Amsterdam, it's a beautiful city. Everyone cycles everywhere, going to work in suits on bicycles, women dressed in their best going out on dates, chatting with their partner as they cycled along, and parents with little wooden carts attached to the front or the back of their bike carrying a young child. I saw lots of angels, of course. At times it looked as if they were cycling the same bicycle.

We sat outside a restaurant on a busy square and had

lunch and watched the world go by. After lunch, Jean said she had a few things to do and we agreed to meet back in the hotel in an hour.

Jean had just left when Angel Michael whispered in my ear, 'Lorna, look up the street.' I did. The street was busy with people walking up and down all the time. About three steps behind each one of them I saw the light of their guardian angel. There were other angels too, and even the occasional soul walking with a person. Then two young men came walking down the street and stopped at the corner about fifteen feet away from me, talking.

Michael whispered in my ear, 'Watch carefully, Lorna.' The two young men stopped talking to each other and the lights of their guardian angels opened up. As they did, everything on the street seemed to stop for a brief moment. One of the men looked quite young, maybe in his early twenties, and the other, who was taller, was about ten years older. It was as if the angels framed the pair of them and drew them closer so I could see better. It was like looking at an enlarged photograph. After a few seconds their guardian angels' lights closed, but the enlarged-photo effect continued.

Michael whispered in my ear. 'Lorna, watch carefully.' There were several angels standing around the two young men. Other angels walked in between them and two angels stood between them. I don't know how the angels found the space because the two men were standing close up. It fascinates me when the angels do this.

The two young men started to talk again, and it was then that I was shown my surprise! The older man's soul moved in his body. This soul came forward and I was shown an appearance of a soldier – not a First or Second World War soldier but from a much earlier time. This young soldier's skin was sallow and clear. His face was oval and he had blue eyes and brown hair. His clothes were of a heavy, grey rough fabric and reached below his knee. His shoes were made of coarse leather and strapped. He had a sword strapped across him and another pointed long weapon tied across his back. I could see there were other weapons, like knives, strapped to his belt. His weapons made him look big and ferocious but I could see that actually by modern standards he was not a very big man.

Michael spoke to me without words. 'This man had a past life. He was a soldier then.' I looked at the man again. I could still see both his current appearance and his past life. They both looked in my direction. His friend stood beside him, but as if the angels had frozen him in time. I understood then that the reason that the two angels were there between them was to shield the younger man from what I was being shown of his friend.

The light of the reincarnated man's guardian angel opened up again. His guardian angel didn't give a very human appearance. It was as if he was a radiant and beautiful swirl moving behind the young man. But I had a definite sense that the guardian angel was male.

Life went back to normal but I continued to see the soldier within this man very prominently. As he said goodbye to his friend he hurried across the road and disappeared down the street. I sat there thinking about reincarnation. I had so many questions to ask Michael about why I had just been shown what I had seen. But I wasn't allowed to.

Up until now I have only been shown about twenty souls who have reincarnated. I remember one particular journalist asking me whether we were all reincarnated as soon as we die. I was a little surprised at the question. I explained that I have never been shown a soul that did not go straight to Heaven after death and I asked, 'If we are in Heaven, why would we want to come back?' I know we like to believe that we would come back because people we loved here are grieving and missing us. That may be, but a soul that has gone to Heaven can do much more for their family from Heaven than they could when they were alive, humanly, on earth. The soul of a loved one can, for example, communicate with you. I am always surprised at how much easier it is for most people to hear a message from a soul, than from an angel. This is because the soul had lived in a human body. Frequently people will tell me that when they had a problem they felt their granny, or some other loved one who is now dead, helping them. They are probably right. This is one of the ways that souls in Heaven can help the living. Another is that they can intercede for us – either with God or with another person – although this latter does require that that person's guardian angel agrees to let them intercede. This is a vast subject, but I will share with you some of what the angels have taught me about it and also what I have experienced myself.

After you have died and gone to Heaven your soul does not want to come back. It is very happy in Heaven. It only returns if God sends it back. When God sends a soul back it may not be into the same family or even nationality. I have been shown this happening only a few times, though as I travel I see more. Occasionally, when I have been out somewhere, even abroad, I am shown someone who has been reincarnated. Then I pray and ask God to help them to fulfil the purpose that they had come for.

I remember when I was about ten, sitting on the floor in the house in Ballymun watching a black and white TV. Angel Elijah was sitting beside me. He told me that the man I was watching on the TV was reincarnated. Here was a soul who had come back to help man to move forward. The man on the television was Martin Luther King. I was shown a vision of his past life. He was white, which will surprise many. He lived in a small rural community. I have no idea when it was or where in the world it was – the one thing I do know is that the language he was speaking wasn't English. It was as if he was the head man, the leader of this small community, but like everyone else he was a worker. I was shown him, along with other men, women and children, clearing rocks from rough but grassy fields. He was telling others what to do as well as working himself. There were green trees around. It was as if they were preparing the land and building a protective wall around the community. I know he – Martin Luther King – was a very spiritually aware man, a man of strong faith, but like any of us he wasn't perfect. God didn't make his life easy, but I could see from what I was shown that he had an enormous strength of character, and a powerful commitment to fight for what was right.

Elijah just reminded me, saying, 'Don't forget, Lorna, God has given man free will and those who are reincarnated also have free will. Sometimes they do not do what they were intended to do, or pass on the wisdom that was intended.'

'Elijah, didn't Martin Luther King fulfil the purpose for which he was reincarnated?' I asked.

'Yes, Lorna, he did. He has given people everywhere a belief in justice and equality – the dignity and courage to fight for what is right. He has given this not only to the family that he was reborn into, and to African Americans, but to all mankind. For generations to come those who are oppressed in any way will gain courage from the life of Martin Luther King. Even today, when people stand up and fight for the elderly or the homeless or the right to work, they are influenced – whether they realise it or not – by what Martin Luther King did. That soul achieved what God sent it back to do. But sometimes a soul succeeds in only a fraction of its purpose. On many occasions people destroy the person.'

When I was about eleven, I was going fishing with my da. We stopped in a little one-street village outside a shop with two petrol pumps. There was a tractor being repaired, and an elderly man outside the shop sitting on a rocking chair smoking his pipe. Piles of firewood were stacked along the wall and near the door there were also rubber tyres and plastic buckets. As Da opened the bonnet of the car he asked me to get water for the radiator. He told me he was going into the shop to get a few things and to ask about the best spots to fish on the river nearby.

Pouring water into the radiator was quite hard for me because I was small. As I was concentrating on this task, Angel Hosus appeared beside me. When I was finished he said, 'Look over at that old man.' I did. The old man was still sitting, smoking his pipe. Every now and then he tapped the pipe on the side of his chair. As I watched, the light of his guardian angel opened up, and I was allowed to see that he had been reincarnated. The old man's soul stepped forward and showed me what he had looked like when he had lived before. He showed me a man with a heavy build and broad shoulders. His long dark hair was tied back, and he had brown eyes and a gentle face. He didn't really look Irish but I have no idea what nationality he may have been. He was dressed in plain dark clothes made of a heavy material, like wool. Everything about his appearance was the opposite of the old man sitting in the chair. The frail, thin old man started to rock in the chair and the old man's guardian angel surrounded him and reached out and took his soul, bringing it forward gently and then setting the soul back down into the old man's body with enormous tenderness and love. The old man seemed to shudder slightly.

The angels have told me that when someone is reincarnated their guardian angel must come back to share their life with them. This is because the guardian is the gatekeeper of that soul.

'Hosus,' I asked, 'why was that old man reincarnated?'

Hosus smiled at me. 'Because that family needed to learn how to love and care for each other.'

'Hosus, that seems very simple!' I said.

'It sometimes is that simple, Lorna, but sometimes people fail to understand it,' he replied. 'Love is a fundamental part of human life. Love is very important. It's one of the most powerful and precious gifts mankind has.'

I looked at the man again. 'Hosus, he looks very frail. Is he going to die soon?'

Hosus looked at me and nodded. 'Don't be sad; his soul will be going back to Heaven shortly. He'll die there in his favourite place – his rocking chair.'

Da came out of the shop and Hosus disappeared. Da closed the bonnet of the car and as we drove away I glanced back at the old man sitting in the chair, and at his guardian angel loving him so tenderly.

On the first evening in Amsterdam I gave a public talk. My first! As I got out of the taxi at the beautiful old church where the talk was to take place, I could see Angel Michael standing at the entrance. I was so glad to see him. He touched my hand as I passed by and filled me with peace and joy. As I entered the hall, there were already people there and the angels around them seemed to be buzzing with excitement.

I spent a little time in peace in an office on my own and then went into the hall. The light of each and every one's guardian angel was extremely bright and there were lots of other angels moving about. I asked silently for the light of the angels to be turned down a little, so as I could see the men and women in front of me clearly. When it was time for questions, I was surprised because each time someone asked a question the light of the guardian angel behind that person opened up, so as I could see their guardian angel clearly. It made me hesitate for a moment each time. Perhaps people thought I was thinking about the right answer!

It is wonderful to see so many people striving to grow spiritually, recognising that they do indeed have a guardian angel who is the gatekeeper of their soul, and that it will never leave them – not for one moment. It was a privilege for me to have been invited to talk to those wonderful men and women. I asked for blessings for each and every one of them in their lives and within their families. The organisers had done a fantastic job.

I hadn't expected at all that I would see another example of reincarnation during my time in Amsterdam. But the angels continued to surprise me and showed me several over the next few days.

Between press interviews I went out with Jean for a walk and some fresh air. Angel Michael whispered in my ear. 'Watch carefully, Lorna, so you'll miss nothing.' A man cycled past on a bicycle pulling a cart with a young boy of seven and a girl of about four in it. I assumed they were father and children. As they passed I was allowed to see that both children were reincarnations. That was astonishing to me. It was just a fleeting glimpse. To my surprise the little girl was the reincarnation of a boy. This was new information to me. Being honest, I had never really thought about whether reincarnations were always the same sex. On reflection, why should they be? If they can be born into different families, nationalities and colour why not into a different sex?

I was shown the little girl's past life as a boy of about seven wearing a black skull cap – so I knew he had been Jewish. He was wearing a white shirt under a little jacket, but I couldn't see the rest of him. The little girl turned and looked in my direction and at the same time so did the past life of the boy within her. He smiled at me with beautiful dark brown eyes. I saw less of the other soul that had been reincarnated. The soul came forward and I was shown a boy a few years younger than the seven-year-old he was in his present life. I didn't get the impression he was Jewish. I really only glimpsed his face before the father cycled out of view. What I did see were eyes that glittered in a rather sallow face, and this face was framed by a big head of dark curls, as if they had grown too long.

There were loads of teenagers around us on that walk in Amsterdam. I commented on it to Jean and she suggested that perhaps it was because of the big shopping centre nearby. I wasn't sure that was the full story, though, because there were so many angels around. One of the angels spoke to me, saying, 'A lot of these young people are here to connect with you spiritually.'

A young teenager, about fourteen with blonde hair, walked past with a few friends. The light of her guardian angel surrounded her, lighting her up so that she stood out from her friends. Her soul moved forward and I was shown that her soul was a reincarnation. I turned to Michael and asked, 'What is going on?' But he put his fingers to his lips, indicating that he wasn't going to answer me. Her soul showed me her as she had been in her past life. For some reason it showed me her sitting down, even though the girl was standing. I was shown a woman of about thirty. She didn't look anything like her present incarnation. Her face was a very pale white and she was dressed in dark, full-length, fitted clothes that showed off a shapely figure. She looked prosperous. Her clothes were good quality and she had a little gold brooch on her dress and a handbag of polished leather. I was told by an angel with her that she was a woman of power and authority within the community in which she lived.

'Michael,' I called silently without words, as I desperately wanted to ask him what was going on. Why was I being shown so many reincarnated young people suddenly? Why was I being shown so many in Amsterdam? Michael answered me. 'No questions, Lorna.'

I was really intrigued and on the walk back to the hotel I pondered the question of reincarnation and what I had been told about it and shown by the angels over the years.

Fortunately Jean didn't seem to feel the need to talk, as I was lost in my thoughts.

Lots of people would like to believe that we are reincarnated as soon as our physical body dies, especially a parent who has lost a child. You sometimes hear a mother saying that their child is a reincarnation of her mother or grandfather, or even a sibling who has died. They will tell you that the child smiles like the dead granny or has the same gestures or turn of phrase. This much may be true but in this case it is probably not that the child is the reincarnation of the granny. It probably means that this child carries a little bit more of the granny's genetic code, passed down through the mother's blood. I understand why we all say these things, especially when we have lost someone we love. All of us look at our children, searching to find characteristics of loved ones that have died and gone back to Heaven. We all must remember that when the time comes for our souls to leave our bodies and go to Heaven it is there that we will meet the loved ones who have gone before us.

I remember when I was a teenager bringing our neighbour's dog Shane for a walk around the estates where we lived. I was a little tired and stopped to sit on a little wall around a green, open area. There were lots of mothers and children out enjoying the sunshine. A few mothers with babies in prams stood near me. Another one walked over and pulled a blanket out from behind her baby's pillow and propped the baby up. Then she sat on the wall. Nearby, some older children were playing and further away in a front garden I could see a mother with a baby in her arms chatting with a neighbour. I watched a beautiful human soul beside the newborn baby. He looked different to other souls I had been shown. He had a more opaque appearance. In fact, although bright and clear like crystal or water, in some ways he looked as if he had been coated in some translucent substance. I could see fewer details of his human appearance than with many souls I have been shown, but he looked male, quite young, tall and well built. He was showing great gentleness and love and was talking ceaselessly to the baby without physically saying any words. I asked the angels what was going on. They didn't answer me.

After a while I got up and continued walking Shane. I headed towards the banks of the river. I could let Shane off his lead there to run around the trees and bushes. I was throwing sticks for Shane when Angel Michael appeared. I was delighted to see him and ran over, but Shane got to him first and lay down on the ground beside him.

'I heard you were asking questions, Lorna,' he said with a smile.

'Yes, Michael. Today when I was sitting on the wall watching that soul talking to the newborn baby, I wondered why there was a soul with that baby? I realise now I have seen babies before with souls talking to them at length, and that these souls look a little different. Who are they and why does this happen to some babies and not others?'

'Lorna, the souls you have seen with newborn babies are souls who have lived previously on this earth. They are talking to the baby to help to give that baby the strength of character it will need to accomplish important challenges during its lifetime. These are teaching souls. This teaching soul could have been a member of that same family, but isn't necessarily so. This teaching soul gives that newborn baby strength of character that they can use in their life if they wish to do so.'

'Michael, I'm not sure if I fully understand,' I said, with a confused look on my face.

'Lorna, you will, as time passes,' Michael replied gently. 'You have already learned so much.'

With a laugh I told him, 'That's because I have the best teachers.' Then I asked, 'What do you mean, Michael, "if they wish to do so"?'

'Lorna, you are always full of questions,' Michael said and smiled at me as he disappeared. I played with the dog for another little while, and then went home.

Years later, again on a fishing trip with Da, I learnt more about the souls that speak to some newborn babies and about reincarnation.

Da invited me to go fishing with him on a Sunday and I was delighted. We got the fishing gear ready and early on Sunday morning, we set off. Two hours later, Da pulled in and parked on a road by a forest. I asked where the river was and Da told me we had to hike. We got all the gear out of the car and headed off through the forest and across a rough rocky area. It turned out to be well worth the hike – the river was beautiful.

Da and I stood by the river fixing our fishing rods. Da suggested that I fish there where we were and that he would go about half a mile upriver. I watched Da walk along the river and disappear out of sight.

I was fishing for about ten minutes when I heard my name being called. I turned around and there was Angel Michael sitting on a rock, dressed like a fisherman. He had wellies that came up over his knees and in his right hand he held a fishing rod. Laughing, I wound up my fishing line and walked over to Michael, asking, 'Did you catch any fish today?' We both laughed as Michael shook his head.

I put the fishing rod down and sat on a rock opposite Michael. 'Lorna,' he started, 'I've come to tell you some more about the teaching souls that you see talking to newborn babies.'

'Yes, Michael,' I replied with interest, 'and I've noticed something else too. As the babies grow and start to speak, that teaching soul is no longer with that baby.'

'Lorna, I haven't explained to you that most newborn babies don't remember what the teaching soul has told them. The most important part of speaking to the newborn baby is to engrave strength of character into the baby's personality. Most times that God allows this to happen it is because leadership is needed. Someone is called for that people can look up to. Sometimes it's leadership within a family – or it might be for a country or even the world, or it might be to help to provide leadership for a cause like justice.'

'Like historical leaders, you mean?' I asked Michael.

'Yes,' he replied, 'that's one example, but there are countless numbers of people – men and women, even children – who have never made it into the history books who have used what a teaching soul gave them to grow, in order to help them to overcome challenges – theirs and others'. God had chosen certain souls that once lived on the earth to become teachers – teacher souls – to tell some newborn babies about their own human life, in order to give this newborn baby strength of character. About one in every few hundred babies will have a teacher soul with them – more when there are particular challenges to be faced. Most of these babies, as I've said, will forget all about what they have been told, even though it will have impacted on their personality. But on very rare occasions a child will retain these memories for a while and talk about what this teacher soul told them, as if they are talking about themselves. The child may even be able to describe details, as if the child had been there to give dates and name, descriptions of places that they have never seen – perhaps that no longer exist – and may even speak a different language. They may even be able to describe how they died in detail, telling of the fatal wound on the battlefield, or starvation or drowning. That is why sometimes adults think that a child like this is a reincarnation. But it's not. This is something completely different.'

'I understand, Michael,' I said. 'I can now understand how adults can think a child is a reincarnation of someone else when something else is happening. I remember that when we talked about a teacher soul before you said something about how they could use this strength of character in their lives if they wished to. Does it mean that God sends us this as help, and then it's up to our free will whether we use it or not?'

'Yes Lorna,' Michael replied and disappeared.

I went back to fishing, thinking about what Michael had told me.

Suddenly I caught a big trout. It weighed about three pounds. I knew my mother would be delighted. I packed my fishing gear and walked along the riverbank. After about fifteen minutes, I saw Da in the distance and called out that I had caught a fish. When I reached him, he opened his bag – he had caught two. We were both delighted. Da lit a fire and boiled a billycan of water to make tea. We enjoyed our tea and sandwiches. When we got home I was exhausted, and Mum was very happy with the fish.

Writing this now, I realise the harm that adults can unintentionally do. Long ago, parents or adults took little notice of what children said, but as we are becoming more spiritually open and aware we are listening to our children more. Nowadays, when a child starts to talk – recalling the life of another soul as if it were their own life – adults are more likely to listen. Sometimes an adult will do some research into it and on discovering some historic truth in what the child has said, will claim that the child had a particular previous incarnation and convince the child that it has had this past life. Such a belief can have a profound effect on how this child develops into an adult. By talking about it and drawing attention to it the adults may cause the child to retain some of the details of what the teacher soul shared with them. This can stop the child from living the life it is meant to live to the full. The child may even retain painful memories of the teacher soul's death, which may traumatise them.

Sometimes people are told by others that they are reincarnated in a way that is harmful. A businesswoman came to see me and told me that she believed that in a past life she had been a ruthless businessman, greedy and without scruples, and that she had unfairly destroyed another man's business and family. She told me this was why all her businesses were failing, why nothing could work out. She told me that a problem over a business lease came about because she had known and damaged the landlord in a previous life.

The angels told me that there was no truth in any of this. She was using it as an excuse, as a reason for her failure. Instead of looking in a realistic and business-like way at what was going on and trying other options she was simply giving up, claiming she was being blocked because of her past life. No one should ever use a past life as an excuse for not living fully here and now.

Sometimes people will also use what they see as the unfairness of life as a rationale for looking forward to another life on this earth. Why, in their family, for example, is there so much sickness? However, it is not our job to judge what is fair or unfair. We have been given this life – not any other – and it is for us to live whatever life we have been given, however long or short it may be, to the full.

Michael did tell me some more about real reincarnation, a year or two later. I was walking down along the canal near my parents' house in Leixlip when Michael appeared and was sitting on a pile of old stones looking out at the old dam on the canal.

'Lorna, God wants me to help you understand a little more about reincarnation,' Michael said. I stood up and Michael took my hand, filling me with the peace of Heaven.

'Lorna, God loves all His human children unconditionally and He has given you all free will. But sometimes God finds it hard to understand why His human children make life so hard for each other, why they destroy each other and the planet God has given them. I know in some ways it's beyond human comprehension to think that God, who knows everything, doesn't fully understand His human children. Lorna, you human beings have so much love and good inside of you all, but you make everything so complicated. God wants to understand you more so as He can give His human children every chance for the future. That's one of the reasons that souls are reincarnated.'

Looking into Michael's eyes, all of a sudden I understood on a spiritual level and put my hand to my mouth, saying, 'O my God!'

'Do you understand, Lorna?' Michael asked. I nodded and Michael continued, 'That's why God sent His Son to earth. His Son is part of God. Out of God walks His Son, and out of God walks the Holy Spirit. The souls that dwell in human bodies are a part of God's body. It is our souls not our bodies that are God's children. God wants to do everything He can to allow a very important part of human evolution to happen. Body and soul are to become one.'

'Michael, I feel a little frightened now, because I think I know what you are going to say next.'

'Yes, Lorna, you do. Say it with me,' Michael said. Michael and I spoke simultaneously: 'If God's human children don't change their ways, God will take our souls from our human bodies and bring them home to Heaven. Without our souls, we as human beings will become no better than the fiercest animal and destroy ourselves.'

I stood there motionless in front of Michael. Michael embraced me, comforting me. After a few moments Michael gave me a gentle smile. 'Lorna, God loves you.'

'Michael, I have to ask you something,' I said urgently. 'God won't give up on us, will He?'

'No, Lorna, and that is the other reason why God sends some of His children back to be reborn humanly. Sometimes, God chooses to reincarnate a soul to right wrongs, to create hope or to build trust, to help to create a better world for mankind.' With that, Michael disappeared.

Neither Michael nor any other angel has answered all the questions that arose for me in Amsterdam about reincarnation. I still don't know why I was shown several reincarnated young people in such a short space of time. Is it something changing in the world, or is it something about Amsterdam? The angels don't always give me the answers when I ask them, but I trust that they will give me the answers as time goes on. I do find that I am growing in my knowledge all the time and this is being helped both by travelling and by meeting people – editors, interviewers, readers – who ask me questions about things I have never thought about before. Remember, before I wrote *Angels in my Hair* there were very few people who knew what I saw, and therefore no one to ask me questions.

I enjoyed my few days in Amsterdam, even though I worked very hard. The angels had been right. They did surprise me, with the reincarnated souls, but also with the pure pleasure of discovering a completely different city. The last night I got to do a boat tour of the canals. It was very beautiful, just getting dark and all the lights of the buildings and bridges were coming on. Some of the canals were so narrow that it took lots of skill from the captain to manoeuvre the boat. He only bumped into the walls of the canal once. The tour guide pointed out a lane called 'The Never-Ending Prayer', apparently so-called because at one time there were so many convents around it. I like the name!

Chapter Thirty-four

The angels of the nations

I was walking along a stretch of the River Nore near Inistioge in Ireland. There are beautiful walks there. I must have walked about half a mile along the riverbank. There were angels walking beside me, but I didn't speak to them or they to me. I was enjoying being alone – well, sort of alone. I stopped and picked up a stick and sat down on a rock at the river's edge. I was tapping the water with my stick when an angel startled me by sitting down on the rock beside me. I nearly fell off the rock in fright. She laughed at me as she reached out and caught me. Her touch was so fine and light, it seemed to pass through me, but I regained my balance.

The angel was beautiful and transparent like the water. She reminded me of an emerald butterfly reflecting colours of green, yellow, blue and red – all the colours you might see reflecting from a river or lake. I could see that her body went all the way down into the river; her feet merged with the water – becoming one with it. It was 'the Spirit of Water'. I was thrilled to see her. She reached out and touched my hand and my hand became wet and warm. I could feel her love. A few moments later, she drew her hand away and the tips of her fingers took every drop of water from my hand, leaving it bone dry. I smiled at her. As I did, I thought of the first glimpses I'd had of her when I was a child out fishing with my da. I would get a glance of her moving through the water, sometimes moving very fast and other times slowly, but no matter what speed she went, it was always very hard to see her. I smiled as I remembered a special time.

I was about six and at the seaside with my family. I was running up and down along the shore through the shallow water, jumping over the little waves. I heard someone calling my name and I had stopped and turned around and looked out to sea. But I couldn't see anything other than the sea and sky. I walked further out into the water up to my waist, hearing my name called all the time, but was still unable to see anyone. My da had always warned me to go no further out into the water than my waist, so I stopped there. Standing there, I stretched my arms and touched the water gently with my hands. Sometimes the waves splashed me in the face and sometimes they were quite calm. Then I saw the Spirit of Water swim by me; she turned around and circled me. She made me laugh so much that I nearly fell in and then she tickled me, which made me laugh even more. Her touch was so gentle and warm. I remember my sister Emer shouting at me, asking what was I laughing at. Then, suddenly, the Spirit of Water disappeared and I headed in towards the beach where Emer and my da were waiting.

I smiled as I recalled it, and the angel of the Spirit of Water smiled with me.

'I must be going now, Lorna,' she said, and she flowed from the rock into the river. I watched her for a brief second before she disappeared completely. I was disappointed she was gone. I turned and looked at the rock beside me. There wasn't one drop of water or any sign of dampness. It was as if she had never been there.

Over the years I have learnt about the Spirit of Water, or the Angel of Water. I have learnt that God has intertwined this angel with water and she is in any place where there is water. She gives me enormous pleasure every time I see her.

There are so many different types of angels, and there is much I want to share with you, and yet I don't want to overwhelm you with too much information. I mentioned that there are angels of the nations when I told you about what happened at the Metropolitan Museum in New York. So let me tell you a bit more.

I was curled up on the sofa in Johnstown watching the television news one night a few years ago. There was film of violent protests, of armed soldiers in riot gear and tanks attacking unarmed people who were holding banners and protesting. Suddenly the picture blurred and the voice of the reporter became distorted and faded. In the middle of the television screen an angel of the nation appeared. I was really shocked to see it.

The angels of the nation are very powerful and forceful angels. They are much more powerful than ancestral angels or guardian angels. In some ways they are like a special type of ancestral angel but appointed to a country instead of a family. They stand guard within the boundaries of that country and like a guardian angel never leave the nation they guard. I only ever see angels of the nations if something is seriously wrong in a country.

I watched the TV screen in distress, looking at this angel of the nation. To be honest, the angels didn't let me know what country he guarded, or what country these riots were in. He, as all angels of the nations I have ever been shown, was dressed in heavy armour, as if ready for war. The armour was so solid and heavy it was as if it were impenetrable, as if even a nuclear bomb couldn't penetrate it. On top of the base armour were metal pieces – reinforcement of different shapes.

The angel of the nation came closer to me on the TV screen and I could see him more clearly. He wore a helmet that came right up around his head but left his face exposed. His expression was authoritative and forbidding. His face was round and glowed; I couldn't see any colour in his eyes.

I heard my name being called in a very deep but clear voice. I jumped. His saying my name startled me and made me even more concerned. I felt great emotion from the angel – great concern for the nation he was guarding. His love for the people was clear to me, as was his deep worry and concern about what was happening in the nation at that time. He spoke – it was as if each word was spoken individually – and told me to pray to God and to ask on his behalf for the nation. Then he disappeared.

I get so frightened and nervous when I see an angel of the nation because it is as if they connect me spiritually with their nation and I feel as if I myself am being torn apart with the pain of what is happening – emotionally, physically and spiritually. I hear the screams of a mother, her despair, the fear of people as they are fired upon, the physical pain as someone is wounded. I would hear the laughter of the people as well as the tears, but unfortunately when an angel of the nation appears to me there are much more tears than laughter.

Angel Michael has told me that the angels of the nations work extremely hard trying to help people, and leaders in particular, to find solutions to problems without going to war. They work across all kinds of issues – jobs, education, environmental, medical. They work to create conditions in each country where people can live in freedom and justice, without poverty, where children can be children and people can follow the religion of their choice. The angels of the nations try and ensure that people elect leaders who are just and have the people's interests at heart. Sometimes I am shown them trying to bring about change – trying to push back soldiers at war, or terrorists, or even multinationals that are exploiting a country. The angel of the nation always seems to be in battle to try and turn things around to the right way, to how they should be. Even giving people courage to fight when there is no other solution left.

I recognise angels of the nations – they are all similar in appearance – all are very powerful looking and wear very heavy armour. But each is different, with different shapes used to reinforce their armour, and they also look different as people do, so I have no problem recognising one from another. Many of these angels of the nations have been there since the beginning of time, but some have been appointed by God in more recent times. I don't really understand how God decides that a particular group of people or a particular place needs a national angel.

Sometimes when I hear something on the news an angel will whisper to me that the people are doing what the angel of the nation has asked them – playing their part, such as standing up looking for justice. Then I feel such joy and ask the angel of the nation to keep inspiring people, to keep giving them the courage to change things for the better in that country and in the world.

Each country, of course, influences others. Angel Michael

has told me that when one country does something right, there is a higher chance that other countries will follow. This is why angels of the nations are in constant contact with each other. They work together – even though they are not allowed to move from their own nation. The people of each country, each and every one of us, can help simply by asking for the angel's help.

Chapter Thirty-five

The Devil's helpers

Megan and I were in Kilkenny one Saturday. It was busy and there were lots of people around. Megan was looking for new jeans and we were having a relaxed time enjoying shopping. Later on, we were standing waiting to cross the road at the traffic lights when suddenly I got a terrible shock. There on the other side of the road, in among a crowd waiting to cross, looking directly at me, was one of what I call the devil's human helpers. He was a tall teenager of about sixteen. He pushed his way through the crowd, acting as if he wanted me to see him, wanted me to see that he was strong and that he wasn't frightened or afraid of me. His eyes were so cold. They just stood out. I shouldn't have been able to see his eyes properly at that distance – but I was allowed to.

The devil's helpers frighten me. I have seen them in Ireland and now that I am travelling to other countries I see them there as well. I feel terrorised when I see one. They seem to know that I can see their evil. I have no idea what the devil's helpers see in me but from their behaviour it's clear that they want my attention, that in some way they are targeting me. If it weren't for the hundreds of angels that surround me every time I see one of these I would be afraid for my own safety. I know that if the time were right they could kill everyone there without a qualm. They frighten me because they know I know this, yet they do not hide.

One of the ways I recognise them is by their eyes. When I see the devil's helpers their eyes seem to change and become very cold and piercing. I have even seen eyes like these looking out at me from a pram.

These people have guardian angels. Everyone has a guardian angel. But it's as if the devil, or Satan, possesses that person and crushes the soul. It's as if the soul is frozen and that person is unable to listen or respond to their guardian angel. I don't believe they have lost their free will, though. They can still turn back to the good. God and the angels present them with opportunities to change, but Satan makes it very attractive for them to stay as they are. Satan will make sure that they get what they need in life. Many of these people can seem to be good, bright and intelligent. Some of them are or will get into positions of power and influence right across the world in every sphere – political, academic, business, educational, entertainment and religious. These are the devil's soldiers.

I have never seen a national leader with these eyes. I hope I never do. I pray that their number is quite small, but based on the number that I have seen, I am quite fearful of how many of them there may be and I don't see glowing babies in the same number. Whether we realise it or not, we are all God's soldiers. Each and every one of us has an important part to play in stopping evil within our world. It's as if everyone must do their bit in the way they live their own life. Everything we do makes a difference. It's the small things that build up to the big. We have to each make sure that in our everyday life we don't give in to Satan's temptation in what might seem like small things. Every time we do, it feeds Satan and makes him stronger – he has won again.

It can be as simple as refraining from saying something hurtful about somebody, deciding to support someone who is being shunned by others, refraining from making judgements – even unspoken – about others, being patient with family members or people in the workplace. Many people go along with what other people are saying even though they don't feel comfortable with it. Not speaking out, even when it's about something that seems trivial, is in fact feeding the devil.

Teenagers in particular need to be careful about not giving in to peer pressure to jeer or bully others. This is so prevalent in our schools today. Hard as it may be for many of you to believe it, Satan has been born humanly into the world. He may be alive and living today. Michael told me this when I was about twelve, when we were talking about good and evil. He didn't use the word 'Antichrist' in that conversation. It was a word I had never heard of. I have heard it used by people to describe Satan born into a human body, but it's not a word that I have heard the angels use. They speak of Satan or the devil. Angel Michael told me some forty-odd years ago that Satan had succeeded in being born humanly, but that it was more than likely he would die as an infant. Angels told me, though, that he would be born and born again until he succeeds in growing up to be an adult. There will be a cycle of rebirth until the Antichrist is allowed to become mature. I have been shown this child, who grows to maturity, being born somewhere in the world other than America, but moving to America at some stage – I don't know what stage – in his life. I have formed the impression from the angels that this will be a long process, but they have never told me how long. Nor have they told me whether Satan is alive today or between births.

Satan was created by God as an angel and God gave him more power and strength than He gave to any other angel, with no exceptions. Satan rebelled and tried to overthrow God, thinking that he was better than Him. He took other angels with him. I don't like to even refer to these as angels anymore and do everything possible to avoid addressing them or even talking about them.

Unlike other angels and archangels Satan has free choice. God gave Satan free choice. God doesn't like to destroy anything He creates. God still works and hopes that Satan will come back to Him. I know that many of you may think that God has this wrong, that He should have wiped out Satan. However, the angels tell me that this is beyond our human comprehension, that we in fact know so little that we can never understand God fully. They assure me that after death we will understand much more. When I am shown visions of the Antichrist – the grown-up human Satan – I always pray to God and his angels, saying, 'Not in my life-time'. I don't want to be here when he comes to power. But the Angel Michael tells me that I will be back and I know from what he has told me that in this life or another I'll be here when he is in power.

We may not be able to stop the Antichrist being born and growing to maturity, but we can reduce the havoc he will be able to wreak. Even now there is a huge battle going on between good and evil and, as I have said, each of us are soldiers in the battle, playing our part with every decision we make in our lives. Many of us think that the battle between good and evil is only fought by world leaders, govern-ments, terrorists, international organisations, armies, or leaders of churches or multinational corporations. We think we can leave it to them, while we get on with our everyday lives. This is not enough – we should all be more concerned and more active in choosing good in everything we do. As I say, we should stand up and be counted and say no to things that don't seem to us to be right – no matter how small they might seem to be.

God wants us to be happy. He has shown me some very positive futures. Man's intended evolution is for the body and soul to become one and for humans to become perfect spiritual beings who will no longer suffer physical illness or die.

The Antichrist will try to stop this evolution. He will appear to give us 'everything'. He will try and fool us into thinking that he is making the world a better place. But he is not! We humans can be very gullible and, if we let Satan get more control of us, he will blind us to the fact that we are much, much more than our bodies and minds. He will wipe out our consciousness that we also have a soul. He will make us forget that we are in fact God's children and are directly connected to God by our souls – that our souls are immortal and never die.

Chapter Thirty-six

We must all play our part

Until the publication of *Angels in my Hair*, few people knew what I was seeing and being told by the angels. To be honest, there is still a lot that the angels have not allowed me to make public. In the years since publication I have for the first time met people with whom I have been able to discuss what I see and hear and this has been fascinating for me. I am constantly surprised by the questions that people ask. I am also constantly being asked questions that I don't know the answer to, so I have been asking Michael and Hosus in particular for lots of answers. Sometimes I get answers, sometimes I don't. But my knowledge and understanding are growing all the time.

One of the things I am often asked about is the future of mankind. I have to explain that I'm not just shown one future by the angels. I'm shown lots of futures and what happens will depend on the decisions mankind makes. I have already told you about some of these possible futures in this book – the human throwback is one. Another future I have been shown is one where children are very rare and precious, where fewer children are being born because women are not able to have them. This has already started to happen. In the future the population of the world will continue to grow a bit more and then will start to reduce. We will make some mistakes and take some wrong turns before we get back on the right path. It's not all bad. I have also been shown children of the future being what the children of the past and the present have not been allowed to be – real children, full of wonder. We may not realise it now, but we treat children abominably. Children of the future will look back to children of the present in their history classes and will cry. They will feel sad that these children of the past didn't know what fun and joy was. These children of the future won't need gadgets or technology. They will get more fun and joy out of the world around them. They will look at a blade of grass or an insect, and see so much more than the children of today do. Their lives will be so different. They will be fascinated by life itself, by nature and all that is around them. And they will love to learn.

I have been shown that if we take the right path, countries will live under the one umbrella, but every country will keep its own individuality and traditions. It would only be on global issues that things will be co-ordinated. Even though we will all be under the one umbrella we will still have our freedom. We are striving towards this good future, but it scares me that we are going in parallel into a bad one, because of wrong decisions that have been made because of the influence of Satan. He wants the whole world under his control with no national tradition, no individuality and no freedom. I pray it doesn't happen, but it's as if the bad side keeps moving forward.

There are tremendous signs of hope. I believe that more and more people are becoming aware of the spiritual part of them, and that this is what God intends for us. As we become more aware, we will realise that we have abilities we never realised we had, and we will learn how to use them. We have not been given these gifts to make loads of money or amass material things. We are given these blessings to help bear fruit for all. We are being given them so that we and those around us can grow happier, healthier and more spiritual. We will, for example, become more telepathic. We won't necessarily be telepathic in relation to everyone but, for example, a mother will be telepathic with her child in school and will know when that child is upset or there is a problem. In fact, it is already happening. Many people are becoming more telepathic, more intuitive. I'm noticing it among young adults in particular. I know business people who have noticed that intuition is stronger in some of the younger men and women working for them. When they make a recommendation – even if it seems to go against conventional wisdom at the time – it often turns out to be right. This can make their boss more open and intuitive too, as long as he or she appreciates and nurtures these young people. This gift is being given to us to help us in our everyday life. I regularly meet people who think that, because they are aware that their intuition is growing, this means they should give up their normal, everyday life and become a clairvoyant or healer. But these gifts are given by God to be used in our normal, everyday life to help us, our families and all around us to live life to its full.

Children will learn how to use spiritual abilities in school as part of normal schoolwork. All children will learn the basics and then a child may decide to specialise in a particular ability. For example, a child interested in plants will develop abilities relevant to plants and might become a gardener. Similarly a child with a love for animals may develop special abilities to do with animals and might use these as a vet. So our abilities in healing and medicine will grow. Doctors may still have to operate, but they may be able to do it without a knife or technology. Although medicine will change, it will have to hold on to some of the old ways of working. The difference will be that there will be no separation between doctors and healers. In the future different individuals will train and specialise in different parts of the body. Some individuals will be able to heal disease by moving the energy or drawing some energy away without even touching the patient. People are working with energy to help healing in this way now, but what they are doing is nothing in comparison with what mankind will be able to do in the future. I've seen some healers out there today doing very good work. In fact, there are many good healers out there. There are, however, some without much ability, many who are not open enough spiritually, or are not doing it for the right reasons. I've been shown a silver bowl full of a liquid, transparent like water only thicker. Some doctors will use this. I've been shown them dipping their fingers in it. I'm not quite sure why. Maybe this substance helps heal or maybe it's to do with cleansing after healing?

Scientists can use these emerging abilities to make the world a better place. As always this requires people to make the right decisions, to decide to use these gifts in a positive way, rather than in a negative, greedy or controlling way.

God wants His earthly children to be happy. He wants what any parent wants for their children. We don't realise that God does everything possible to please us. The only imperfect thing He has given us is our body. The body is designed to be born and, for now, to die. The soul lives forever.

In a future scenario I have been shown that we will become so evolved that physically everyone will be perfect. Our bodies will not get sick and will not suffer from wear and tear. This doesn't mean that we will lose life's challenge. There will still be lots of challenges, but they will be different to the ones we face today.

I remember being shown a group of children in the future. They were standing by a road then suddenly they disappeared and appeared somewhere else. They were able to transport themselves in this way. I was also shown a child crossing a river. He didn't need to use a bridge. It was as if he floated across.

I know that in the future God wants people to be able to see angels. For me it's always been natural to see them. When I'm allowed to see God's chosen future, angels are a part of the family. Children in the future will regard their guardian angel as a friend, a constant companion. If we were parents in this future, we wouldn't be surprised to hear our child talking to their guardian angel. We will also see other people's guardian angels. In this future the guardian angel will need to guide us less.

In His chosen future God will be able to open up other worlds to us. Mankind doesn't understand how big the universe is. It's never-ending. What's out there is beyond us in our present form. This is hard for us to understand, as we like to put a beginning and an end to things. But God has made other planets, other 'worlds'. Some of them are inhabited by God's children. Some of these children are more evolved than us, some less evolved. There are also planets where there are intelligent beings that don't have souls and therefore are not in that sense God's children. I don't know why God has created them. Some of these intelligent beings may be more easily influenced by the other side.

But I also believe that the decisions we make about the future on this earth will not only affect our planet – they will affect the universe. In both good and bad futures I see us going to other planets. If mankind has taken the right decisions, our going to other planets will be a part of human evolution and the evolution of those inhabiting those planets. We will travel to other planets and we will bring back people from other planets to earth. The angels who accompany the humans who undertake this travel will have the task of guiding those who are far away, so that they don't get distracted from what it is they are supposed to be doing. But if we have failed to make the right decisions, I see the human race going to other planets because we have to, because we have destroyed so much of this earth. We will go to other planets with the intention of stripping and leaving them bare. We will become the terrorists of the universe.

At a certain stage in evolution people will not die. We will have a perfect body, which will be more like our soul. It will be as if body and soul are intertwined. When we die now we go straight to Heaven, but we leave our body behind. In this future our body and soul will be united, so both will go to Heaven together.

I have been shown a future where God the creator comes and asks a very spiritually evolved human race, 'Do you want to stay here or do you want to come to Heaven?' and humanity replies, 'No, we'd like to stay,' secure in the knowledge that God will invite them again. God will be quite happy for them to stay for a while. The human race will then continue – for at least a while – enjoying living and working on creating a perfect glimpse of Heaven on earth, making life here more and more like life in Heaven.

But I don't see Heaven and earth ever merging. The barrier between earth and Heaven will always remain. The earth will only end if all mankind says yes to God's invitation to go to Heaven. God would love us to do that – but only when we are ready and have evolved as we are meant to do. To evolve in the way God wants us to requires that each and every one of us plays our part.

Appendix – Prayer of Thy Healing Angels

In *Angels in my Hair* I tell the story of the evening that Archangel Michael gave this prayer to me, and from that day on I have given it to people who come looking for help. All angels do healing work, but there is a particular group of angels called 'healing angels', which are called in by guardian angels when healing is required. There are literally millions of healing angels, and God is pouring healing angels on the world all the time. All we have to do is ask for their help.

We must always remember that the healing will happen in the way that God knows is best for us. Sometimes we may not recognise that healing has occurred, as it may not be the healing we have asked for – it may be emotional or spiritual healing rather than physical. We need to watch out for healing and recognise when it has been granted. Often healing can seem small: perhaps somebody who has been depressed for a long time smiles or laughs; maybe someone who was in a lot of physical distress feels a lot better; or maybe a mother who has been stressed out and unable to cope suddenly feels happiness and joy.

Many people have told me that the healing angels have helped in response to this prayer and over the years I have been told a lot of stories of people believing they, or those they loved, were helped by this prayer. Many people have told me they have written out the prayer to carry it around with them, or to give it to someone else.

Prayer of Thy Healing Angels,
That is carried from God by Michael, Thy Archangel.
Pour out, Thy Healing Angels,
Thy Heavenly Host upon me,
And upon those that I love,
Let me feel the beam of Thy
Healing Angels upon me,
The light of Your Healing Hands.
I will let Thy Healing begin,
Whatever way God grants it,
Amen.

To find out more
about Lorna Byrne go to
www.lornabyrne.com

Here you can:

Add your wishes and prayers to Lorna's prayer scroll.

'Years ago the Angels handed me a prayer scroll and told me that when I was praying I should hold it in my hand and that the Angels would join me in praying for everything contained within it.

When I'm in a meditative state of prayer I hold in my hand this spiritual scroll with every name and every request written on it and I hand this scroll to God.

I invite you to send me your thoughts, joys and worries so as they can be included.

I won't be able to reply individually to your notes but be assured I will make sure they are included in the prayer scroll and in my and the Angel's prayers. There is naturally no charge and everything is treated with confidence.'

Lorna

Sign up to receive Lorna's quarterly email newsletter.

Read more of the wisdom that Lorna has been given by the angels.

See where Lorna is speaking and doing signings

Watch videos and read interviews with Lorna

10% of the author's royalties from the sale of this book are being donated to charity. For details of the charities benefiting see www.lornabyrne.com

ALSO BY LORNA BYRNE

Angels in my Hair

Angels in my Hair is the autobiography of a modern-day mystic, an Irish woman with powers of the saints of old.

When she was a child, people thought Lorna was 'retarded' because she did not seem to be focusing on the world around her, instead Lorna was seeing angels and spirits.

As Lorna tells the story of her life, the reader meets, as she did, the creatures from the spirit worlds who also inhabit our own – mostly angels of an astonishing beauty and variety – including the prophet Elijah and an Archangel – but also the spirits of people who have died.

This remarkable book is the testimony of a woman who sees things beyond the range of our everyday experience.

'Those who see angels are close to being angels. In this book, Lorna beautifully and graphically describes angels and how they work.'
William Roache, MBE, author of *Soul on the Street*

'Nobody is going to argue with her underlying message of love and compassion and forgiveness and her hopes for "peace among nations and peace in families".'
Irish Times

'The world has discovered a modest mystic that it might do well to listen to.'
Daily Mail

'*Angels in my Hair* is a very simply and softly written narrative, one that managed to grip me emotionally (tears were shed) and made me reflect.'
Sunday Independent

'*Angels in my Hair* is an amazing book by an incredible woman.'
Jim Corr, The Corrs

Published by Arrow Books

arrow books